P?~ . GILDING is an international thought leader and advocate for
~ ~ability. He has served as head of Greenpeace International, built
~ d two companies, and advised both Fortune 500 corporations and
~ unity-based NGOs. A member of the core faculty for Cambridge
~ rsity's Programme for Sustainability Leadership, he blogs at
~ ~ paulgilding.com, and his newsletter, *The Cockatoo Chronicles*, has
~ ribers around the world.

THE GREAT DISRUPTION

*How the Climate Crisis Will
Transform the Global Economy*

PAUL GILDING

BLOOMSBURY
LONDON · BERLIN · NEW YORK · SYDNEY

First published in Great Britain 2011
This paperback edition published 2012

Bloomsbury Publishing Plc
50 Bedford Square
London WC1B 3DP

www.bloomsbury.com

Bloomsbury Publishing, London, Berlin, New York and Sydney

A CIP catalogue record of this book is available from the British Library

ISBN 978 1 4088 2218 0

1 3 5 7 9 10 8 6 4 2

Typeset by Westchester Book Group

Printed in Great Britain by Clays Ltd, St Ives Plc

To the prescient pioneers of sustainability of the 1960s and 1970s who spent their lives alerting us to what was coming: Rachel Carson, Donella and Dennis Meadows, Jorgen Randers, Paul Ehrlich, E. F. Schumacher, Denis Hayes, Steward Brand, and many others. And to those who have and will follow in their footsteps as we decide to realize their hopes, instead of their fears. I salute you all.

Contents

Foreword to the Paperback Edition

When I first wrote about the inevitability of a global economic and ecological crisis in 2005, the response was largely skeptical. The free market system was fundamentally seen as self-correcting and would surely be able to solve any problem thrown at it. Just three years later, after the wake up call of 2008's financial crisis, the market didn't look so invincible. Those who saw the potential for a global crisis started to grow in number. Now, with a further three years of evidence, you can almost *hear* the world waking up as the bubbles of delusion burst.

In the last year, experts from many fields have published conclusions that align with mine. Peak oil expert Richard Heinberg's book *The End of Growth* argued that in addition to severe environmental and resource constraints, we face financial system overload: a world weighed down by debt. He concludes growth, as an economic system, is basically finished. Chandran Nair from Hong Kong has given us *Consumptionomics*, a devastating analysis that explains why Asia can't possibly follow the Western model of growth. He argues that Asia has to lead the way to a new economic model and is the only group of countries now likely to do so. Jeremy Grantham, the legendary fund manager, has explained all this to us in numbers, showing how commodity prices have hit a new and permanently higher level as supply constraints are tested by the global growth.

Occupy Wall Street has now thrust these issues into the mainstream, provoking serious questioning of the dangers of extreme inequality and of the role of the financial sector in the economy. People have woken up to what I argue in Chapter 18 is "Ineffective Inequality"—levels that aren't just morally suspect but don't even benefit the economy. But why have these protests been so successful and why now? Because Occupy

Wall Street is like the kid in the fairy story, saying what everyone knows but is afraid to say: The emperor has no clothes. They've given focus to what people were already seeing and feeling; that our problem is not just debt, or inequality, or a recession, or corporate influence, or ecological damage. It's the whole package—the system is profoundly broken and beyond incremental reform.

Meanwhile, physical and economic indicators of crisis have continued to mount. The year 2011 saw more extreme weather, with droughts, floods, and wildfires breaking records across the United States, while famine gripped the Horn of Africa. The United Kingdom faced widespread rioting, global stock markets saw unprecedented volatility, and more countries teetered on the edge of debt default. To top it off, food prices hit record highs while Arctic sea-ice volumes hit record lows.

People who believe that markets always self-correct are getting harder to find. Every day, people e-mail me with questions: Is this it? Is this the beginning of the crisis your book argues will come?

The answer depends on when you ask that question. If you ask today, "Are we facing a civilization-threatening global crisis?" the answer you will get from most commentators is no—things are not *that* bad. They have explanations for each event. Yes, the climate is changing, but these are just extreme years in a gentler warming trend. The African famine is climate influenced, but it's more about poor governance and conflict. Debt is a serious issue, but we'll get growth back on track soon. Food prices are high, but it's as much about market speculation as fundamental limits. They're all a bit right. But in the big picture, they are very, very wrong, as *The Great Disruption* explains.

If, however, you ask the same question in the future, the answer will be very clear indeed. As Tom Friedman wrote in the *New York Times* in a column about this book: "You really do have to wonder whether a few years from now we'll look back at the first decade of the 21st century—when food prices spiked, energy prices soared, world population surged, tornados plowed through cities, floods and droughts set records, populations were displaced and governments were threatened by the confluence of it all—and ask ourselves: What were we thinking? How did we not panic when the evidence was so obvious . . ."

So, yes, the world is a complex place, and many factors drive any crisis, but the overall situation is now clear. We have hit the limits in these past three years, and reality can no longer be explained away.

So what *are* we thinking? If the signs of crisis are so clear, why don't we see them? Why aren't we declaring a state of emergency and responding? Why are we doing the opposite—arguing about climate science while borrowing more money from our children to boost illusory economic growth? Why are we the first generation that, rather than sacrificing ourselves for our children's future, are sacrificing our children's future for ourselves?

The answer is surprisingly simple and surprisingly good news. When you are confronted with a problem so big that it requires you to change profoundly, denial is the natural response. Acceptance requires change, and change is difficult. So the stronger the evidence becomes, the stronger the denial must become.

The reason this is good news is that the path denial takes is predictable. Denial gets stronger and stronger as the evidence of the need for change increases, as we are witnessing now, and then it collapses, usually suddenly. Exactly how and when it collapses is unpredictable but that the fact that *it will collapse* is clear.

For now we are stuck, bouncing against the limits of what I call the debt/growth trap. Here's how that works. Remember back in 2008, before the financial meltdown? Food prices and oil prices both hit record highs with resulting riots and political unrest gripping many countries. Then the global financial crunch came. Economies shrank and oil and food prices fell. In response, we borrowed massively, determined to do whatever it took to get growth back on track. On the surface, this worked. Major government stimulus packages and interventions around the world kept the global economy from collapsing, and now the economy is growing again, at least in the developing world. So isn't this good news? Aren't we on track again?

No, and this is the trap. As we've started to grow, commodity prices have risen, as they did when the economy was growing in 2008. Food prices have hit new record highs, and oil is trending upward. As you will read in this book, commodity prices are one of the key indicators that we are hitting the limits to growth. On this issue, Jeremy Grantham is blunt. Of rising commodity prices, he says "we are in the midst of one of the giant inflection points in economic history" calling it "perhaps the most important economic event since the Industrial Revolution.

"From now on, price pressure and shortages of resources will be a permanent feature of our lives . . . The world is using up its natural resources at an alarming rate, and this has caused a permanent shift in their value."

The interesting thing about Grantham is that he approaches scarcity as an investor. He dispassionately analyzes the data and comes to conclusions similar to what you'll read in this book, warning us that "if we maintain our desperate focus on growth, we will run out of everything and crash."

This context frames the debt/growth trap. We borrowed massively to get ourselves out of the last financial crisis, and the only way the resulting debt can be paid off is if we have significant economic growth. Yet such growth, Grantham explains, will lead to commodity price rises that will stop economic growth. So we're stuck. Grow and face resource constraints; don't grow and drown in debt.

Yet as I've traveled the world in the last year sharing the message of *The Great Disruption*, my optimism about our future has not been dented but rather reinforced. Yes, the crisis is coming toward us faster and faster, but the world has never been more ready for it. I've spoken to countless audiences, large and small, from local community groups to gatherings of CEOs. Many have challenged the wisdom of my optimism, pointing to the attacks on science, to the inability of many governments to act on these issues, to the paralysis in the U.S. political system, to the rapid melting of the polar icecaps and the droughts and extreme weather around the world.

I acknowledge all this, but I see the world differently. I see the boom in the global solar market, with dramatic falls in prices as that industry rapidly scales for what's coming—building annual manufacturing capacity to 50,000 megawatts up from just 100 megawatts in 2000. I see China and other developing countries leading this, investing heavily in a cleaner, low-carbon economy, deciding they will grab hold of the economic opportunity presented to them by the West's indifferent response. I see the largest civil disobedience campaign in a generation as young people organize peaceful protests against the Tar Sands pipeline, and do so with a smile, choosing hope over fear. I hear conversations at the top of our defense establishments preparing for the inevitable global crises over resource limits. I hear both young entrepreneurs and senior corporate leaders talking about how they are getting their companies ready for a future of endless possibility in transformational change and new business opportunities.

But mostly, I'm optimistic because I see denial coming to a crescendo of absurdity. I see such extreme antiscience views taking hold, I quickly go from despair to laughter. It feels like I'm talking to a drunken alcoholic, telling me they don't have a problem and they really like it down there in the gutter. So I know this moment will pass. It will pass because we're better than that. And when it does, those who are ready, like the solar industry and like the young climate activists, will seize the day.

Yes, we have a big task ahead of us. We have to thread our civilization through the eye of a needle. The capacity of the earth to provide for our needs is declining through our overuse and abuse of resources, while our demand for those resources keeps accelerating. That's a recipe for a big squeeze, with much pain and suffering. But out the other side, when we have accepted that our only option is to build an economy that meets human needs while reducing global resource use, when we all live with less stuff and more time for things that matter, then we will see a world of limitless possibility. A world we are quite capable of building: An economy that feeds, clothes, and houses all of our people, that gives everyone the opportunity to lead fulfilling lives, that treats the planet like it's the only one we've got. That is where we are heading, and I wrote this book for the people who want to be part of *that* future.

—Paul Gilding
September 2011

CHAPTER 1

An Economic and Social Hurricane

The earth is full.

In fact our human society and economy is now *so* large we have passed the limits of our planet's capacity to support us and it is overflowing. Our current model of economic growth is driving this system, the one we rely upon for our present and future prosperity, over the cliff. This in itself presents a major problem. It becomes a much larger challenge when we consider that billions of people are living desperate lives in appalling poverty and need their personal "economy" to rapidly grow to alleviate their suffering. But there is no room left.

This means things are going to change. Not because we will choose change out of philosophical or political preference, but because if we don't transform our society and economy, we risk social and economic collapse and the descent into chaos. The science on this is now clear and accepted by any rational observer. While an initial look at the public debate may suggest controversy, any serious examination of the peer-reviewed conclusions of leading science bodies shows the core direction we are heading in is now clear. Things do not look good.

These challenges and the facts behind them are well-known by experts and leaders around the world and have been for decades. But despite this understanding, that we would at some point pass the limits to growth, it has been continually filed away to the back of our mind and the back of our drawers, with the label "Interesting—For Consideration Later" prominently attached. Well, later has arrived.

This is because the passing of the limits is not philosophical but physical and rooted in the rules of physics, chemistry, and biology. So passing the limits has consequences.

If you cut down more trees than you grow, you run out of trees. If you put additional nitrogen into a water system, you change the type and quantity of life that water can support. If you thicken the earth's CO_2 blanket, the earth gets warmer. If you do all these and many more things at once, you change the way the whole system of planet Earth behaves, with social, economic, and life support impacts. This is not speculation, this is high school science.

In all this though, there is a surprising case for optimism. As a species, we are good in a crisis, and passing the limits will certainly be the biggest crisis our species has ever faced. Our backs will be up against the wall, and in that situation we have proven ourselves to be extraordinary. As the full scale of the imminent crisis hits us, our response will be proportionally dramatic, mobilizing as we do in war. We will change at a scale and speed we can barely imagine today, completely transforming our economy, including our energy and transport industries, in just a few short decades. Perhaps most surprisingly we will also learn there is more to life than shopping. We will break our addiction to growth, accept that more stuff is not making our lives better and focus instead on what does.

This is why we shouldn't despair in the face of what the science is telling us—it is precisely the severity of the problem that will drive a response that is overwhelming in scale and speed and will go right to the core of our societies. It is the crisis itself that will push humanity to its next stage of development and allow us to realize our evolutionary potential. It will be a rough ride, but in the end, we will arrive at a better place.

This is the story we will tell here. It is a story that starts in the past, passes through the present, and extends into the future. The past is the story of warnings issued and decisions made. The present, the story of today, is the factual result of our failure to heed those warnings. But rather than a platform for issuing recriminations, our present situation is the foundation for our future story, a story of great challenges and comparably great opportunity.

This is *our* story. It is about our world, what has been happening in it, the state it is currently in, and what is going to happen next. It is not, however, a passive commentary about the world we live in. It is a call to arms—a call to decide what kind of world we want to live in and what kind of contribution we can each make to define that. It is about a future we must choose.

By coincidence, this story also spans my lifetime. As I was being born in Australia in 1959, the start of this dramatic story was unfolding in the United States. The U.S. Department of Agriculture banned the sale of cranberries, just before Thanksgiving, due to the poisoning of the national crop by the excessive use of inadequately controlled pesticides.

It was what I consider the beginning of modern environmental awareness. It was the moment people on a large scale started to wake up to the fact that there were limits to the earth's capacity to cope with our abuse, that we had grown so powerful as a species that we had "now acquired a fateful power to destroy nature," as scientist Rachel Carson stated. It was when people came to realize that while we had for ten thousand years learned to control nature around our houses, villages, and farms for our immediate benefit, the scale of our impact had now changed the game.

Our story will go through this period to give us context for our present situation, where we find we have ignored earlier warnings and have now exceeded the limits, breaking the rules on which our system and its stability is based.

As you read this history, you may share the angst many feel about the lack of response to the decades of warnings. Environmentalists like myself also have to acknowledge a sobering reality in this. Given that we were unsuccessful in convincing society to respond to the challenge that was coming, there must have been failings in the approach we took. While I too lament the result and wonder what we could have done differently, I have now moved on. It is what it is. We can only change the future.

In that sense, this is a kind of guidebook to that future. While my views are shaped by decades of experience and a thorough analysis of the facts, they are of course my views. I hope they will help you come to your own conclusions on where we are and where we are going and, most important, how you personally are going to respond.

Before we start the journey, though, let's consider our starting point. If you're one of the billion or so people at the top of the global economic tree,[1] and if you're reading this, then you probably are, then how good is this? We get a good meal whenever we want it. We all have housing that prevents us from being exposed to the elements. Most of us rarely face violence in our day-to-day lives, and if we do, we can get a response that pretty much reduces the threat to a manageable level. We generally get basic health care needs met, with even the poorer-quality care light-years ahead of what the average person received just a few generations ago.

And this quality of life is no longer just for those in Western countries, as it largely was a few decades ago. There are now many hundreds of millions of people in China, India, South America, and other developing countries who live this relatively luxurious life.

We, the lucky billion, now spend most of our lives seeking ever-greater and subtler refinements in what we perceive to be our quality of life: nicer clothes, better music, more comfortable furniture, more interesting holidays, more convenient technology, more unusual variations of food, a more secure retirement. It doesn't get much better than this.

Our grandparents, let alone the generations prior to them, would look at us in amazement. They would see us living like kings and pharaohs, with every convenience dealt with, every basic human need met, and our arguments on what needs to improve going to ever-greater refinements to all of this. They would hear us complain about interest rates, not being able to afford a larger house or a renovation, and having a degree of uncertainty that we will be able to live this lifestyle when we stop working. A few generations ago, no one stopped working unless they were dead, let alone spent their latter years in physical comfort with decent health care.

Humanity has on balance performed extraordinarily well. As we've swept across the world in just ten thousand years, we have established a quality of life for billions of people that was unimaginable at this scale even just a few hundred years ago.

Of course, still left behind are many more billions, many of whom live in grinding, soul-destroying poverty. While we strive for larger televisions, DVD screens in our cars, and the perfectly grilled tender steak, they die for a glass of clean water or a bowl of rice. We will return to this cancer on humanity's soul, but for now let's stay with those of us who are, by comparison, filthy, stinking rich.

We have done well. Our needs are met. We have the capacity not just to make our lives comfortable, but to explore space, to develop extraordinary scientific knowledge, to cure diseases, to invent amazing technologies that will help us and future generations live even better lives. We can now connect to one another instantaneously and globally to share our hopes, our dreams, and what we had for breakfast. It is an amazing point in human history.

You all know where I'm heading with this, don't you. That's the really interesting point here. We all know where we're heading.

When I started presenting the ideas in this book five years ago, the thing that struck me most was how little push-back I got on the basic situation we were in. Most audiences, whether activist, corporate, or government, agreed that the path we were on was, in summary, completely unsustainable, that we wouldn't change until the crisis hit, and then it would be a big, bloody mess.

So question time became a discussion about whether or not this would lead to the collapse of the economy, whether the population would crash to one billion or fewer, and how ugly the descent could be. Then everyone would have a cup of tea and go back to their lives.

We all know where we're heading. We know it from the science, we know it from the politics, and we know it in our hearts. That's why I get so little push-back. We know.

We've been borrowing from the future, and the debt has fallen due. We have reached or passed the limits of our current economic model of consumer-driven material economic growth. We are heading for a social and economic hurricane that will cause great damage, sweep away much of our current economy and our assumptions about the future, and cause a great crisis that will impact the whole world and to which there will be a dramatic response. We know this to be true.

The science says we have physically entered a period of great change, a synchronized, related crash of the economy and the ecosystem, with food shortages, climate catastrophes, massive economic change, and global geopolitical instability. It has been forecast for decades, and the moment has now arrived.

I use the analogy of a hurricane because we need to understand this is not a forecast of a hurricane season, but a forecast of a category six hurricane that is clearly heading for our coastline—and every time the forecast is revised, the category goes up one level. It is already higher than the rating system allows.

We now need to get ready. We *can* manage our way through the hurricane, but only if we acknowledge it's coming and are clear first on how we will survive it and then on what our recovery plan is.

Despite the evidence and the straightforward logic of the crisis being here now, or at least soon, denial is still the dominant response. I say this not in despair, but as a fact. This doesn't mean we should see the cause as hopeless. It just means we should accept that we won't change at scale until the crisis is full-blown and undeniable, until the wind really kicks up speed. But we will then change. And we need to get ready for that as well.

This is where the story gets really interesting, not to mention a lot more cheerful and uplifting!

We are an extraordinary species, and we are capable of great things. History is full of evidence that when our backs are against the wall, all the great qualities of humanity, our compassion, our drive, our technical brilliance, and our ability to make things happen on a massive global scale, come strongly to the fore.

Yes, it is also true we have a shadow side, left over in our reptilian brains, that can take us to a bad place, where fear and anger reside. In the circumstances now emerging, this kind of response could lead to the breakdown of society. So, yes, we could choose to have a dog-eat-dog response drive us into ever-smaller conflicting groups of regions, nations, and communities—of defensive and scared people fighting over what's left, fighting for physical survival. In that scenario, we would lose hundreds of thousands of years of human development and have to effectively start again, just hoping the cycle won't repeat itself.

I don't believe we will do this. Given our natural survival instincts, our history as a species, our new global connectedness, and the scale of the threat, I believe we will instead choose to consciously overcome that tendency, as we have many times in the past. We will draw on what is great about being human and dig deep to express our highest potential— the potential that can take us through the coming crisis and out the other side to a stronger, safer, and more advanced society.

This story will describe that journey we have now embarked on and the choices we face.

I will tell you what I think this journey will look like, what it means for you, and how you can be involved in helping us all get where we need to go. We all have a role, as individuals, in companies, in government, in our communities, and in our families. The good news is that the things I'm going to suggest we all do now to help us get where we need to be in the long term are going to make our lives better and our communities, companies, and countries stronger in the short term as well.

It is true that the crisis coming will almost certainly see great conflict among nations over resources and refugees, mass suffering, and some difficult situations emerge as fear and nationalism rear their ugly heads. We need to plan for all of this. However, we will also see the best humanity can offer, great compassion, extraordinary innovation, and millions of people digging deep and finding their capacity for brilliance and innovation. This is because scientists, researchers, business leaders, community organizers, policy makers, entrepreneurs, and youth are all out there now, building the future we need. They just need our permission and support to take their work to mass scale.

The Great Disruption will ultimately take human society to a higher evolutionary state, where we will address centuries-old challenges left over from our lower-order animal state—like poverty, consumerism, and conflict. We have the opportunity to build a society that represents our highest capacities, with extreme poverty eliminated; great technology that works *with* rather than against nature and provides us with abundant energy and resources; a closed-loop economy with no waste; communities that work and support one another; happiness, satisfaction, and service as the central organizing principles of our economy and society, rather than our current approach of "money = happier people."

We will do all this not just because we can, but, more important, because we have to. The alternative is no longer an option. The ecological-system changes now under way present a significant risk of global economic and social collapse. So the choice we need to make is not a philosophical one.

The good news gets better. The global nature of the problem means only a global solution can fix it, and that means we are going to come together as a people like never before. Protecting national interest will have to be confined to the sporting field. Again, not just because we might choose to, but because it is the only way we can address the challenges we face.

Getting through to the good side of this crisis, however, is going to require us *all* to engage. That's why I'm writing this book. We are going to have to change our expectations about our material lifestyles, about the nature and focus of our work and career, about our expectations of government, and about how we all behave in our communities and our companies. The good news is that most of these changes are going to make us happier anyway.

This crisis presents what may be a "once in a civilization" opportunity for a step change in human evolution, but one driven consciously rather than biologically.

So this is your story. There is no one else. We are the people we've been waiting for. This is the time. This is our time.

Let's get to work.

CHAPTER 2

The Scream—We Are Their Children's Children

To understand where we are and where we are going, we first have to understand where we've come from. In 2005, when I first wrote about the impending ecological system crash, I called the paper "Scream Crash Boom."[1] In summary it argued that the Scream—the call to action that had been under way since the late 1950s—was coming to an end; the Crash—of the ecosystem and economy—was beginning; and the Boom—a response of extraordinary speed and scale—was not far behind.

The reason I called the first phase the Scream was that it conveyed both the practical notion of warning—seeking to draw attention to a problem—and a healthy dose of fear—evoking the classic image of Edvard Munch's painting. While many have accused environmentalists of "fearmongering" over the decades, when you see a threat, the right thing to do is to warn those around you. In hindsight, we now see clearly that the fears of the early environmentalists were well-founded indeed. Those who argued we would be okay were, to say the least, overly optimistic about society's capacity to deal with the threats involved in a timely fashion.

I want to tell the story of the Scream for three reasons. First, we need to understand the full depth and complexity of the issues we are facing. As I will explain, we face a fundamental systemwide challenge that needs fixing from the ground up. This challenge goes to philosophy, science, economics, and personal values. Knowing the history can inform our knowledge of the subtleties and complexities of that challenge, so we are more likely to get the solutions right.

Second, given that most people have seriously focused on this area only recently, we should remember that many in science, business, government, and the community have been focused on it for decades. They have developed a great deal of experience and understanding of what works and what doesn't. This knowledge can help us decide how to move forward and avoid duplicating effort.

Third, it's a great story of enormous significance to humanity's progress.

There are many views as to what signifies the "start" of the Scream or of the environmental movement. While I think this was around the late 1950s, there were certainly many people dedicated to the conservation of nature prior to this.

However, their views on the environment tended to position them as "conservationists," focused on the protection of nature or wilderness as a separate place, an untouched place. They perceived that humans didn't live in nature—it was somewhere we went on the weekend if we were lucky. In contrast, the modern environmentalists, who made up the Scream, saw nature as a system of which humans were an intimate and inseparable part.

A notable early exception to this thinking was the American writer Henry David Thoreau (1817–1862). While perhaps best remembered for his retreat to the Walden Woods, Thoreau understood the relationship between humans and nature in a profound way. Thoreau famously recognized that "in wildness is the preservation of the world." Rather than seeing nature as something to be conserved and valued for its own sake or beauty, he recognized that human society was part of nature and dependent upon it. In Thoreau's words, "It is in vain to dream of a wildness distant from ourselves." He sought "to regard man as an inhabitant, or a part and parcel of Nature, rather than a member of society."[2]

So while such thinking has been around for a long time, it was in the realm of philosophy rather than mainstream opinion. For me, the start of the Scream is best symbolized by the controversy over pesticide use in America in the late 1950s. While I lay on my cot in Adelaide, Australia, just ten months old, a debate erupted in the United States that would start the slow, multidecade process of reshaping popular thinking. Just weeks before Thanksgiving in 1959, the U.S. government announced it had found dangerous levels of the chemical weed killer aminotriazole in cranberries from Washington and Oregon. The timing of the result could hardly have been more dramatic. Consumers across the country stopped buying cranberries, several areas banned their sale completely, and Thanksgiving meals were largely cranberry-free. Tapping into the popular mood, the group Robert Williams & the Groovers even released a pop song entitled "Cranberry Blues," urging listeners that "if you want to be sure not to get sick, don't touch a cranberry with a ten-foot stick!"

This brought the issues around environmental protection into people's living rooms and kitchens, and so began our awakening to the interconnectedness of life. We began to realize the environment was not just a wild place we visited for spiritual nourishment and recreation, but the place we lived, the source of our food and our physical health, and the foundation of our economy and prosperity.

This controversy led in part to Rachel Carson's seminal 1962 book, *Silent Spring*. A serious and well-qualified scientist as well as a bestselling writer, Carson had become an active environmental campaigner in response to the excessive use of pesticides.

Her book gave birth to a way of thinking that put humans *in* the environment as part of a single system. She also established that scientists could be strong advocates on these issues and that their scientific knowledge gave them credibility to do so.

While many were already debating these issues, Carson's literary skill helped to inspire many people to join the cause with her powerful metaphor of "the silent spring":

> There was once a town in the heart of America where all life seemed to live in harmony with its surroundings. . . . Then a strange blight crept over the area and everything began to change. . . . There was a strange stillness. . . . The few birds seen anywhere were moribund; they trembled violently and could not fly. It was a spring without voices. On the mornings that had once throbbed with the dawn chorus of scores of bird voices there was now no sound; only silence lay over the fields and woods and marsh.

While Carson's book and writing were focused primarily on the environmental impacts of pesticide use, the reason for her historical importance was her ability to draw in the deeper implications of this behavior for human society. As she argued in *Silent Spring*:

> The "control of nature" is a phrase conceived in arrogance, born
> of the Neanderthal age of biology and philosophy, when it was
> supposed that nature exists for the convenience of man.

The industry reaction to Carson's *Silent Spring* was immediate and fierce, led by Monsanto and other chemical giants and backed up by the Department of Agriculture. When threats of lawsuits to prevent publication failed, industry resorted to a public smear campaign in an attempt to counteract Carson.[3]

These attacks were personal, with clear sexist overtones. Carson was labeled a "hysterical woman" rather than the calm and careful scientist she really was, and her argument was called "emotional" rather than scientific.

There are clear parallels with those who today criticize climate scientists for being "political," for overstepping their role. In fact, what these contemporary scientists and Carson have in common is that they saw the clear message of science and felt a moral and professional obligation to use their knowledge to passionately advocate for this science to be heard and acted on.

Another parallel to today's debate is that critics took Carson's moderate and careful argument to the point of absurdity. An example found in a chemistry industry newsletter argued that Carson's vision meant "the end of all human progress, reversion to a passive social state devoid of technology, scientific medicine, agriculture, sanitation, or education. It means disease, epidemics, starvation, misery, and suffering incomparable and intolerable to modern man."[4] Of course, it meant nothing of the sort. A common rejoinder to Carson's work in 1963 and 1964 was to assert that there seemed to be plenty of birds that year, a deliberate manipulation of Carson's metaphor of the silent spring.[5] Again, the parallels to the reception of climate science are clear.

Monsanto even published in its company magazine a widely distributed article called "The Desolate Year," which parodied *Silent Spring* by describing a world overrun by insects and pests in the absence of pesticides.[6]

The industry tactics backfired, however, and public opinion quickly swung firmly behind Carson. Their attacks served only to give more attention to Carson and her bestselling book. Caught in the public storm, President Kennedy ordered his Science Advisory Committee to investigate the claims made by Carson. Within the year, they had returned a report that substantially accepted and agreed with Carson's findings. Shortly after this, Carson was called to testify before Congress on the issue and was well received.[7]

Carson continued her work, giving us an analysis that maintains relevance to this day. For example, in a CBS documentary in April 1963 she said:

> We still talk in terms of conquest. We still haven't become mature enough to think of ourselves as only a tiny part of a vast and incredible universe. Man's attitude towards nature is today critically important simply because we have now acquired a fateful power to destroy nature. But man is part of nature and his war against nature is inevitably a war against himself.

While she died of cancer in 1964, just two years after publishing *Silent Spring*, Carson was subsequently widely recognized as one of the main inspirations for the modern environmental movement. Her work helped to establish the idea that we needed to control and regulate human behavior and led to crucial developments, including the 1970 establishment of the U.S. Environmental Protection Agency (EPA), which soon acted to ban the pesticide DDT and enforce other controls on the market.

Actions like this enshrined the idea that protection of the environment was an essential part of the regulatory framework *within which* the market had to operate. Time has further vindicated Carson's work, and she was posthumously awarded the Presidential Medal of Freedom in 1980.

The 1960s ended with a powerful signal of the risks of inadequate regulation. On June 22, 1969, the Cuyahoga River in Cleveland, Ohio, caught fire when a potent mix of oil and chemicals that had been discharged in the river spontaneously and spectacularly burst into flame. While it wasn't the first time this had happened, this event received widespread public attention, with *Time* magazine referring to it as the river where a person "does not drown but decays."[8]

From 1970 on, the action started to come thick and fast. Around the world, other countries were tracking similar paths to that of the United States, with many governments acting at the national level. It was already clear to many, however, that these issues couldn't be addressed just nationally and that a global focus would be needed.

In 1972, two important events occurred. The first was the United Nations Conference on the Human Environment, held in Stockholm. This meeting was chaired by Canadian Maurice Strong, who went on to become a powerful and positive force in corporate sustainability, particularly with the establishment of the Business Council for Sustainable Development (now known as the WBCSD).

While no decisions of great practical significance were made, the conference was a clear indicator of the rapidly increasing political importance of environmental issues in the international community. It laid the foundations for the decades to come, inspiring a series of international government-to-government meetings. These gatherings have become key milestones measuring society's progress on sustainability, or the lack of it, with a recent example being the Climate Conference in Copenhagen.

The 1972 Stockholm Conference also established various global and regional scientific monitoring processes that helped provide the data scientists now use to measure the changing state of the global ecosystem. And in case you thought climate change was a recent issue, it was addressed at this meeting nearly forty years ago!

The second key event of 1972 was the publication of *The Limits to Growth*. While commissioned by the Club of Rome, an international group of intellectuals and industrialists, the report was produced by MIT experts who were focused on system dynamics—taking the behavior of systems, rather than environmental issues, as their starting point. What they modeled was the interaction between exponential growth and a world with finite resources.

What *The Limits to Growth* argued is now obvious to most rational people, but nearly forty years ago it completely challenged the then dominant worldview. It modeled, in twelve possible futures, the consequences of ongoing growth in population and the economy in the context of limited resources, including the limited capacity of the earth to "absorb pollution." In doing so, it spelled out our true relationship with the world around us.

The computer model World3, at the heart of the report, recognized that human activity interacts with and affects the natural world. Not only are we completely dependent upon this natural world for our survival and prosperity, but in the language of *Limits to Growth* we are capable of "inducing its collapse." The report concluded that such a physical collapse was inevitable if observed trends in humanity's growing ecological footprint continued, and with it would come a dramatic decline in our wealth. *Limits to Growth* argued that while forward-looking policy could avoid humanity "overshooting" the earth's limits, delays in political and economic decision making meant this would be challenging. Once the earth was in overshoot, the only options would be to initiate a "managed decline" of our footprint or accept the coming collapse.

The *Limits to Growth* report quickly obtained notoriety because when it was released, attacks on the work were fast and furious and came from many quarters. Famously, Yale economist Henry C. Wallich called it "irresponsible nonsense."[9] Why such a strong response? The book was a fundamental challenge to those who believed the market was a self-correcting system that could continue to grow indefinitely. The ideas in it threatened the global assumption that the consumer capitalism model of the time would inevitably and indefinitely continue its march across the world. It was like a grenade thrown into a glasshouse.

The work was so effectively vilified that it has become accepted wisdom that the book got it wrong. In fact, the book got it close to exactly right.

The most famous and effective attacks centered on one scenario from World3 where nonrenewable resources are depleted without any societal or market response. This was a clearly unrealistic scenario, as explained in the book, but in modeling it is useful to create extreme scenarios for comparison purposes. World3 was in fact used to generate a range of scenarios, many of which—including the "business as usual" scenario—saw collapse by the middle of the twenty-first century.

Despite the lack of rigor in the attacks, they soon became accepted, and for many even today *The Limits to Growth* simply got it wrong and is lumped in the same category as the earlier Malthusian forecasts of a global famine. Denial is a powerful thing.

In fact, *The Limits to Growth* has proven to be surprisingly accurate, not just conceptually as we'll explore over coming chapters, but numerically as well. In 2008, a study was done into the modeling by Graham Turner from Australia's national science body, the Commonwealth Scientific and Industrial Research Organization, in a paper entitled "A Comparison of 'The Limits to Growth' with Thirty Years of Reality."[10]

It examined the past thirty years of actual results against the suite of scenarios in the *Limits to Growth* report and found that changes in industrial production, food production, and pollution up to 2000 compare well with the report's business-as-usual scenario—called the "World3 standard run." Interestingly, this scenario includes economic and societal collapse around the middle of the twenty-first century!

Of course, it was never the point of *Limits* to precisely forecast the future for one hundred years, a clearly impossible task. The objective was actually far simpler—namely, to establish the obvious and commonsense conclusion that if you insist on growing your footprint exponentially within finite limits, this will unavoidably lead to a crash, unless you decide to stop the growth before it is too late.

The fact that the book's forecasts are broadly on track is a remarkable outcome and a testament to the author's technical competence and system insights.

This work clearly indicated that what we were facing was not just an energy crisis, or a population problem, or a climate crisis. Rather, it was a system design problem, with "the system" being our model of consumption-based, quantitative economic growth. This meant a system design change would be needed to solve it. The work sold many millions of copies and along with *Silent Spring* was one of the defining environmental treatises of all time.

The book also triggered widespread media coverage of these issues. I clearly remember as a thirteen year old in 1972, sitting in the morning sunshine on the back veranda of the family home in Australia and being captivated as I read a newspaper series about the future of humanity. It painted a bleak picture of global crises around shortages of resources and food and forecast a society creaking under the burdens of population growth and pollution.

I recognized this was my future and that, if it unfolded as predicted, this would be a very bleak future indeed. Little did I know how deeply these ideas had entered my young mind. This was probably the moment my life's direction was set.

Some thirty years later I became good friends with one of the authors, Professor Jorgen Randers, when we both joined the faculty of the Cambridge Programme for Sustainability Leadership and taught together on the Prince of Wales's Business and the Environment Program.

When I discussed with Jorgen recently why and how he became a lifelong environmentalist, he explained that he joined the team that produced World3 and wrote the *Limits to Growth* report while completing his PhD at MIT. He did so out of intellectual curiosity about system dynamics rather than out of any initial interest in environmental issues. It was only when their analysis showed the consequences of exponential growth that his life changed track. He then became focused on advocacy to prevent what he learned from their modeling was the otherwise inevitable crash of the global economy and society, through pollution and resource depletion.

Nearly forty years later, Jorgen still maintains his passionate advocacy of the need for change, cheerfully lecturing around the world in his thick Norwegian accent and indulging his passion for visiting areas of great biodiversity that he believes will soon be largely gone.

Despite the lack of real action, from 1972 on the environmental movement built strongly. Greenpeace was founded, along with many other environmental organizations, and around the world people engaged in these issues at a broad and deep level. Greenpeace's arrival was important both practically and symbolically. It symbolized the arrival into the mainstream of global nongovernmental organizations (NGOs)—nonaligned agencies that provide a global check and balance to the behavior of governments and multinational corporations. Greenpeace also provided a practical accountability and monitoring capacity with courageous and daring confrontations, bringing environmentally destructive behavior into the living rooms of ordinary people through its powerful use of the global media.

In the face of growing public concern that was mobilized largely by these groups, strong action by regulators like the various national EPAs and their equivalents during the 1970s saw significant steps taken to address city air quality, water pollution, and other such impacts. As a result, there was considerable improvement in many Western countries, and many incorrectly saw this as the problems being addressed. Certainly it was good that rivers stopped bursting into flame, but the problems ran much deeper.

Around this time I became an activist, at the age of fifteen, focusing on issues surrounding human rights and various independence struggles, such as that in East Timor. In the mid-1970s, I became very involved in antiapartheid campaigns. I had been heavily influenced in my thinking by the massacre in Soweto, South Africa, where children even younger than me were shot and killed when protesting against not being taught in their own language. The concept of sacrificing your life for your beliefs had a deep influence on my understanding of what it meant to be an activist and how lucky I was to live in Australia.

This led to my first involvement in direct action protests, chaining myself to the gates of the South African embassy in Canberra, Australia, at the age of seventeen. I remember being a very nervous young person taking action that could lead to my being arrested. However, I was acutely aware that with the people I was supporting in South Africa being shot for their beliefs, the risks to me paled by comparison. It was an exciting time for a young seventeen-year-old, being interviewed on national radio and TV about the outrageous abuses of human rights in South Africa while I stood there chained to the gates of the embassy's main entrance. I believed I was making a difference, and it felt good.

I also remember very clearly, though rather embarrassingly, a day in 1977 when the International Whaling Commission was meeting in Canberra. On our way from an antiapartheid protest, we drove past a much larger protest against whaling by Greenpeace and others. The conversation in the car was one of moral outrage that so many people cared about whales more than they cared about people. "Why aren't they joining our protest, which is about people being oppressed and killed?" we asked. "Who cares about whales when people are dying?"

Looking back, I can see that, like most people at that time, I failed to understand Carson's argument about the interconnectedness of life and the arrogance of humanity. I saw people as superior and more important beings, from which whales were a separate and an unrelated distraction; I failed to see that protecting ocean life was about protecting the complex system that supported us. I didn't yet understand that with the whales went the watchers.

I probably should have spent more time reading Henry Thoreau and less time reading Chairman Mao!

My personal head space took a profound shift in 1979 with the birth of my first child, Callan. Even though I was just twenty years old at the time, my span of interest suddenly catapulted way into the future. Many first-time parents say this happens. You realize that along with newfound responsibility is a newfound understanding of the implications of life being handed down to future generations, not just in theory but with *your* genes being passed on to experience whatever the future holds. Once you cross that line, the future becomes a lot more personal, and so it did for me when Callan was born.

So there was a lot going on in the 1970s. Despite these efforts, the 1980s was characterized mainly by environmental disasters, including some with global impact.

During the night of December 2–3, 1984, the American-owned Union Carbide pesticide plant in Bhopal, India, released tons of toxic gases into the local atmosphere in the world's worst industrial disaster. Thousands were killed immediately, from the gases or in the panicked stampede to escape. Best estimates suggest that over fifteen thousand people ultimately lost their lives.[11] In many ways, the disaster was emblematic of the 1980s. As developed countries raised their own standards, industry in developing countries continued to implement lower standards—to make products for rich countries. Accidents like that in Bhopal put this issue of Western companies' behavior in the developing world firmly on the agenda.

On April 26, 1986, the irrelevance of borders to environmental pollution was catapulted into public consciousness. At 1:23 a.m. that day, two explosions occurred at the Chernobyl nuclear plant. A power surge had ruptured the uranium fuel rods, while a steam explosion created a huge fireball, causing the reactor's dome-shaped roof to be blown off and the contents to erupt outward. Air was sucked into the shattered reactor, igniting flammable carbon monoxide gas that caused a reactor fire that burned for nine days.

The resulting radioactive plume blanketed the nearby city of Pripyat. The cloud moved on to the north and west, contaminating land in neighboring Belarus, then drifted across Eastern Europe and over Scandinavia. While monitoring stations in Scandinavia began reporting abnormally high levels of radioactivity, there was silence from the Soviet authorities. They took three days to acknowledge there had even been an accident.

Many parts of Europe were dramatically affected by radiation poisoning drifting across the continent. Swedish food authorities recommended that moose hunters eat moose or fish no more than once a month owing to significant levels of radioactive contamination. Mushrooms, berries, and honey from the north of Sweden—where the weather had carried the radiation—could not be sold. In the years following, hundreds of thousands of culled reindeers were rejected in testing due to radiation contamination. Reindeer herding and the sale of reindeer meat largely sustains the indigenous Saami population of northern Scandinavia. The stories of this incident are still told and resonate in Sweden to this day. As well as locking in public skepticism of the safety of nuclear power, people had been given a palpable example of global interconnectedness.

The 1980s also brought one of the world's most famous oil spills by the world's least favorite oil company, when the *Exxon Valdez* spilled 250,000 barrels of oil into the pristine waters of Alaska in 1989. A legal battle followed to hold Exxon accountable for the damage—they had placed in charge of the tanker a known alcoholic, who was drunk and not on the bridge at the time the vessel ran aground. At the initial trial, a jury levied $5 billion in punitive damages against Exxon. With their enormous resources and so much money at stake, Exxon managed to drag the legal process on for decades, until in 2008 the Supreme Court cut punitive damages to just $507 million. That same year, Exxon filed a record profit of over $40 billion.

With the *Valdez* incident and the corporation's strident opposition to action on climate change, including actively financing antiscience climate skepticism to this day, ExxonMobil has earned the well-deserved nickname of the Death Star among many environmentalists.[12]

There was one significant positive development in the 1980s when the world adopted a key global environmental agreement to phase out chlorofluorocarbons (CFCs), which were creating a hole in the ozone layer. This agreement in 1987, supported by the conservative governments of

Margaret Thatcher and Ronald Reagan, remains the classic example of denial and delay by industry being followed by decisive global action once denial ends. UN chief Kofi Annan described this agreement as "perhaps the single most successful international agreement to date," and it remains a shining example of how action can be taken when business and governments decide to do so.

Some years later, as an adviser to the DuPont Company, I heard the inside view on this shift from the executives there. When DuPont's own scientists came to the conclusion that CFCs were definitely the cause of ozone depletion, the company faced an ugly reality that a whole area of their business was effectively finished. DuPont, despite being accurately targeted by Greenpeace at one stage as the "World's Biggest Polluter," has a strong ethical culture. When their scientists agreed with the problem, DuPont agreed to close down that business and cease production, well ahead of what the agreement required. This was a tough decision, as it was not yet then clear to DuPont whether they could participate in the market for alternative products.

The executives I spoke to were proud of this decisive ethical action by their company. Mind you, at the time the decision wasn't just about ethics, with DuPont correctly seeing this as a serious business issue. As DuPont's Joseph Glas said, "When you have $3 billion of CFCs sold worldwide and 70 percent of that is about to be regulated out of existence, there is a tremendous market potential."

The politics and divisions within the business community around such shifts in direction are often complex and fascinating. So whereas in 1980 DuPont had spearheaded the creation of the Alliance for Responsible CFC Policy, a lobby group fighting against regulation of CFCs, in 1986 with their change of heart they switched sides and lobbied the Reagan administration for action to ban them. DuPont's efforts culminated in the Montreal Protocol, a treaty President Reagan described as "a monumental achievement."

Some argued this was primarily about business rather than ethics. The reality is it was both. Mostafa Tolba, executive director of the UN Environment Programme, said, "The difficulties in negotiating the Montreal Protocol had nothing whatever to do with whether the environment was damaged or not. It was all about who was going to gain an edge over who; whether DuPont would have an advantage over the European companies or not." I can well believe the negotiations at this point had become intensely commercial, with governments supporting their national companies' positions. U.S. and European companies were racing one another to capture the market for substitutes, but the business decisions involved were complex. DuPont, for example, had to commit to around $500 million of investment, so timing and competitive position would have been critical business questions.

This offers a very good example of the messy reality of business in relation to environmental decision making. There *are* deeply ethical issues involved, *and* they have enormous commercial consequences. This reflects the reality of how markets behave. Businesses often have a genuine, principled commitment to ethical behavior, but the evidence suggests it is only when change is profitable and in line with market reward that they shift behavior on a significant scale. This complexity continues today with climate change, where we see constantly shifting positions by companies and industries as they come to accept that change is both necessary and inevitable but then seek to gain commercial advantage by either accelerating or slowing down the transition.

As the CFC debate raged in the mid- to late 1980s, it helped trigger the rise of the corporate sustainability movement. Many companies like DuPont realized that resistance to the emerging world of increased environmental concern was both futile and poor business strategy. Such companies decided to get ahead of the curve and be proactive in pursuing better practices.

The 1980s also saw the spectacular growth of environmental organizations around the world and strong campaigning against corporate pollution, with individual companies targeted rather than just a general push for regulation. This was the birth of campaigns targeting brands, with activists deliberately using a company's focus on its brand as a point of vulnerability, as they did with Nike over sweatshops. Writer Naomi Klein noted: "Brand image, the source of so much corporate wealth, is also, it turns out, the corporate Achilles' heel."[13] The more a company is a brand image, the more vulnerable it becomes to activist campaigns targeting that image.

This was also the era when the seriousness of fighting for environmental protection came into sharp focus, with the murder of a Greenpeace activist by a Western government. On July 10, 1985, agents from the French government's intelligence agency, the Direction Générale de la Sécurité Extérieure, acting with the approval of French president François Mitterrand, bombed the Greenpeace vessel *Rainbow Warrior* in Auckland, New Zealand. The ship was about to sail for protests against nuclear weapons tests in the South Pacific. The bombing killed crew member Fernando Pereira, photographer and father of two young children.

There had previously been many cases in the developing world where environmental activists were killed by criminal elements or secret police. However, this case, where a Western democratic government murdered an activist in a friendly Western democratic country, was a stark reminder for environmentalists everywhere of what was at stake. It was also evidence of protest groups' ability to have a significant impact on corporate and national reputation. Relatively small groups could now mobilize public opinion on a large scale with the clever use of the increasingly globalized media.

The *Rainbow Warrior* bombing and the broader public debate on the prospects for a nuclear war led me to reengage in activism from my then role as a serving member of the Australian military. I had joined the Royal Australian Air Force in 1983.

Prior to that, I had worked as labor union organizer for a Communist-led trade union, the Builders Labourers Federation, in Sydney. While I felt I was making a contribution to society by protecting workers' rights and safe working conditions, in what was at that stage a pretty shoddy industry, I soon became disaffected with the ideological obsession of the leadership and their blind support of their political beliefs. There were too many examples where the leadership was focused more on the power and influence of the union rather than on the interests of the workers. At one stage, I even spent several weeks on a picket line in a dispute with another union over who covered the workers on that site. So I left that role in 1981, and after a year of unemployment (it being quite hard to land a job when your last one was as a labor organizer!), I joined the military.

This was a great surprise to my friends and family, who assumed my political leanings would prevent such a life turn. For me it was a consistent move. I was pursuing a life of making a contribution to society, and I saw the Australian military as doing just that.

While in the military and now with my second child, Asher, born, I became very concerned about the threat of nuclear war. Being in the military naturally led to great interest in matters of national and global security—after all, this was the 1980s, with Ronald Reagan, Star Wars, and a massive global movement against nuclear weapons.

I particularly remember a newspaper story from a science conference at the time reporting that an alarming proportion of teenagers believed there would be literally no future for them, as nuclear war was inevitable. They therefore felt there was no point in working toward a better life. It struck me that whether that assumption was accurate or not, the fact that we had a generation growing up with such a view was of great concern to me as a young parent.

I believe this period of global focus on the nuclear issue, when many came to understand that we had the capacity to destroy most of life on earth with a nuclear holocaust, was critical to later developments in society's collective thinking. It provided a deep and direct understanding of the idea of intergenerational impact and that we humans could easily and irreversibly affect the entire planetary system. I think some people today still struggle to believe we really have the power to damage the earth's environment as a whole. Sure, we could destroy a river here and a forest there, but the planet is *so* big, surely we couldn't wreck it all?

The prospects of a nuclear winter—a sudden global cooling triggered by a massive nuclear holocaust coating the planet with fine dust particles—showed that in fact, yes, we could, and with just a few buttons and phone calls. It was a sobering time. We had learned to understand the implications of Rachel Carson's comment that we had "now acquired a fateful power to destroy nature."

Motivated by this threat to my children's future, I was by 1985 still serving in the military but spending my personal time active in waterborne protests conducted by an activist group, the Sydney Peace Squadron, on Sydney Harbour against visits by nuclear-armed warships from the United States and the United Kingdom. At that time, I still enjoyed serving in the military and continue to this day to have great respect for our armed forces.

While the Australia military exists in a clear democratic framework and was surprisingly tolerant of what I did on my own time, we did in the end agree that a long-term career in the military was probably not compatible with a personal life as an antinuclear campaigner, especially since our protests were against allied countries' ships. After some interesting (!) conversations with military intelligence, who came to check out my threat level, we amicably agreed to part company in 1986. I then committed myself full-time to my antinuclear campaigning; by that stage I was separated from my first wife and living with my two children.

Not being able to afford housing, the children and I occupied an abandoned government-owned house. It was badly dilapidated so we had to first rebuild the roof and put in doors and windows from scrap materials we collected. My income came from supportive activist friends and the government social-welfare payment for single parents. None of this posed a challenge as I was happily pursuing my life's purpose.

The anti–nuclear weapons movement had a great influence on the environmental debate, as it helped connect the dots on many levels. For example, it exposed the many linkages between the government military and security apparatus and the civilian nuclear power industry. It was perfect fodder for conspiracy stories and for dramatizations like the BBC's iconic TV series *The Edge of Darkness*, helping a whole generation grow up deeply skeptical about whose interests were being served by government.

After several years as an independent activist, I joined Greenpeace in late 1989 at a time when a great wave of growth had swept the U.S. and European environmental movements. Perhaps driven by the controversy around CFCs and the ozone hole on the back of the antinuclear campaigns, environmentalism had taken off in all Western countries. Membership and influence boomed as public awareness and media coverage exploded.

Companies ducked for cover as consumers railed against irresponsible behavior. This was the time when companies like Nike suddenly and unexpectedly found themselves embroiled in controversy. Nike thought their task was to make trainers and money but suddenly found themselves being expected to deal with complex social issues around social equity, workers' rights in developing countries, and different cultural expectations about the appropriate working age. It was becoming clear that some new competencies were going to be required to make money in the future.

Up until this time, environmental issues had been seen primarily as concerns in developed countries, where public support was high and regulation tightening. As a result, many companies had thought they could operate in developing countries where environmental standards were lax and wages cheap. But as the 1980s progressed, companies found that the globalization they liked because it lowered their costs was also creating a new interconnected world. Activists were joining together as a connected network, with cheap technology enabling anyone to send a message to corporate headquarters via the media. So suddenly behavior anywhere was public everywhere.

The best organization in the world at doing this in the late 1980s was without doubt Greenpeace. I joined them in 1989 to lead the Clean Waters Clean Seas campaign in Australia, which focused on exposing the more outrageous examples of corporate pollution. It was a classic Greenpeace pipe-plugging campaign, with our first direct action being to send divers to plug up the underwater discharge pipes that an oil refinery used to discharge toxic waste into the ocean. In Australia at the time, there was little effective regulation of industrial pollution. Our team secretly took samples from companies' discharge points that variously went into rivers, creeks, sewers, and oceans. Almost every discharge point we tested had levels of toxic waste way in excess of the legal limits specified in the companies' license agreements.

These were heady days for Greenpeace, with the media loving the combination of exciting and bold direct actions and the exposure of what we called "illegal toxic waste dumping" and the companies called "discharges temporarily in excess of license limits." Our political influence skyrocketed, and our direct actions captured the public imagination. It was firmly positioning us as the environmental good guys against the corporate polluting bad guys.

Most of the companies involved were clueless in their response. An infamous highlight was when the corporate PR guy from BHP, Australia's biggest company at the time, put his hand across the lens of the TV cameras to prevent them from filming and had the journalists removed from the site by the police. This of course guaranteed sympathetic media for us, with blanket coverage of our protests, including our slogan rebranding BHP as Australia's "Big Horrible Polluter"! This incident became the classic case study at PR conferences over the next decade in how not to respond to environmental protests.

While our intentions were honorable and the company's behavior clearly wrong, not to mention illegal, I often grimace in hindsight at the delight I took in confronting corporate leaders on national television and humiliating them with the evidence of their "corporate vandalism." Many of these were decent people caught by surprise with rapidly changing public expectations.

While most companies' responses were incredibly naive, one corporate CEO, Dr. Michael Deeley from the chemical giant ICI, called one day and asked if he could come and chat with me (I was by this stage CEO of Greenpeace Australia). It was a surprising move, and I immediately agreed. ICI was a key target of ours, as their Sydney chemical plant was an appalling example of poor environmental practices.

It was a fascinating meeting and started to shift my attitudes to the corporate sector and more broadly to the role of the market. It was a private meeting, and we were both candid about our situations. Deeley explained that while Greenpeace's campaigns were an issue for him, the much larger challenge was getting his organization to change its attitude toward environmental issues and to give them more priority. He talked about the old guard's attitude and the complexities of modernizing an old organizational culture.

He was clearly a decent man, and while it didn't stop us from campaigning hard against ICI over the years that followed, it certainly gave me an important insight into corporate behavior. It also made me think deeply about the dangerous psychology of "demonizing the enemy" as we had been doing to great effect. I understood he was coming to see me to avoid this, in his company's self-interest, but I started to doubt the ethics of what we were doing as well. I thought perhaps we needed to focus more on attacking the behavior and less on attacking the morality of the people behind it.

While I was still at Greenpeace Australia in 1992, one of the most important historical environmental conferences was held, the Rio Earth Summit. This conference came at a new high point in global political awareness of these issues and was attended by 108 heads of state, including George H. W. Bush. This conference started the process of global climate agreements with the adoption by consensus of a treaty agreeing to prevent dangerous climate change—the UN Framework Convention on Climate Change (UNFCCC).

I have attended many such international meetings, including the Conference of the Parties to the UNFCCC in Kyoto in 1997, which led to the Kyoto Protocol and the Earth Summit +5 in New York, also in 1997. These events are better understood as "festivals of debate" rather than meetings, with thousands of lobby groups of all persuasions battling for media and political attention on their particular agendas.

They are also important examples of our immature global governance structures. They are generally great gatherings of the elite of environmental decision making, with business, NGOs, and government representatives getting together to lament the lack of progress—like a great collective confessional!

When I attended the Earth Summit +5 review in New York in 1997, a special UN General Assembly meeting, world leaders got up one after the other and gave speeches on how appalling it was that so little progress had been made in the five years since the 1992 Rio Earth Summit. It was a strange thing to witness, as the most powerful people in the world gathered but then behaved as if they were observers of the process and had little power to influence it. Five years later in 2002, the whole process occurred again in Johannesburg at the Earth Summit 2002.

At each of these meetings over two decades, increasingly earnest speeches have been made, I'm sure mostly genuinely felt, about the critical risks that humanity faces and the urgent need for action. From the outside, it looks as though all the important people are in the room and all the power required to change the world is there, ready and able to act. Yet on the inside, what actually happens is that pretty much no one is in charge, because as we'll discuss later, the system has become so large that no one can be.

Over the fifty years of the Scream, we've learned that in reality global change is much more a bottom-up process. Our political leaders, with rare exceptions, respond at best to what they think the politics allows them to do rather than what they feel they should do. As we saw in Copenhagen, even when our political leaders are personally convinced of the need to act, the strategy of keeping one eye on what is politically acceptable at home and the other eye on protecting national economic interest merges with an immature and chaotic global decision-making process to make progress glacial.

So critically for our story, and the good news here, is that while little happened over these decades at the upper ends of political power, except for a greater understanding of the challenge, enormous strides were taken in the bottom-up process. Many, many millions have joined the ranks of the passionate and committed people working as activists, scientists, entrepreneurs, policy makers, corporate sustainability champions, and ordinary citizens. They have slowly but surely changed the way we all think, so that today everyone's an environmentalist.

When the history of environmentalism is written, 2010 will be the point when pretty much everyone was on board and has agreed: "Someone should do something!" Now all we have to do is work out who that's going to be. We'll return to this at the end of the story.

However, despite the extraordinary levels of activity, the millions of people and billions of dollars focused on the effort, nothing of any real systemwide consequence has happened in response. We have all agreed the science is clear and indicates a major problem. We have fixed this river and that town, we have saved forests here and there, we have banned numerous toxic and dangerous chemicals, and we have become highly knowledgeable, now being able to monitor the total earth system as never before.

But where have we got to in the system as a whole?

That's the next part of the story. For fifty years we've been saying we have to act on these issues or our children's children will suffer the consequences. Well, we are their children's children. So what's going to happen?

To quote Winston Churchill (November 12, 1936):

> They go on in strange paradox, decided only to be undecided, resolved to be irresolute, adamant for drift, solid for fluidity, all-powerful to be impotent. . . . Owing to past neglect, in the face of the plainest warnings, we have entered upon a period of danger. The era of procrastination, of half measures, of soothing and baffling expedience of delays, is coming to its close. In its place we are entering a period of consequences. . . . We cannot avoid this period, we are in it now. . . .

CHAPTER 3

A Very Big Problem

I have argued that humanity, the economy, and the planet's ecosystem operate as a single interdependent system and that this system is in serious trouble. We will now look at the scientific and economic evidence for this.

Our story now moves from the past to the present. This means we need to understand the condition the planet's ecosystem is currently in. What is our starting point?

At the Rio Earth Summit nearly twenty years ago, our leaders—representatives from 172 countries, including 108 heads of state—gathered in a momentous meeting that agreed protecting the environment was critical to sustained prosperity for humanity. The resulting declaration recognized many important principles that remain relevant today, such as the "precautionary principle":

> Where there are threats of serious or irreversible damage, lack
> of full scientific certainty shall not be used as a reason for post-
> poning cost-effective measures to prevent environmental deg-
> radation.[1]

They also signed on to the UNFCCC, which committed them to "preventing dangerous anthropogenic interference with Earth's climate system."[2]

So in 1992, a road map for the subsequent decades of action was set. How did we do?

Any analysis of the state of the world's capacity to support human society must be based on the physical sciences—measurement and trend analysis of actual physical activity based on our understanding of physics, biology, and chemistry. Therefore, I first want to make some comments on how nonscientists (people like me and most readers) can approach such information. I am often asked by people not involved in these issues day-to-day: "So how am I supposed to come to a view in these debates? I hear this side and that, and it just seems very confusing."

The way through this confusion lies in a combination of a basic understanding of the scientific process and some good old common sense. In explaining this, I will use climate change as an example to make my point, but the principles apply across the board to all areas of sustainability-related science, which is my focus here.

As our starting point, it is critical to understand that the scientific process is deliberately designed to encourage the questioning and challenging of ideas. This is good. Otherwise our progress to greater knowledge would be much slower and ideas that are wrong would not be exposed as quickly. Humans in general, scientists included, get attached to ideas and ways of thinking, so skepticism is healthy as it pushes against this attachment and therefore should be encouraged. This makes genuine skepticism useful in life but especially in the scientific process.

The problem comes when people with a particular agenda use the debate this healthy skepticism creates to cherry-pick science that supports their position. It gets worse when they then use that narrow piece of science as supposed "evidence" that a whole area of analysis should be in doubt. The climate debate is very challenging in this regard because that process, which occurs anyway, is further driven by powerful and well-funded interests in a systematic and deliberate way. The book *The Merchants of Doubt* explores the way this has become endemic across many issues, from tobacco to climate change.[3] A recent example on climate change would be Koch Industries, a U.S. oil and chemical giant with $100 billion in annual sales that has spent almost $25 million funding organizations involved in spreading climate denialism.[4]

The way past all this for the non-specialist is a simple one. In considering the complexity involved, you should be comfortable that no single scientist understands all the detail, either. They can't, because they have one or a small number of scientific disciplines, whereas understanding something with the complexity of the global ecosystem requires many disciplines to be considered together. Any one individual who claims to understand it all in full detail, including a number of prominent skeptics, clearly doesn't and should be treated with caution.

For this reason, the science already has a process embedded in it to deal with the challenge of cross-discipline issues and the inherent uncertainty they involve. This is important because we use scientific conclusions to guide everything from approval for medical processes and drugs to the design of bridges and the safety of airplanes. What happens is scientists come together and intellectually fight it out to reach what they call "consensus positions." Scientific bodies, either within a discipline or across a number of disciplines as appropriate to the task, analyze an area of debate, rigorously peer-review the data, argue out the uncertainties, and come to a considered, collective view based on the balance of evidence. The process also plays itself out in the peer-reviewed journals, conferences, and other academic discussions, allowing a common view to emerge over time. This is what is meant by the term *consensus*. It is inappropriately named because it implies 100 percent agreement, which it isn't, but it does represent the considered integrated view of qualified scientific experts.

It is a good example of where the collective mind is greater than the individual one. What these "consensus" positions effectively say is: "We have considered all the debate and the uncertainties, and we acknowledge them. We know what we know, but we also know where the uncertainties lie. Therefore the considered view of the top experts in the world on this topic is XYZ, and we have an ABC percent level of certainty in that view. So if you want to make a decision, this is the best advice on balance that can be provided by the science."

Because so much of the process is internal, those inside the scientific community may recognize a consensus more easily than those outside it. That is why the important scientific organizations, which work internally but also communicate externally, can be particularly useful.

When this approach is applied to climate change, it is interesting to note that *every* major grouping of qualified scientists that has analyzed the issue comes to the same conclusion and has done so consistently over time and around the world. Examples include national science academies, which are the peak science bodies across all disciplines in a given country, or major international subsets of the scientific community, such as atmospheric scientists or, at the highest and most comprehensive level globally, the Intergovernmental Panel on Climate Change (IPCC). The broad conclusion they all come to is that we face a significant risk of major change that undermines society's prosperity and stability, we are a substantial contributor to the risk, and to reduce the level of risk we should dramatically reduce emissions of the pollution that causes the problem. As with most issues in sustainability, defining the problem and the solutions is really very simple.

This "consensus position" on climate change is also reflected in the rigorously peer-reviewed journals in which research is presented and issues are debated. One study by Naomi Oreskes published in the journal *Science* demonstrated that of the papers whose abstract contained the keywords *global climate change* between 1993 and 2003, none questioned the consensus position—not one.[5] Oreskes's subsequent book *Merchants of Doubt* interestingly reveals how many of the figures who fronted the tobacco industry's antiscience campaign to deny the link between smoking and lung cancer are also now prominent and vocal climate skeptics.

A more recent study in *The Proceedings of the National Academy of Sciences* used a data set of 1,372 published climate researchers and their publication and citation history, finding that 97 to 98 percent of those climate researchers publishing most actively on the topic agreed with the tenets of climate change as identified by the IPCC. They also found the expertise and prominence of the scientists who agreed with the IPCC findings to be substantially higher than that of the scientists who did not.[6]

Of course, there are always outliers who hold a different view regarding the level of consensus on an issue, and that is good. In the case of climate change, though, this uncertainty, where it is genuine, applies to detailed subissues such as regional variations or speed of change, not to the basic conclusion. There is organized skepticism, but it comes primarily from small groups that have banded together specifically for the purpose of promoting uncertainty, as opposed to the scientific bodies that are structured to apply their expertise objectively across a scientific discipline. These organized groups leap on any mistake, such as those detailed in the so-called Climategate e-mails, and pretend it has some greater significance regarding the whole process and conclusions, even though numerous

independent reports and investigations concluded the Climategate
e-mails did nothing to question the science of climate change.[7]

So it is important to separate the two types of skepticism. On the
one hand, we have the scientific process, where outliers have a healthy
role to play in challenging dominant views and seeking to find holes in
consensus positions. On the other, we have an ideologically or commercially driven process, which deliberately seeks to undermine a viewpoint
for political or commercial gain rather than scientific inquiry. These are
increasingly called "deniers" or the "antiscience crowd," to separate them
from those genuine scientists engaged in healthy skepticism.

This separation is important to the health of science. It is dangerous
to dismiss all counterarguments to the consensus on climate science as
coming from climate denialists or as representing corrupt science driven
by coal or oil industry funding. This is not to say the latter doesn't exist,
but there is alongside it a healthy skepticism that we should celebrate
as being at the core of good science. We should be aware that discourag-
ing people who challenge the consensus risks undermining good science.

This is where common sense comes in. You should not be overwhelmed
by scientific complexity. The experts are capable of sifting that and telling us what we need to know. An inquiring mind and common sense
are all you need to draw your own conclusions.

So how do we apply this to our task with common sense?

First we need to think about how and where the science is being applied. Science at the scientific research level is about finding the "truth."
That process is generally about narrowing uncertainties until we know
with a high degree of certainty how something works and how it will
behave in different situations. This high degree of certainty is the right
approach to take when the field of inquiry or application is narrow. Examples include designing a chemical plant or a nuclear power station,
where the consequences of failure are catastrophic and immediate and
the uncertainties can be narrowed to a manageable level.

We get into trouble when we take this approach of requiring certainty and apply it to the worlds of broad policy and business strategy.
Doing so often translates into "We're not sure, so we shouldn't change
anything."

In those worlds, the commonsense approach is to get solid advice
that informs us *on balance* what is likely to happen and what the levels of

risk are in different paths. It therefore requires not certainty but broad general agreement as to direction, an understanding of where the uncertainties lie, and an analysis of what the consequences might be if those uncertainties lead to different outcomes.

It is through this framework of common sense that I view the science of sustainability. I am comfortable with a degree of uncertainty, and I recognize that we cannot know everything we'd like to know about how things will unfold.

I am uncomfortable, however, with those who argue that the uncertainties are justification for delay and inaction; that because we're not sure, we should stay on our current path. The reason this is so dangerous is that we are not dealing with normal policy or economic challenges here, where error can generally be later rectified and the course altered in response to new information. We are dealing with changes that are in some cases irreversible, at least in time frames meaningful to humanity. Failure in this particular set of issues is unforgiving.

A commonly used analogy to explain this is the medical one. If you were told you had a serious heart problem, a clogged artery that posed a very high risk of a fatal heart attack, you would respond dramatically. There would still be uncertainty, but if a doctor said you had a 25 to 50 percent chance of a fatal event in the next five years, you would not respond with, "Oh well, let me know when you're 100 percent certain and then I'll consider surgery or taking medicine." You would respond immediately, because a 25 to 50 percent chance of catastrophic failure (death) is a very high likelihood.

In summary, what this means is we should not look for certainty in our assessment of the science of sustainability, because certainty will not be found until it is too late to influence the outcome. You can't measure the future. We need instead to take a commonsense or precautionary approach—what are the scientists collectively telling us about the level of risk that we face, what are the consequences of acting early or late, and what is the right strategy to follow in response?

So in that context, let me move on to answer the first of those questions: What is the science telling us about the state of the global ecosystem and how much risk we face? Just how serious are the challenges, and what would failure in this context look like?

There have been many studies published concerning the state of the global ecosystem. As we discussed earlier, however, the danger with considering something as abstract as the "global ecosystem" is that we tend to see it as a system "over there," the place we visit on occasion. While of course Rachel Carson and others have long demonstrated the fallacy of such a view, we still struggle with it. Therefore the best way to consider the science from a human impact point of view is to take the "ecosystem services" approach—to look at those things in the ecosystem that we draw on every day for our human society and economy.

Probably the best and most comprehensive work done to date in this approach is the *Millennium Ecosystem Assessment* (*MEA*), a 2004 report that resulted from an investigation by 1,300 scientists who were commissioned by the UN to comprehensively analyze the state of the global environment.[8] The report took a human point of view by looking at the planet's ability to provide the services we take from it to nourish our lives, from basic requirements like food to the various resources we need to feed the global economy, like fiber.

This is why the *MEA* was so important. It clearly assessed the ecosystem as the underpinning of the *human* economy and society.

What the *MEA* did was to identify twenty-five ecosystem services, or categories of activity that humans use. They then assessed the peer-reviewed, quality science that analyzes the state of those services around the world and concluded how sustainable our level of use was. These included recreational and spiritual services such as tourism and the pleasure we get from nature, but the report focused mainly on direct services like fish to eat, land to grow food on, forests to provide fiber, regulation of the climate, the cleaning and provision of water, and so on.

The report's conclusion was that sixteen of those twenty-five services were being used unsustainably and, in summary:

> At the heart of this assessment is a stark warning. Human activity is putting such strain on the natural functions of Earth that the ability of the planet's ecosystems to sustain future generations can no longer be taken for granted.

I think it is important to clarify at this point the use of the words *sustainable* and *unsustainable*. They have been used so much, they have lost some of their meaning, becoming almost philosophical views rather than the literal logical terms they are.

In this case, if a system is being used unsustainably and behavior doesn't change, then it will no longer be available to use. This is a practical issue; if we don't have enough fiber, food, or water, or if we don't have a stable climate, then we simply won't have the economy or society we have now. So through this and other studies, we can now define and measure what Rachel Carson argued forty-five years ago: We are part of the environment, and our economy, health, and lives all depend upon it.

For decades in my work, I approached this issue from a values or philosophical perspective. It was my view, instinctively held, that messing with the environment was a bad idea. It was a place of extraordinary wonder and beauty, something way more impressive than anything humanity had ever created. So not looking after it was just dumb. The issue that brought this home to me most strongly was biodiversity, particularly through the lens of time. It had taken billions of years for the amazing diversity of life on earth to develop in all its dazzling complexity, brilliant design, and joyful wonder. So the idea that we were on track to wipe out 50 percent or more of all that amazing creation through our actions over just a few short centuries, for the sake of material distraction and fleeting satisfaction, was incredibly stupid. Not to mention breathtaking in its arrogance.

So for decades I presented countless speeches and workshops on these issues, appealing to people's humanity, sense of obligation, and morality to bring them along to the cause. Generally my audiences, often businesspeople, agreed with genuine earnest endorsement, but little actually changed in their lives, their organizations, or the broader community.

Then in 2005 I changed tack. When the ideas laid out in this book first became clear to me—that this issue was going to have a direct, short-term economic impact—I decided to communicate that instead.

I remember very clearly, when I presented this to a U.K. seminar of senior business executives at Cambridge University, how my new approach generated an entirely different response. I no longer argued that this was about the destruction of ecological systems or the arrogance of humanity's disrespect for nature; rather, I warned my listeners that the global economy was at risk of sudden collapse and with it their pension funds, their personal wealth, and their companies. The level of engagement in response was a quantum leap from what I had seen previously. It wasn't a wholly positive response, as I'd witnessed when I had presented on the risk to the environment. This was more sharply personal. People found the threat to the economy and to economic growth far more challenging than the threat to our planet.

My first reaction was critical, that these people cared so much about money and so little about the world. On reflection, however, I realized the criticism should be on me and my kind, that we had failed previously to communicate these issues in a way that engaged people in their lives; instead, we had preferred to stay on the ground of ethics and righteousness, perhaps believing that put us in some kind of higher moral position.

Whatever the rights or wrongs of previous approaches, what was now clear was that we had arrived at a point in history when these issues had become practical and very real. The time frame between assessment of the problem and direct economic and personal impact on people's lives had shrunk from forty years to ten or even less, and the level of engagement would now increase commensurately.

The *Milllennium Ecosystem Assessment* communicates this shift clearly. We now face threats that are not philosophical but intensely practical and personal. They are not about the balance *between* environmental protection and economic growth, but about the *causal* relationship between them. We face threats to our food supply because of excessive degradation of land and changing rainfall patterns brought about by climate change. We face further risks to food supply because of the potential collapse of fisheries both through overfishing and through broader damage to ocean ecosystems. Billions of people face increasingly urgent issues about access to fresh and clean water, both for everyday consumption and to supply industrial and agricultural processes. These and many other issues will have a direct impact on economic growth, on geopolitical and domestic security, and on our quality of life. The flow on effects of any one of these trends, let alone a number of them in combination, will be dramatic. It is important to emphasize this point—that environmental damage means economic loss—because many still don't fully accept the connection.

With fisheries, for example, the science suggests that with our current growth trajectory all global fisheries are on the path to collapse—

indeed 30 percent of them already have. A study published in *Science* in 2009 concluded that every type of fish currently consumed by people will have collapsed by 2048, defined as catches having dropped by 90 percent. When they say collapsed, they mean just that—the end of the fishing industry. With five hundred million people[9] in families that depend upon the direct and indirect income of fisheries and around one billion people relying on fish as their prime source of animal protein, the economic and social implications of collapse are profound, as the *MEA* demonstrates. We're already feeling the impact, with a World Bank study of 2008 finding that overfishing was already costing the industry $50 billion a year.[10]

We can get an idea of what this would look like by considering the smaller case study of the collapse of the Newfoundland cod in Canadian waters in the early 1990s due to overfishing. In a haunting example of sudden, nonlinear change, the catch size dropped from hundreds of thousands of tons a year to close to zero in the space of just a few years, despite a failed last-minute attempt to save the stock through the imposition of catch quotas. Along with the loss of a valuable industry, the collapse led to the loss of thirty thousand jobs and a cost to taxpayers of $2 billion in income support and retraining. If sustainable fishing had been practiced instead, the industry would today be worth $900 million a year.

Aquaculture is often proposed as a solution to declining catches. While aquaculture has theoretical potential, current practices suggest that the ecosystem economics is questionable there as well. Farmed fish species such as salmon and tuna have to be fed many times their body weight in wild fish meal, increasing inefficiency and diverting cheap fish protein catches away from local populations. The loss of ecosystem services in establishing aquaculture farms can also be huge. A 2001 study of mangroves in Thailand referenced by the *MEA* found that protecting mangroves and their existing uses returned between $1,000 and $36,000 per hectare, whereas conversion to shrimp farming returned just $200 per hectare.

When thinking of water systems and economics, we often gravitate toward the oceans, but inland water systems are tremendously important as well, and under particular strain. An estimated 50 percent of them were lost in the twentieth century. Even after this loss, the ecosystem services provided by inland water systems have been estimated at between $2 trillion and $5 trillion annually. As an example of direct human losses following environmental change, we need look no further than the Aral Sea, an inland sea and one of the world's four largest lakes, located between Kazakhstan and Uzbekistan.

Severe overirrigation originating in the Soviet era literally drained the once massive lake, so that by 2007 it had been reduced to 10 percent of its former size. Around thirty-five million people were dependent upon the lake for water, fish, and transport—services it no longer provides. The loss of water has dramatically changed the climate and is quickly turning the area into a desert, with hotter, drier summers and colder winters. With declining water quality and availability, increased dust storms, and a host of other associated problems, the region has seen its rates of a whole range of diseases increase dramatically, along with the number of children born with birth defects. Once again, environmental problems caused direct human and economic loss with surprisingly broad systemwide impacts.

The ongoing TEEB Report—*The Economics of Ecosystems and Biodiversity*—builds upon the work of the *MEA* to provide an up-to-date and quantified understanding of the value of ecosystem services. One example they provide looks at the case of deforestation in China between 1950 and 1998, where a massive increase in the logging of natural forests provided the backbone for the construction industry in a rapidly expanding economy. This period of growth has vastly improved the lives of hundreds of millions of Chinese, but it has not been without a cost. In this case, the study concluded that the loss of ecosystem services, in the form of flood damage, drought, lost nutrients, and so on, amounted to an economic loss of $12.2 billion annually. This loss amounted to almost double the market value of the timber over the same time period. For every $1 of timber sold in China, $1.78 of ecosystem services were lost.[11]

These are just a few examples of how ecosystem breakdown has far-reaching economic impacts. With ecosystem change and breakdown now under way globally, I draw two conclusions. First is that the economic impacts will be global and system threatening, and second is that these threats are no longer to our children's children, but to us. They are hitting on our watch.

So if this is the case, why have we not responded? Why do we ignore such pressing global environmental challenges yet respond so dramatically to economic ones, as we did in 2008 during the financial crisis?

The answer is that despite the overwhelming evidence, we still don't see these issues as economic ones. People hear and accept the environmental arguments, but they don't fully accept their economic impacts. So I'm often told something like this:

> Look, I get these issues are really important and I care about them deeply, but while the loss of rainforests and coral reefs would be tragic, it won't directly affect us that much in our day-to-day lives.

This is a common assertion, which I understand looking at the history of the debate. It is the legacy of environmentalists and scientists focusing for decades on the ecological impacts, framing the issues as one of protecting "the environment."

Most people still don't think they live in "the environment" but rather see that as "somewhere else," so they connect to environmental protection in an abstract way. I don't mean they think this literally and logically—people get the basic science of where humans fit into the ecosystem and evolution. I'm referring more to a kind of cultural context and resulting subconscious response.

This view is deeply ingrained. For thousands of years, humans have sought to distance themselves from "nature," which historically was a difficult environment in which to live, with many sources of discomfort and danger, from extreme weather to dangerous animals. So we have been steadily moving our society away from it and into air-conditioned houses, sealed buildings, massive sprawling cities, large comfortable "climate-controlled" cars, and so on. Not everyone can afford this, but even those who can't mostly aspire to.

So in this context, many people have engaged with environmental protection in an abstract way, separating it from their lives in both space and time. They see the threat being to the environment, as in nature—forests, polar bears, orangutans, and whales—and to the future, as in their children's children.

This natural cultural tendency has been caught in a self-reinforcing loop with what works for advocates of change. At Greenpeace we were acutely aware that our membership was more responsive to the need to "save the environment" when it was positioned as saving whales, especially if they were being killed by foreigners a long way away. In the 1990s, asking them to give up their cars was rather less popular than asking for $50 to stop foreigners from butchering whales!

All this is interesting historically but unfortunately is no longer relevant. As articulated by studies into the economic linkages to ecosystem breakdown and resource constraint, the economic impacts will be dramatic and have direct global and personal impact.

On the global scale, studies like that by Sir Nicholas Stern have put numbers on this impact in just the narrow case of climate change. In Stern's study, he concluded that unchecked climate change could lead to a 20 percent decline in gross domestic product (GDP), an estimate that appears increasingly conservative as the science progresses.

The economic implications aren't just about the direct costs of systems failing. We also need to consider the costs of creating the required alternative economic infrastructure. These costs are often put forward as a reason for delay. In fact the opposite is the case, because Mother Nature doesn't wait for us to get around to it, so the impacts keep marching on and therefore the response becomes more expensive. Again taking the example of climate change, the International Energy Agency (IEA) has concluded that every year of delay on climate change increases the cost of building the new energy infrastructure required because the necessary rate of reduction gets steeper and steeper, stranding capital assets. They estimate *every year* of delay means we will pay an extra $500 billion.[12]

The system complexity of the economic impacts of ecosystem degradation is considerable, however, explaining further why it's hard for us to incorporate it into decision making.

This complexity is brought to the fore in studies like the Stockholm Resilience Centre's report into planetary boundaries. Their innovative approach was to identify key natural systems that were critical to human civilization as it has developed and thrived. Where possible, they then defined absolute limits to changes in those systems, limits that could not be crossed without endangering our prosperity and stability. The results were summarized in the scientific journal *Nature*.[13] The study identified nine such boundaries and found that we had already crossed three of them—climate change, biodiversity loss, and nitrogen levels—and were approaching several others.

The study provides numerous examples of the interlinkages between ecosystem health and economic prosperity. For example, it showed how our efforts to increase agricultural productivity have led to us dramatically exceeding the earth's capacity to absorb our emissions of nitrogen.

Nutrients in the form of nitrogen are added to the land as fertilizer to boost crop production. However, when they are washed into the oceans, they have the opposite effect, as they encourage algal blooms and deplete oxygen levels to the point where nothing else can survive. So while in this case significant economic benefit comes from higher food productivity, significant economic loss comes from loss of drinking water, loss of fisheries, and dead rivers. It was estimated that the total economic losses from freshwater eutrophication in the United States was $2.2 billion in 2009 alone.[14]

Other studies have put a number on the total value of all ecosystem services to the economy. The most comprehensive attempt to do so was published in *Nature* in 1997 and has been cited thousands of times subsequently.[15] Based upon a thorough literature review and compilation, the team of scientists and economists who produced the report estimated that the total value of ecosystem services was between $16 trillion and $54 trillion annually, with an average of $33 trillion. They noted the uncertainties but took a conservative approach and stressed that "this must be considered a minimum estimate." Versus this figure, they noted that total global gross national product (GNP) in 1997 was around half that at $18 trillion. Recent work done by the TEEB project, led by Deutsche Bank's Pavan Sukhdev, provides valuable tools that business and policy makers can use to integrate this way of thinking into their work. While different studies will produce different numbers and details, the core conclusions are always the same. What we get from nature is fundamental to our economy, and without these inputs we would in fact produce nothing. Yet most political debates are still framed in the context of environmental protection being "nice to have" if we can afford it.

What all this means is we have clearly moved beyond needing to protect what environmentalists call "charismatic megafauna" like polar bears and pandas. We are now firmly in the space of needing to protect rather less charismatic creatures, like you and me. Let there be no doubt that if the environment crashes, the economy will go with it.

So while it is clear that environmental damage leads to economic loss, how certain are we of the underlying assessment of the environmental damage? Good science, like good business strategy, requires us to check our conclusions against other sources. In scientific language, we need multiple independent lines of evidence. In the case of the global sustainability challenge, we are fortunate to have a plethora of them.

One of the more famous, because it provides such a beautifully simple way to communicate a complex problem, is the work of the Global Footprint Network.[16] This group of scientists, under the supervision of an eminent global advisory board, takes the complexity of the various ecological services such as those detailed in the *MEA* and translates them into the area of the earth's surface needed to sustain them. To quote from their report, they take "5,400 data points for each country, each year, derived from internationally recognized sources to determine the area required to produce the biological resources a country uses and to absorb its wastes, and to compare this with the area available."

In other words, they work out how much land we would need to support our economy and lifestyle and then compare that with how much suitable land we have available to do so. By analyzing this globally, they show us how many "planets" we need to sustain our current economy—either how much more we can still grow the economy if the answer is less than one planet, or how far past sustainable capacity we are if the answer is more than one. The answer on a global scale is that in 2009, we needed 140 percent of the available land, or 1.4 planets.[17] It was just 1986 when we first went past the earth's capacity, and we've been exceeding this capacity ever since. This means we are using up our capital every day now just to survive.

It is often easier to understand the implications of this by thinking about it in terms of personal finance or of running a business.

Suppose you ran your life or your company with all your money coming from two bank accounts, one with the capital—the amount you start with—and one with income—the interest you earn from your capital. You can't obtain any more capital except by transferring it back from your interest account. For humanity, the earth is our capital: We can't create any more planet.

Each year on January 1, the interest you have earned on your capital balance is transferred into your income account, representing in our comparison all the services we take from the earth.

If you ran your life in 2009 the way we run the earth, you would have spent your whole year's interest income by September 25 and the balance would then be zero. However, you'd still have expenses after that date, so you would draw cash from your capital account from September 25 until December 31. This would decrease the balance there, but your lifestyle wouldn't be affected yet because you would have all the cash you needed. You wouldn't yet notice any difference day-to-day.

Then the next year, on January 1, 2010, your interest would be transferred into your income account again, but it would be less than last year because the balance in your capital account would be lower after your withdrawals over the last three months of 2009. In 2010, however, you would have greater need for cash (representing our growing economy), so you would have both less income *and* greater costs. As a result, in 2010 the interest income would be all gone earlier, meaning you would need to draw *more* cash from your capital account than you did in 2009.

Unfortunately, you won't be able to borrow any money to pay back in future. Why not? Because the bank would have noted that your spending was already 40 percent greater than your income and getting worse each year, so there'd be no way you could pay any loan back. Even more fundamental, if your capital account balance represents the planet, there's nothing else to lend you.

Nevertheless, in our comparison, this still works for you for a while. In fact, each year your lifestyle *appears* to get better because your expenditure is growing and you can buy more stuff, representing our growing economy. Things feel good day-to-day.

But then one year there isn't enough money in the capital account to top up your income account. It doesn't happen slowly, it all happens on the day the money runs out. Then suddenly the game is up and your personal economy falls over. You can't pay your bills and you can't buy your food. This is system collapse.

Every time a group of qualified scientists reviews the situation using different approaches, they reach comparable conclusions. In the absence of a monthly statement from the bank, these conclusions are the closest thing we have to a planetary income balance sheet. Their conclusion is we are trading insolvently.

As Joe Romm of ClimateProgress.com has observed, what this means is that the global economy is basically a giant Ponzi scheme. We are using our capital to pay out income to the investors (us), and then one day the capital will run out and the scheme will suddenly fall over.

The question in this comparison becomes, how long do we have? Is it possible to cut back our spending enough to prevent the capital from running out? Can we act to restore our capital by restoring the damage we have already done to the earth? I will answer these questions in the following chapters.

A critical approach taken by the Stockholm Resilience Centre, and one that needs to be given much more prominence, is that there are tipping points in the system that when passed can lead to systemic breakdown that self-accelerates and is irreversible. Fisheries are a good example of this. This risk requires us to set boundaries that allow for a margin of error, something we always do when we apply risk assessments to engineering design tasks. We don't, for example, define the stress levels when a plane will fall apart and then design it to operate at that limit; we allow for a large margin for error because failure is catastrophic.

The crucial significance in all these studies is not the conclusions drawn in each particular report. In the context of the scientific process discussed earlier, the significance is that *whenever* a group of credible scientists analyzes these global issues from their particular perspective, they *all* draw the same basic conclusions—we are using the earth's resources at a rate that cannot be sustained, and if we don't change, the system will at some point face a crisis, most probably a nonlinear one characterized by a disruptive, relatively sudden shift in the state of the global ecosystem.

In order to relate to these issues, people often focus on local impacts of extreme weather or natural climatic disasters. There's no shortage of examples of this playing out today, with direct human and economic impacts. In my home country, Australia, we have in recent years experienced many of them. We've had the worst drought on record, with serious impacts on our food production and collapsing river systems. We've had to urgently build expensive and energy-intensive desalination plants when we faced the prospect that some of our largest cities could run out of water. We've had the most intense wildfires on record, with hundreds killed, and we've had record heat waves that have led to hundreds more fatalities, like the heat wave (the kind that hits just once every *three thousand* years) that ravaged my hometown of Adelaide in March 2008.

As I write this book, new heat records are being set all around the world and in global averages. Pakistan is facing instability and widespread suffering from extraordinary floods. Russia has banned wheat exports after record-breaking temperatures and a severe drought threatened food supplies. Each time a record is broken or new extreme weather impacts are observed, it is easy and understandable to focus on them. However, the science says don't pay too much attention to individual events or years, focus on the global system and trends as a whole, as we've covered. This is what should concern us most.

Despite all this evidence, when I present on this topic, one of the questions I often get is something along the lines of "Surely it's not *that* bad? I understand it's serious, but environmentalists and scientists need to shock us into action, so they exaggerate, don't they?"

In response, I often refer to what a nice day it is outside, what a pleasant and safe walk I had to the venue, what a good breakfast we all had that morning after a good night's sleep in a comfortable home or hotel. My point is to acknowledge that it is really hard, in the face of all this, to internalize that the global ecosystem is on the brink of crisis, or perhaps already in one, when we don't directly feel or see the signals around us.

This is a human response based on instincts we have developed over millions of years. We respond to danger that is physically close and immediate in time. This response has served us well, when the neighboring tribe attacked or when there was a tiger at the cave entrance.

So here we are in the modern era with the same instincts. For most readers, things are good, life is interesting, our needs are met, and the environment we see every day seems pretty good. Sure, there are issues, but it doesn't feel as if we're on the verge of systemic collapse, that's for sure. We focus instead on tonight's dinner, the project we have due at work, or the challenge we're facing in our relationship.

The problem is that we don't sense any danger in our physical, instinctive senses. Those who do, such as those facing wildfire, drought, or flood, respond to that immediate challenge, focusing on their personal safety and protecting their friends and family.

To understand the threat we face here, we have to resort to global ecosystem science, an area most people find intimidating and confusing. However, we simply have no choice. Given the time it takes to change human instincts, we are going to have to work with what we've got!

So my response to this question is that you either accept the science, articulated by groups of experts and based on a rational assessment, or you don't. This is the way it is, because most of us don't see, and critically *won't* see, sufficient physical manifestations of ecosystem collapse in our lives until the process is well and truly under way.

So the answer is yes, it really is that bad, and as we covered earlier, the scientific consensus is clear on that point.

So to summarize, this is our baseline, the place from where we can start to discuss how the future is likely to unfold. We have a problem, a Very Big Problem, because we have already passed the limits of the planet's capacity to support our economy. Limits that when crossed are unforgiving and will impact us directly.

So what happens next?

Here we must first dive deeper into the problem, but don't worry, I promise I will bring you back out again. So stay with me for the whole ride!

CHAPTER 4

Beyond the Limits—
The Great Disruption

The plans we have been making for our economies, our companies, and our lives have all been based on a key assumption that is clearly wrong. This assumption is that our current economic model will carry on unless we *choose* to change it—in other words, no action means more of the same.

This is not surprising. For fifty years, eminent scientists, economists, and philosophers have correctly presented these issues as a warning rather than a forecast—*if* we don't change, *this* will be the result. In this context, *choice* has framed the debate—the choice to change before the consequences become serious.

That has led to endless debates, scientific, philosophical, ideological, and political. Many argued the warnings were wrong, or at least exaggerated. Others argued the warnings were right but that we would comfortably address them in the natural course of events. They argued humans are smart and always come up with new technologies and behaviors through the market. We would fix the problems and so avoid the consequences we would otherwise face. Others have argued that consumerism is a bad culture for humanity—that it leads to bad social outcomes and lives without meaning—so we should try to develop a better economic model for society in order to enhance our quality of life.

Many of these debates continue today. My message is that you can now leave them all behind. They are of relevance only to historians. We didn't change. So now change will be forced upon us by actual physical consequences. Here's why.

It's all about the math, and it's simple math at that. We have an economy, tightly integrated into an ecosystem that is already operating at about 140 percent of capacity, as we discussed earlier. While different studies have variations in the details, at its core this conclusion is not conjecture; it is scientific fact.

Now we plan to run that economy faster and harder. First we plan to increase the population to over 9 billion by 2050. The UN high projection sees a population of 10.5 billion, but let's work with the medium projection of just over 9 billion.[1] This amounts to an average annual growth rate of about 0.7 percent over the coming decades. Even under the UN's most optimistic projection, we'll still be dealing with a staggering 8 billion. So going forward, we can assume an increase in population of approximately a third. So that gives us a Very Big Problem times 1.33. That would by itself present a Very, Very Big Problem, but that's just the beginning.

We also plan to grow per capita income around the world even faster than we are growing the population. According to International Monetary Fund (IMF) and Australian Treasury estimates, by 2050 we can expect global output per capita to be three times the size of output per capita in 2005.[2] This amounts to a growth of around 2.5 percent each year. Let's make this clear—this means that year after year, each individual produces and consumes 2.5 percent more than the year before, meaning that by 2050, the world economy would be around three times larger than that of 2005—*even if the population didn't grow at all*.

Goldman Sachs has another set of data and predictions that reach similar conclusions. They forecast that while per capita GDP will approximately double in the G7 developed economies by 2050, the real growth in per capita income will occur in the BRIC (Brazil, Russia, India, and China) and N-11 (Next Eleven, the large developing economies that along with the BRIC have the potential to overtake the G7 as the world's largest economies this century). In these economies, Goldman Sachs sees per capita income increasing on average by almost ten times between 2006 and 2050.[3] These countries already are (in the case of China) or are rapidly becoming the world's major economies.

When we add population increases to per capita income increases, we can see a world in 2050 where the economy is many times the size of today's. According to the IMF and Australian Treasury figures, it will be five times larger. According to accounting firm PricewaterhouseCoopers (PwC), we can forecast an average global growth rate of 3.2 percent a year in purchasing power terms until 2050, which over forty years means an economy more than 3.5 times larger than today's.[4]

So now we have a Very Big Problem times 3.5 or maybe times 5. That's a planet now running at 140 percent of capacity that will subsequently run at somewhere between 500 and 700 percent of capacity. Yes, it is true, that there is potential for significant efficiency gains that will decrease resource use and pollution per dollar of output, but that has a natural limit—we can make things lighter and cleaner, but in the end we still have to make them. This combined with the fact that we keep making more of them means efficiency gains will not even come close to compensating for the growth we plan for. Consider the following.

Over the thirty years to 2009, world resource use per unit of GDP decreased by 30 percent. That means that each year on average, we have used our resources 1.2 percent more efficiently than the year before.[5] This trend in the use of general resources has largely been matched in the particular case of energy use, with energy use per unit of GDP declining 33 percent between 1970 and 2007, or about 1.1 percent per year.[6] If such trends continue, we'll be using resources 38 percent more efficiently by 2050. This seems like good progress.

And yet as suggested by the earlier numbers, such "decoupling" or efficiency gains have been far offset by rising per capita incomes and population growth—in fact, as we'll come back to, increased efficiency seems to actually encourage increased consumption. So since 1990, the Kyoto Protocol base year, emissions have risen 40 percent despite these efficiency gains. When each of us demands and expects our incomes to increase 2.5 percent a year, using 1.2 percent less resource per dollar of income doesn't avoid the overwhelming logic—our environmental impact continues to grow and grow. Today, as a global average, an individual consumes 22 kg of resources each day—but regionally, consumption ranges from just 10 kg for the average African to 100 kg for the average Australian. On current trends, we can expect that to continue rising.

Putting the numbers together, including continued efficiency gains, we plan to create an economy which in 2050 is running at somewhere between 300 percent and 400 percent of capacity. Based on their own data sets and projections, the Global Footprint Network has warned that we are on course to be running at 200% of capacity by the early 2030s—two planets' worth.[7] Having only one planet makes this a rather significant problem.

Consider as well that when I say we plan to grow the economy by this amount, this is not just a casual forecast or the current policy. This is the absolute underpinning idea behind the global economy and society and is pursued by virtually all participants with steely determination and political focus. With few exceptions, every government regardless of its political system believes it must deliver economic growth to its constituents or it will be removed from power. So even taking the lower PwC estimate, our economy will be 3.5 times bigger than today's. That's the overwhelming logic of compound growth—a seemingly small growth of 3.2 percent in purchasing power each year produces a global economy that doubles in size *every* twenty-two years. So if we start at 140 percent of capacity in 2009, then twenty-two years takes us to 280 percent of capacity in 2031 and forty-four years takes us to 560 percent in 2053.

It is *not* going to happen.

Not because it's economically, environmentally, and politically challenging. Not because we don't want it to happen. Not because doing so would damage the environment. It's not going to happen because achieving it would defy the laws of physics, biology, and chemistry or of mathematics. Those laws are firmly established and are not negotiable.

This means the assumptions we are all making about global society—that we will bring the poor out of poverty, that we will carry on creating jobs, food, and basic needs for the more than two billion new global citizens and the existing seven billion or so, that we in the West will continue to increase our financial and material standard of living, that the world, despite conflicts here and there, will carry on in relative stability—are a grand delusion.

I repeat—it's not going to happen.

So what will? We will face the Great Disruption. First, the economy will simply not grow. The earth is full; there is nowhere to put an economy that is twice the size of the earth, let alone five times the size. We will try hard to grow it; indeed, we will throw everything we have at the task, as we did when growth stalled in 2008. We will have some success, and growth will occur in individual countries and companies, and at different times it will occur globally for periods. But it will not happen on a significant scale or for sustained periods, for many decades to come. It will be prevented from doing so by the physical constraints of resource availability and the physical response of the global ecosystem, particularly the climate, on which our economy depends.

The faster we grow, the faster we will hit the limits and the harder and more dangerously we will bounce off them. So ironically, our obsession with economic growth will force the end of economic growth.

While our economy overall stagnates within this cycle of growing and shrinking for several decades, with all the associated political, social, and economic challenges that will present, we will also have to deal with the human and economic consequences of the systemic breakdown of the environment on which we depend.

In combination, this means we are entering a period of economic stagnation, geopolitical instability, and ecological chaos, during which we will need to both cope with all of that *and* begin the process of reinventing the global economic and political model under which we operate. I am confident that the latter will be part of the mix because there are only two ways this can unfold.

As happens with any system facing its limits, we will either shift to a higher order of existence or break down to a lower-order system. In other words, we will either evolve to a more intelligent, conscious, and stable civilization or we will enter what James Lovelock believes is inevitable, our terminal decline, or what Jared Diamond would call collapse. Either way, we're now, in my view, inevitably going to pass through a rough patch on the way there, and in the geopolitical, economic, and climate chaos involved I expect we'll tragically lose a few billion people.

Mmm. A moment for reflection . . . maybe a few moments. . . .

At this point, everyone who confronts this logic will have one or more of the following emotional responses. A common response is despair and a sense of the utter hopelessness of it all. Understandable. Some go to anger, either at themselves for being part of this idiotic behavior or at the world and those in charge for leading us here. Others go into denial, either "Oh, we've heard all this before, we always sort it out and we will again" or "What a lot of rubbish, the science is wrong, your analysis is flawed." Personally, I've had all of these responses, even the last one, and considered them each carefully.

In the end, I have always come back to the overwhelming logic of the math, the science, and the rigor of the scientific process. People will always argue about different models, numbers, and forecasts. They will do different analyses and present alternative scenarios. The problem we face is not affected by such disputes because the scale of the problem is so clear. Running at 140 percent of capacity, then trying to increase output to even just 200 percent of capacity, let alone to 500 percent or 700 percent of capacity, means we are going to hit the wall.

Over the past five years, I have presented these ideas to business, political, and community audiences around the world and answered thousands of questions in response. The most common responses, other than stunned silence, are the "Yes, but what about . . ." questions.

So let's deal with these questions first, while you're working through the emotional responses to the inevitability of what I'm arguing. We'll return to the latter, including why I now live with great hope, after you've had a little time for your right brain to process your emotional responses while your left brain is reading! I separate these two types of responses because we need to consider our situation with our whole being and give legitimacy to both logical *and* emotional responses.

Applying logical, rational thinking helps ensure we don't live in artificial hope or become misled by our ideological beliefs or what we *want* to be the case.

I find this is best done using the mathematical equation famously expressed by Paul Ehrlich and others some forty years ago.[8] The Ehrlich equation, $I = P \times A \times T$, states that environmental impact (I) of human activity is a product of the size of the population (P) times the affluence or income level per person (A) times the technological intensity of economic output or the impact associated with each dollar we spend (T).

What this says is that only three core things drive our environmental impact: population, affluence, and technology (including our behavior with it). This means we have only three levers we can pull to lower our environmental impact. We can have fewer people, we can have less affluence, or we can have lower impact per dollar spent, through either better technology or change in our behavior with that technology.

Remembering this equation helps us analyze the issue based on the data rather than on what we want to be true.

Within the context of those three levers, I will give you my answers to the three questions I am most often asked when I present these arguments.

1. The problem is population. There are just too many people, so we should focus on that.

2. When the impact hits we'll respond and fix it. It will be difficult, but it won't be a crisis. Markets and technology are remarkable.

3. We can just grow the economy in a different way, with fewer materials, less energy, and more renewable resources.

The first question is very popular, especially in Western countries. It's usually something like "So the problem is population, isn't it? There're too many people, so we should just fix that!"

This is a consistent response to these issues and has been for decades. The answer lies in the numbers of the mathematics and the politics of reality.

First to the mathematics, remembering the critical equation $I = P \times A \times T$. What this shows is that while population is a lever we could pull, even if we did, the impact, while certainly helpful, would not solve the problem. The UN forecasts for world population increases reflect an average growth rate of around 0.7 percent over coming decades, to reach a peak population of just over nine billion by 2050 under the medium projection. So the nature of compound growth means that even a substantial reduction in the population growth rate would soon be overwhelmed by economic growth on a per capita basis, predicted to grow by about 2.5 percent each year, thus outrunning population growth rates considerably. I will give you an example of the comparative impact shortly.

The second challenge, of course, is the politics. While individual nations (most notably China) can and have acted on their own populations, there is no realistic chance that we could reach a global agreement to slow global population growth in the countries we need to in any meaningful way. We should remember here the comparison between growth rates in per capita wealth vs. growth rates in population. What they mean is that even a 50 percent reduction in the population growth rate, which would require a herculean effort, would actually have only a small impact on the trends we're discussing.

To really have a substantial impact on the forecast environmental impact, we would need to dramatically *reduce* the global population by a significant percentage from what it is now. Given that we struggle even to slow the rate of *growth*, a deliberate strategy to reduce the population is not going to happen. We will return to whether it might happen involuntarily, but it certainly won't be a strategy we deliberately pursue to avoid the crisis. It's also worth bearing in mind that with 2050 less than forty years away and average world life expectancy now almost seventy years, many of the people of 2050 are already around today or soon will be.

So back to our core equation; the population lever is clearly broken, and pulling it would have little impact.

The most common question I get to my arguments from those who disagree is something along the lines of "Surely when the impact becomes clear for all to see, we can then change quickly and fix this without a major crisis. After all, haven't we fixed many of our environmental and social problems in the past?"

Or it's put as "There's always been doom-and-gloom forecasts, but we always make it through. Markets and technology are remarkable and will deliver again."

I have some sympathy for this view, and I have really challenged myself on this one. It's always seemed to be the most likely reason I was wrong. After all, history has seen humanity face many crises and respond effectively. There have also been a remarkable series of extraordinary technological breakthroughs, often surprising ones, that have reshaped society and/or have addressed what would otherwise have caused a monumental crisis. Take the examples of World War II, which we will consider later; the agricultural green revolution of the 1960s onward, which saw food production in developing countries more than double;[9] and the rapid growth of information and communications technology.

It is also true there are some remarkable and exciting technologies and business models both under research and in the process of commercialization that could have massive impacts on the "T" in our equation.

But even if technology could fix the underlying problem, it cannot prevent a major crisis from happening first. I will explain why in a moment.

Nor do I approach this philosophically as a person opposed to technology or to markets. Indeed, I have now spent fifteen years advocating the power of markets to drive change in this area and running companies delivering that change. So my natural sympathies are in that direction because I recognize the enormous potential to drive change at speed and scale globally through well-directed markets.

However, a sensible and calm analysis of the idea, applying not belief or hope but mathematics and science, gives us the answer to the question of whether markets and technology can save us from the crisis. The answer is, in short: "No, not this time."

There are two reasons, one of which (around the scale and speed of the change required) I'll come back to. The most important reason, however, is based in science. It is the lag between the action of emitting pollution or causing other ecosystem damage and the impact on the system of those emissions or damage. This of course also translates into a lag between reducing those emissions or impact and there being a benefit to, or restoration of, the global ecosystem.

While we work in an economic system of annual targets, quarterly profits, and twenty-four-hour news cycles, the planet works in longer and more complex cycles. And, as U.S. senator Gaylord Nelson reminded us, "the economy is a wholly owned subsidiary of the environment, not the other way around."

For example, the consequences we are seeing in the climate today are being caused largely by pollution emitted decades ago. As greenhouse gases trap heat in the atmosphere, much of that energy is absorbed in the upper layers of the ocean, meaning that temperatures are not immediately observed to increase. It's only after the ocean has warmed up that we start noticing the impact of that CO_2 on the climate and land-based ecosystems, a delay that is measured in decades. This observation caused the National Academy of Sciences to caution as early as 1979 that "we may not be given a warning until the CO_2 loading is such that an appreciable climate change is inevitable."[10]

Once we start noticing this warming, a lot more of it is already locked in given how long CO_2 sticks around in the atmosphere, with some remaining there for over a thousand years after release.[11] And it keeps warming the planet the whole time.

This principle applies to many environmental issues, making this lag an ecosystemwide problem, not just a climatic one. Examples include the acidification of the oceans (that at some point can prevent coral reefs from being formed and stop shellfish from having shells) and the ozone layer, which kept deteriorating long after we addressed the causes and may take until the next century to recover. Furthermore, many of these systems tend to act in nonlinear ways. They resist change while trying to absorb our impact, and then approach a tipping point, where they change rapidly or collapse. Likewise when we address the causes, recovery can take a very long time, if it occurs at all.

This means when we look around now and see the arctic sea ice melting, the glaciers disappearing, food supplies diminishing, and wildfires causing death and destruction, Mother Nature would like you to know "You ain't seen nothing yet." This is just the warm-up act.

What this means as a system tendency is that even if we had a dramatic societal response, which we will at some point, the momentum for change already built into the physical processes of the earth's ecosystem means the impacts would continue for decades to come. To slow this down, we would not only have to reduce our impact (for example, cut CO_2 emissions), but also actively restore the system (actually remove CO_2 from the atmosphere so our net impact was to *reduce* concentrations). Doing so in the case of CO_2 is imaginable, though very challenging. Doing so across the whole range of global ecosystem services at sufficient speed to overcome the various lags is stretching probability. I wouldn't rate it as impossible, but I certainly wouldn't be betting our future on it.

This doesn't mean we can't do anything. In fact, it means we must and will do even *more* extraordinary things. And when we do respond, it will be with breathtaking speed and scale, and it will drive the biggest economic and industrial transformation in history. This is the fun part we come to later in our story.

My point on technology as the solution is simple. It's not that technology is not crucial; it most certainly is. It's just highly unlikely that it will be physically possible to drive new technology and its adoption fast enough to overcome the inertia for ecological change already in the system—sufficiently to prevent an economic and social crisis.

This is particularly so given that the challenge is not primarily a technical "is it possible" one, but more a political/economic one. In this context, what the lag means is that we will be fixing the causes of future problems (such as reducing current emissions) while also dealing with the economic and social consequences of yesterday's behavior (for example, dealing with rapid climate change, famine, and the like). This need to respond to past behavior will undermine our economic and political capacity to reduce future impact. An example might be the collapse of the global insurance industry in the face of rapid changes in the physical climate.

The momentum driving ecological change in the system is just too powerful to overcome smoothly. When the scale of change required to keep the issue from becoming a crisis is translated into arithmetic, as we'll do shortly, it defies belief that it can be achieved. So, yes, I believe in markets, I just don't believe in miracles that ignore the laws of physics and mathematics.

The final straw clutched at by market-focused technology optimists is that we can avoid the crisis by decoupling material and energy growth from economic growth. This has long been the holy grail of corporate sustainability experts and has been advocated by many, including myself until five years ago, as the solution to the growth dilemma.

The idea is that we can shift the structure of the economy away from stuff and pollution. We would move to renewable energy and resources and drive dramatic resource efficiency improvements, thereby using less and cleaner material and energy per unit of economic output. It assumes we can do so at sufficient speed and scale that economic growth can occur while total absolute environmental impact is dramatically reduced.

It is a good idea, and it is the right direction for the economy. Indeed, the focus on the concept has led to some very good business ideas that are being implemented around the world, like a shift from selling physical products to selling services. A good real-world example is the idea that we should buy the service of air-conditioning rather than the equipment. The logic is that we don't want to own a machine, we want the air at a certain temperature and humidity, so we buy that service. The company we buy it from then owns the machine and pays the energy bill, so they would be encouraged to design it for longevity, recyclability, and efficiency because the company rather than the customer would bear the costs of repair, disposal, and energy consumed. The company would be incentivized to improve these, as they would get the resulting savings. This approach has long been applied in commercial photocopiers, where you can pay by the page.

Another example is the sustainability-focused carpet company Interface, led by the legendary sustainability-focused CEO Ray Anderson. They promote an "Evergreen Carpet" lease, where the customer pays for the service of having their floors covered. Interface is then incentivized to produce the carpet in a way that minimizes life cycle costs, including making the materials recyclable and hard wearing.

So why can't we pursue decoupling by putting in place structures like these that incentivize efficiency? We can and will. The challenge is that we again face the problem of the math. Returning to Ehrlich's formula, we are in this case dealing with the T in $I = P \times A \times T$.

An excellent study on this topic was published in 2009 by the U.K. government's Sustainable Development Commission. Initiated under the chairmanship of my friend Sir Jonathon Porritt, this study, *Prosperity Without Growth*, was led by Professor Tim Jackson and offers an outstanding summary of the issues.[12]

The report presents some fascinating scenarios to 2050, using just the challenge of decoupling economic growth from CO_2 emissions to achieve 450 parts per million (ppm) of CO_2 concentrations. Keep in mind when reading these numbers that most scientists regard 450 ppm as an inadequate target, so the actual challenge is much greater than that expressed here.

It should also be noted that CO_2 is one of the *easiest* decoupling challenges because energy can be produced with no CO_2, whereas making cars without metals or plastics, for example, would be more difficult.

The study used the measure of grams of CO_2 emissions per dollar of economic output to compare across the scenarios. In 2007, this measure was 768 g of CO_2 per dollar globally. They give four potential scenarios going forward to show the scale of change required in this, the *easiest* decoupling challenge:

1. Under the midrange forecast of nine billion people and assuming economic growth continues as it has since 1990 at 1.4 percent per annum, we would require CO_2/$ to decrease from 768 g CO_2/$ today to 36 g CO_2/$ in 2050, representing a 95 percent reduction.

2. With the upper forecast of eleven billion people, it would require a reduction to $30\,g\ CO_2/\$$.

3. If we assume that we deal with poverty and have nine billion people in 2050 at a per capita income equivalent to that in the European Union in 2007 (that is, no further per capita growth in the West), the target drops to $14\,g\ CO_2/\$$.

4. If we assume every country is broadly equal and the standard of living is based on the EU in 2007 but grows globally at just 2 percent per year, then we need to achieve a reduction from $768\,g/\$$ to $6\,g/\$$, or a reduction of around 99.2 percent.

There are a few key lessons from these numbers.

First, they strongly reinforce that population growth, while material, is not the key driver of the problem compared with per capita economic growth.

Second, they show that the scale of change required is quite extraordinary. Even scenario three with a midrange population and equal incomes with *no* further growth in the developed world requires an improvement in efficiency of 9 percent *every* year for forty years and results in an economy *six times* as large as today's!

Third and most important, this is just the herculean task required to achieve action on climate with a growth economy. That is clearly the *easiest* challenge compared with finding the forest, land, fish, food, transport, minerals, and water to feed an economy six times the size of today's.

Further complicating this strategy is what is known as "the rebound effect." What happens when products become more efficient is that we use more of them. So as cars become more fuel-efficient through better engine technology, we make our cars heavier; as home appliances become more efficient in power use, we buy bigger ones; as air-conditioning becomes more efficient and therefore cheaper, we air-condition more homes. This means that as long as we consider only technology, rather than also considering per capita consumption, we'll keep bouncing back and hitting the limits again.

As I said earlier, the *Prosperity Without Growth* scenarios consider only CO_2 emissions, a significant challenge but still possible. But given that decoupling is about every resource that feeds the modern economy and we're operating at 140 percent of capacity now, there is no conceivable decoupling scenario involving economic growth that sees us bringing the situation under control in time to avoid a crisis.

As the report itself concludes:

> The truth is that there is as yet no credible, socially just, ecologically sustainable scenario of continually growing incomes for a world of nine billion people. In this context, simplistic assumptions that capitalism's propensity for efficiency will allow us to stabilise the climate or protect against resource scarcity are nothing short of delusional.
>
> Those who promote decoupling as an escape route from the dilemma of growth need to take a closer look at the historical evidence—and at the basic arithmetic of growth. Resource efficiency, renewable energy, and reductions in material throughput all have a vital role to play in ensuring the sustainability of economic activity. But the analysis in this chapter suggests that it is entirely fanciful to suppose that "deep" emission and resource cuts can be achieved without confronting the structure of market economies.

I'm most certainly not dismissing the core idea of decoupling or greater resource efficiency. There are enormous benefits on offer in such a strategy, and we will have to pursue it vigorously. My question at this point is simply, "Can we avoid a systemwide crisis?" and my conclusion is that decoupling and efficiency will not come close to that objective, even though they must be pursued for other reasons.

To summarize where we are at this stage:

- We have established that the challenge we face is clear, logical, scientifically based, and broadly accepted.

- We have identified that bringing the earth's economy within its operating limits is a herculean task with the size of our present economy.

- The math indicates it is an inconceivable task if we carry on growing the economy even modestly.

- It is clear that markets and technology will not be capable of adjusting at the scale required.

- We have observed that despite all this evidence, humanity is not yet responding with any substantial action at the global scale, let alone with the massive warlike intervention we clearly need.

- The science tells us that the lag in the ecosystem between emissions and impact means there is now great momentum racing through the system toward us.

- The lack of response to date indicates that the inertia against change in human society and the global economy is very powerful. Given that the change we need to make is much, much greater than the change we're already resisting, it is clear this resistance will continue and probably strengthen.

- This means any hope that we can mobilize the massive intervention required to *avert* the crisis is a false hope.

In combination, this evidence all points to one conclusion. We cannot now avoid the crisis of the Great Disruption.

How will this manifest?

If you thought the financial situation in 2008 was a crisis, and if you thought climate change was a cultural, economic, and political challenge, then hold on for the ride. We are about to witness humanity deal with its biggest crisis ever, something that will shake it to the core—the end of economic growth.

CHAPTER 5

Addicted to Growth

> The global economy is almost five times the size it was half a century ago. If it continues to grow at the same rate the economy will be 80 times that size by the year 2100.

So explains Professor Tim Jackson, who is being joined around the world by a chorus of experts now arguing that we have to question economic growth. It seems so obvious to question growth. Indeed, as argued by economist Kenneth Boulding: "Anyone who believes exponential growth can go on forever in a finite world is either a madman or an economist." Yet growth is the underlying driver behind all economic policy and a sacred tenet of global capitalism.

The numbers referred to by Jackson and others clearly show we will inevitably see an end to economic growth at some point. While there is debate on the timing and the trigger, it is hard to argue that growth can continue forever. As we showed earlier, dramatically increasing efficiency or decoupling material growth from economic growth may at best buy us a bit of time. However, at some point we are going to have to face the reality that we live in a finite world.

So does this really pose a challenge? Can't we just transition with a few bumps along the road to a new model, recognizing the game is up on the old one?

Yes, we will transition, but the bumps will be more like earthquakes and the transition will shake us to the core, forcing a substantial rearrangement of human values, political systems, and our physical lives. There are two reasons for this. One is that we won't change until we're forced to by actually hitting the physical limits, meaning we'll change rapidly and through a crisis. The second reason is that growth is interwoven into the fabric of modern society. We'll come to crisis later, but first let's take a good look at growth.

I mentioned earlier that a few years ago I shifted the focus of my speeches from the unfolding global ecological tragedy to the short-term economic implications of ecosystem breakdown and resource scarcity. I particularly focused on the inevitable end of economic growth. As a result, the response of my audiences shifted from earnest concern and broad agreement to genuine engagement and serious controversy.

Then and since, the issue that grabs attention about my Great Disruption thesis is not the demise of 50 percent of global biodiversity, or the civilization-threatening changes to the global ecosystem over the coming century, or the potential for the reshaping of the global geopolitical landscape. No, what grabs attention is the prospect that we are facing the immediate end of economic growth.

We just love growth; it frames the political and economic strategy of every government in the world, democratic or not. It frames the strategy of every company and certainly determines the longevity of board directors, CEOs, and corporate executives in their roles. It is not, however, just about "those in charge," it is for most people one of the key measurements of progress through life. We generally consider our success over time in the context of whether we see growth in our levels of assets, income, and financial security along with all the material manifestations of this, in our homes, cars, and lifestyles. We have also linked this to our emotional security and sense of self-worth.

So because growth is so closely entwined with our economic system and our personal and political expectations the end of growth is not going to be a smooth process. As population grows, we need more jobs, and that requires growth. That becomes more difficult because technological efficiency and productivity improvements drive down the number of people needed to create the goods we produce. If the economy doesn't grow fast enough to overcome these efficiency improvements and deal with population growth, unemployment goes up, spending goes down, fewer products are produced, and fewer jobs are created. So growth gives us a high when it's happening and a nasty crash when it's not. It's an addictive cycle that will be hard to kick.

Our addiction to growth is a complex phenomenon, one that can't be blamed on a single economic model or philosophy. It is not the fault of capitalism or Western democracy, and it is not a conspiracy of the global corporate sector or of the rich. It is not a bad idea that emerged in economics, and it is not the result of free market fundamentalism that emerged in the 1980s with globalization. While each of those factors is involved, it is too simple and convenient to blame any of them as the main driver. Growth goes to the core of the society we have built because it is the result of who we are and what we have decided to value.

So the fact that it is finished, at least in its current material form and indeed in any form for some decades to come, is going to strike at the heart of modern society. While the end of growth is actually a symptom of the underlying crisis—the crash of the global ecosystem—it is this symptom that will be seen as the actual crisis, at least initially.

This is because a growth-based economy has gone well beyond being a policy, a desire, or a mode of operating that is judged to be superior to the alternatives. As we have seen, growth is now an addiction—and addicts resist change with increasingly complicated, desperate, and (in the end) delusional excuses. Anyone who has dealt with an alcoholic or other addict knows that denial, in the face of mounting evidence, slips slowly into lies and deceit. The justifications as to why the addiction is not an addiction and why the consequences are not as bad as they seem get more and more bizarre and separated from any objective reality.

It changes only when the consequences of the addiction become so overwhelming, direct, and all-encompassing that self-delusion can no longer be maintained and a decision to change breaks through the fog of denial.

This is how it will be with economic growth.

I want to be crystal clear here that I am not arguing *in favor of* the end of economic growth. I certainly could do so because there are credible arguments that economic growth no longer serves its own purposes of improving the quality of life for those out of poverty. We will return to this later. The desirability of growth is largely irrelevant to the coming crisis because that will not be the driver of change.

What I am arguing is that growth has effectively ended for reasons that are now locked in. We need to adjust to this new reality because it will trigger a global crisis, and how we respond to this crisis will determine the future of humanity, not to mention the planet's ecosystem.

But first, back to the addiction. The idea and motivation behind growth is not bad. It's probably comparable to the use of alcohol. People drink for various relatively healthy and socially acceptable reasons: the desire to socialize and share an experience, the wish to break down barriers, the enjoyment of the taste, or a delight with the whole cultural package of production, flavor, and socializing such as that experienced by wine lovers. None of these things are bad or destructive in themselves. However, the death and tragedy caused by drunk driving, the health impacts to an alcoholic of excessive consumption, or the alcohol-fueled violence and abuse of family members can all be truly devastating.

Likewise with growth: There are many drivers behind it, and many results of pursuing it, that are good and have served humanity well. While it can be argued that it no longer serves us well, the original motivation was not bad. There is nothing wrong with wanting to improve your quality of life, to enhance your comfort, to increase your financial security in later years, or to enjoy quality entertainment.

Extreme poverty, by comparison, has no redeeming features. I make a distinction here between poverty and living a simple life, which some argue has inherent value. For others, simplicity is chosen from a religious belief that the lack of possessions enhances the clarity and focus of spirituality. But neither of those is poverty; both are lifestyle choices or belief systems.

True poverty stinks and the alleviation of it for many millions of people has been one of the great outcomes of economic growth over recent decades and has enhanced many people's lives. Likewise, going further back, economic growth enabled greater food security and urbanization and gave humanity the freedom for some people to specialize in roles that have considerably enhanced the quality of life for all of us. Examples include health services, energy technologies, and reliable food supply, along with sources of joy and insight such as music, art, and literature. Many of these developments have increased the true prosperity of our lives.

So the problem is not the idea of prosperity or its pursuit; the problem is the abuse and addiction of the drug at the center of our current economic model. This drug and the artificial "high" it delivers corrupts the reasonable and sensible pursuit of prosperity. This drug is the idea that increasing wealth, and in particular the material possessions bought with that wealth, is at the core of improving our prosperity.

The good news is that while we have an addiction problem, there are treatments in the advanced stages of development that are currently undergoing clinical trials. We now know when and how real quality of life improves and what causes these improvements. There has been extensive research and investigation under way around the world, the results of which we will return to. In summary, what it tells us is that we are pursuing economic growth aggressively without significant improvements in our lives, with the notable exception of those who are being brought out of extreme poverty.

However, despite the good news that we understand the problem and are on the way to defining solutions, we must be clear that we are definitely not yet ready as a society to face up to reality. Furthermore, the sustained period of continuing denial we are now in will not be easy. We are in the endgame, but we are not at the end.

Evidence of the scale of the challenge in accepting growth's limits was seen in the response to the global financial crisis in 2008. While there were some interesting measures to focus stimulus packages on environmental initiatives, particularly clean energy, the fundamental and overwhelming focus was to get economic growth going again at all costs. Governments around the world of all persuasions, from liberal leaders like President Barack Obama and Prime Minister Kevin Rudd in Australia to conservatives like Angela Merkel in Germany to Communists like President Hu Jintao in China, all threw money at the economy to get it growing. No significant political or corporate leader questioned this approach or the urgency of it.

This was despite the ample evidence that our obsessive focus on growth was actually one of the causes of the crisis. The provision of cheap credit to feed our addiction led to irresponsible investment by banks and irresponsible consumption by consumers, which in turn drove global environmental impact and accelerated resource constraint, all while delivering increasing inequity between the rich and poor. Our solution to the failure of this approach was to quickly get back to doing it again.

Karl Marx argued that religion was the opiate of the masses, but religion has largely faded in its effect in this regard. Perhaps the new opiate of the masses is material consumption, delivered to us all without regard for ideology, in the two decades leading up to the 2008 financial crash, by the likes of Chairman Hu of China and President George W. Bush of America.

Now that we are addicted to endless increases in material wealth, governments are trapped. They recognize that if they don't keep up the supply, there is a serious danger of rapid, unsupervised withdrawal leading to revolution, or at least of lost elections!

The reason I want to establish the level of addiction is to enable us to understand what's coming. You see, even though the evidence is all around us that growth is driving us off the cliff, we will now go into ever more fanciful explanations as to why it is not. We will not let go easily. Such is the nature of addiction.

Mind you, a certain level of resistance is understandable. While I am arguing that continued growth is impossible because it would have to defy the laws of physics, an unplanned lack of growth or economic contraction is very unappealing and socially destabilizing. We are to an extent trapped. Our current system is designed for growth; that's what keeps us employed, keeps services flowing from government via taxes, and keeps the poor believing that they can escape from poverty. Without growth or at least without the end of growth being carefully managed, there is a danger that the whole house of cards will come crashing down.

That's why we need to understand that growth is finished and that we must plan the transition to a new approach carefully. Leaving it to unfold by itself is a risky strategy.

Yet despite the current system being in a cycle of growth dependency, this was not a design feature put there by early economists; on the contrary, they understood the limits of growth.

John Stuart Mill, one of the founding fathers of economics, recognized both the necessity and the desirability of moving eventually toward a "stationary state of capital and wealth," suggesting that it "implies no stationary state of human improvement."[1] Even one of history's most influential economists, John Maynard Keynes, assumed that the time would come when the "economic problem" would be solved and that society would then "prefer to devote our further energies to non-economic purposes."

The problem we face is that we've conveniently ignored both the desirability and the inevitability of the end of growth, and as a result we haven't planned for it. So not only do we have an addiction to the drug of material consumption, we have also entwined our lives, our culture, our political systems, and our economic structures in such a complex web with the growth monster that separation is going to be complex and traumatic.

We will cover many of the arguments as to why growth is failing us anyway and what we should pursue instead. As we do, however, remember this is relevant only to what comes after the crash. We face the end of economic growth regardless of our intentions, for reasons of physical constraint. When five hundred million people lose their livelihoods and one billion people their protein because fisheries collapse, growth for them will be a fading dream. If we have to eliminate the fossil-fuel industry to cut CO_2 emissions, we will have lost $3 trillion of economic activity. If we don't eliminate them, we will face runaway climate change with the potential for the loss of the insurance industry, the collapse of the food supply, and geopolitical crises and instability over water and refugees. If we get growth back on track as it was before 2008, then we will face peak oil and food shortages with prices soaring to new highs that stop growth again.

The issue is not therefore whether growth is stopping, the issue is *how* it will stop, *when* we will accept that it has, and *how* we will then adjust to our new reality. So when you hear arguments in defense of growth, consider them not as the case against ending it, because this is not a decision we will get to make. Think of them as more evidence of how challenging its inevitable end will be.

This cloud does have a silver lining, however. Economic growth has not been delivering on its promise of increased prosperity anyway, not once people are out of poverty. What the numbers from numerous studies show is that once societies move past approximately $15,000 per capita income, neither objective measures of quality of life nor subjective measures like life satisfaction show any material improvement. This applies across the board in all political systems and cultures with only minor variations. It even applies to such basic measures as life expectancy, infant mortality, education, and health—areas where you'd think money would buy progress.[2]

In measures of life satisfaction, the story is even more interesting. The evidence ranges from growth having no positive impact after basic needs are met to growth actually having negative impacts on some important aspects of prosperity.

As the *Prosperity Without Growth* report argued:

> For example, in British society since the early 1970s incomes have on average doubled. But the "loneliness index" increased in every single region measured. In fact, according to one of the report's authors, "even the weakest communities in 1971 were stronger than any community now." "Increased wealth and improved access to transport has made it easier for people to move for work, for retirement, for schools, for a new life," reports the BBC. . . . In other words, some degree of responsibility for the change appears to be attributable to growth itself.

We all have personal experience of this phenomenon—how wealth has increased but quality of life hasn't.

While the data on lack of improvement for society overall is clear, there is one important and interesting exception to the lack of a wealth/happiness link and one that explains a core driver of the market's success at motivating personal effort.

Having more or less income than those we compare ourselves with, at the local or societal level, does have an impact on perceived life satisfaction. This explains why people work hard to get ahead and compete within their organizations and society. While on the one hand this seems like a useful attribute, motivating people to work hard and strive to better their lives, it means that our focus on growing the economy, with the associated pollution and environmental damage, delivers no net gain for society as a whole. We just change positions on the dance floor. This is a rather profound design flaw.

Of course, many have argued for a long time that consumerism is socially unhealthy. Not just environmentalists, but religious leaders, economists, philosophers, and artists. They point to the destructive physical impacts of consumerism, but also to the negative social and values impacts of the pursuit of material sources of satisfaction rather than more meaningful ones.

Many of them blame capitalism and in particular corporate marketers. This has some validity in explaining the extreme consumerism of recent decades, but it is hard to argue that this is the underlying cause.

As Professor Tim Jackson argues, consumerism runs deep:

> Material goods continue to entrance us, long past the point our material needs are met. The clue to the puzzle lies in our tendency to imbue material things with social and psychological meanings. A wealth of evidence from consumer research and anthropology now supports this point. And the insight is devastating. Consumer goods provide a symbolic language in which we communicate continually with each other, not just about raw stuff, but about what really matters to us: family, friendship, sense of belonging, community, identity, social status, meaning and purpose in life.
>
> . . . The "language of goods" allows us to communicate with each other—most obviously about social status, but also about identity, social affiliation, and even—through giving and receiving gifts, for example—about our feelings for each other.

It is certainly true that corporate marketers build on and at times abuse this tendency, encouraging behavior that can become bizarre at the extremities: personal vehicles the size of small homes, equipped with multiple TV screens and refrigerators; family homes big enough to house a small community with TVs in every room; food consumption and wastage that goes so far beyond meeting needs that it borders on the obscene. All these are examples of marketing gone mad, and encouraging such behavior is unethical marketing, hiding behind consumers' right to choose. As much as we like to find people to blame—and in this case they're easy to find—the underlying causes are in us and the choices we make about our lives.

However, growth is about far more than consumerism. It is a complex system of interlocking processes.

One of these processes ensures that efficiency will never address the underlying problems of growth's ecological impact. Efficiency, while hard to argue against given the obvious ecological benefits of less stuff and the consumer benefit of lower costs, actually just re-creates the problem it solves.

Market-driven efficiency reduces the resources and labor used to create goods. This lowers costs, thereby increasing demand and enabling people to buy greater quantities of the more efficiently produced goods. This is well understood in the experience of recent decades. The money gained through energy savings, for example, is often used to buy more energy-using appliances and services. Dramatically more efficient car engines over the 1970s to 1990s led to heavier cars laden with new features and accessories.

The system in the end feeds upon itself and, like many addictions, creates its own cycle of dependency. We want more stuff to communicate with one another, to fill the void of meaning, and to compete to show we are successful relative to others. Our companies and countries then compete to deliver these products by becoming more efficient, thus lowering costs and enabling more consumption, but creating less employment. We then need to grow the economy to keep employment up so people can keep buying these more efficiently produced goods and to avoid the political instability widespread unemployment would otherwise lead to. Unemployment would lead to lower life satisfaction because lack of money prevents citizens effectively engaging in a society driven by consumerism, as in the earlier example from the United Kingdom of loneliness levels increasing with societal wealth.

It is a system both pathological, because it doesn't work, and incredibly effective at driving itself in a cycle of reinforcement.

Prosperity Without Growth again:

> These understandings provide us with our clearest insight yet into the enormity of the challenge implied in delivering a truly sustainable form of prosperity. Perhaps first and foremost, that challenge compels us to develop a different kind of economic structure. But it's clear that this task isn't sufficient. We also have to find a way through the institutional and social constraints that lock us into a failing system. In particular, we need to identify

opportunities for change within society—changes in values, changes in lifestyles, changes in social structure—that will free us from the damaging social logic of consumerism.

So we have a system design problem. The problem we face now is not that we can't redesign it and find ways to address all these challenges. We can certainly do so, and the work to define those changes we need to make is well under way. They are challenging and complex changes, particularly in transition, but they are realistic and achievable. We will come back to these ways forward, and there is much good news to have on this front, including immediate actions we can take in our own lives.

No, the problem is not the lack of a way forward; the problem is that the system is so comprehensive and self-reinforcing, we will resist the need for change until we have no choice. Until we're in the gutter, we won't face up to our addiction.

A realistic comparison is to observe our response to the relatively easier challenge of climate change. Despite forty years of research and twenty years of very clear science and economic logic and the fact the transition to a net zero carbon economy will create many winners, we have failed almost completely to deliberately initiate change ahead of the crisis.

So when it comes to the transition to a steady-state economy, letting go of growth and consumerism, confronting the challenge of how we address the cancer of global poverty without the total pie getting any bigger, *and* dealing with the sustainability-driven transformation of the entire global economy, the system is going to resist change and do so fiercely. It will take a serious crisis to force the issue, and that's why that crisis is inevitably coming.

In summary, growth is deeply ingrained in our global political, economic, and cultural systems. While change is inevitable, growth is so ingrained that this transition will not come easily. So even when growth stops, we will try hard to get it moving again, as we did in 2008. As a result, we will see growth return and then we'll argue, "See, we can still grow!" Then we'll hit the wall again because of the ecological damage and resource constraints that growth creates, and we'll bounce off the growth limits and shrink again. Each time we'll argue it was some other cause and we can fix it with a narrowly focused solution. We will stay in this cycle of denial for a while, denying the reality that we have a system design problem.

We will basically keep trying to treat our drug addiction with the provision of more drugs. We will do this until we're in the gutter.

The financial crisis of 2008 was a case in point, a taste of what's to come. As a talk-back radio caller I heard in the middle of the crisis said in response to the Australian government sending a check for $900 to most citizens as part of the national stimulus package:

> So we have this crisis caused by people using money they don't have, to buy stuff they don't need, and in doing so helping to drive the planet to the edge of collapse. Now the best our government can do in response is to give us more money that they haven't got, so we can do more of the same. Is that really the best we can do? Is that how far we've come?[3]

CHAPTER 6

Global Foreshock—The Year That Growth Stopped

When it first became clear to me in 2005 that we were heading for an ecological and economic crash, I wanted to test the idea with a broad audience. So I wrote up the arguments in a letter called "Scream Crash Boom," and sent it to my network. Over the months that followed, I received hundreds of responses from around the world as it spread virally to thousands of people. It had clearly struck a chord, with responses from CEOs to government ministers to grassroots activists. Many people sensed that the endgame for our current economic model had begun.

As a result of the interest the letter sparked, I was invited to present my arguments around the world. I spoke to groups of business executives at corporate retreats, to activists, to policy makers, to university seminars, and so on.

The general response was one of reluctant acceptance of the potential accuracy of my thesis but it was a kind of removed acceptance. When I spoke as an invited guest at corporate retreats, I often felt as if I were there for "intellectual entertainment" rather than for the arguments being considered in the context of business strategy. This surprised me a little, given I was arguing there would be discontinuous change in the market at some point, probably in less than a decade—a meaningful time frame for senior executives.

The reason why became clearer when I more methodically tested the response through my work on the core faculty of the Prince of Wales's Business and Sustainability Programme (BSP), run by the Cambridge

University Programme for Sustainability Leadership. I was able to test the thesis over three years with a broad cross section of leaders from dozens of countries and from all sectors of society and business. These executives generally had little prior knowledge of sustainability issues, and the BSP seminars ran for four days, giving me a chance to go deeper in exploring their reactions.

The responses were wide-ranging and gave a number of insights into how the collective corporate mind works and why change is hard to achieve. One of the most significant insights was the sense of power-lessness in the face of big-picture trends. While some rejected the thesis completely, those who accepted it generally responded with a passive-ness that I still find surprising. It was kind of, "Oh well, we can't do anything about that so we'll just have to observe it unfold." Many of them, however, separated this quite clearly as their professional, ana-lytical reaction. Alongside it, usually in the bar, they articulated a per-sonal, emotional response of concern for the future, particularly for their family and their personal career choices.

For three years I traveled the world, arguing the case that we were in a slow-motion global car crash; that we were hitting the ecological and resource limits of the global economy, and the resulting economic crisis was inevitable and imminent.

Then in early 2008, it started to become clear that the moment had arrived. What I had seen from mid-2006 to mid-2008 was the emer-gence of the two "crash indicators" I had been arguing would show the economy had clearly outgrown the earth's limits. The two indicators I had been looking for were: 1) resource constraints forcing prices up and 2) ecosystem changes accelerating at a scale suggesting that sys-temic shifts and tipping points were under way.

I saw both of these clearly emerging by early 2008. At the time, though, most of my audiences saw the global economy going gangbusters with spectacular growth, particularly in China and other parts of the developing world. The Dow had recently been trading in the 12,000 to 14,000 range, and while it had backed off to the lower end of that because of problems in the finance sector, they could see no signs of imminent danger to the global economy. So my argument—that this spectacular growth was driving us into the wall and would soon stop as a direct and causal result—was a difficult proposition for them to internalize.

It was particularly challenging for those operating daily in the global market economy. I remember one BSP seminar at Cambridge University in the United Kingdom in April 2008 with fifty delegates, mostly senior executives from global companies, with some from government and NGOs. I presented my case, with the economic consequences being put particularly firmly. I said economic collapse was now inevitable and with it the value of both their retirement savings and the companies that employed them. When I asked who agreed with the basic direction of my thesis, only three people out of fifty raised their hands! The questioning was aggressive and particularly dismissive of the idea that these ecological trends, which were generally accepted, would have this level of economic impact. They mostly wrote me off as an extremist and a merchant of doom.

The faculty at these seminars met daily to take a temperature check of the delegates' mood and the seminar's progress, so we discussed this reaction the next morning. While we were surprised by the strength of their response, on reflection we could see what was behind it. These business executives were deeply enmeshed in the global market, with their careers and personal lives firmly wrapped up in the system. Every day they were surrounded by people who accepted that economic growth was good for the world. To them, this view was not a political belief, but a simple fact.

They also believed that spreading the gospel of economic growth across the global economy was the only way to address the deep and grinding poverty we had addressed earlier in the seminar; poverty was in sharp contrast with their personal lives, and they genuinely felt it must be addressed.

As a result of all this, accepting my argument would require them to question their lives at a deep level. These were good people who had chosen to attend a seminar about global sustainability and social issues out of concern for the world and their role in it. So accepting the idea that the market they were driving, the machine they spent every day maintaining and expanding, was going to fail to deliver people out of poverty, destroy the global environment, wreck their children's future, and in the process cost them their personal financial security was never going to be easy.

I always found such push-back personally challenging. Even putting aside the ego challenge of being rounded on by a room of highly educated, successful people, it always made me question again whether my analysis and assumptions were right. I recognized that in general when you think you're right and everyone else in the room is wrong, you may well be slightly mad!

In my case, I have often been the only one in the room who believed what I was saying, but that was because I chose to go to that room to spread the message. I also have the good fortune to have regular contact in my work with the Cambridge faculty and elsewhere, with some of the world's top scientists, economists, and technology experts, who by 2008 largely agreed with the logic of my view, with the major question being timing.

So while I challenged myself constantly in case I was missing something, the evidence that reinforced my case continued to mount. The scientific evidence over late 2007 to early 2008 had been particularly distressing. The most dramatic was the accelerated melting of the northern polar ice cap. In the summer melt season of 2007, the arctic sea ice reached a new record low, with more than one million square kilometers less ice than the previous record low set only in 2005, and 41 percent below the 1978–2000 average.[1]

The IPCC climate models had predicted consistent melting, but this was so far ahead of their forecasts that it sent shock waves through the science community. Professor Mark Serreze, director of the U.S. National Snow and Ice Data Center and an arctic ice expert, reported his shock at how the ice levels had "simply fallen off a cliff." Along with others, he argued that if trends continued, all summer ice might disappear by 2030, a full seventy years earlier than many of the models had predicted. We were and are witnessing a classic feedback cycle—recent research suggests that one of the greatest causes of the warming arctic is the *lack of ice* itself, as seawater reflects less solar radiation than ice.[2] As there is less ice, so there will be even less in following years.

To me this was just one of a number of indications of the emerging breakdown of the planet's ecological systems. While individual glaciers, droughts, and floods all give some indication of direction, something as large and significant as the northern polar ice caps was an indication of a systemwide shift. It was also a positive-feedback risk globally, with dark blue water absorbing heat whereas ice reflected it. This meant local melting led to local and global warming, leading to more melting, and so on.

Other scientific reports around that time showed more early signs of acceleration and systemwide impact. Examples included the reports of methane bubbling to the surface in lakes of meltwater in the massive area of frozen tundra. This frozen earth keeps billions of tons of methane locked out of the atmosphere, and its release is perhaps the single biggest tipping-point risk. The methane involved is such a powerful greenhouse gas and is there in such large quantities that its release could dwarf human emissions and accelerate warming beyond anything we could control.

On the broader issues of systemic change, the oceans were showing signs of major shifts as well. A series of reports indicated the oceans were acidifying with unexpected speed. This process, caused by the oceans absorbing excessive CO_2 in the atmosphere, has two impacts. First, it becomes a self-reinforcing climate feedback loop because it threatens the ocean ecosystem's ability to absorb CO_2, leaving more in the atmosphere to heat the planet. Second, it has the potential to wreak havoc on the global marine ecosystem by preventing marine creatures like prawns from producing hard shells and slowing coral growth, threatening changes across the whole marine food chain.

Making these individual signs worse was that every global parameter we could measure was tracking at or worse than the upper end of the IPCC forecasts that create the basis for policy. These included the amount of sea level rise, the rate of sea level rise, the volume of emissions, the levels of CO_2 concentrations in the atmosphere, the recorded increases in average global temperatures, and so on. This meant we had two things happening in parallel: The causes of the problem were worse than expected, and the response of the ecosystem was worse than expected. It was a sobering period.

I knew, however, from previous experience that while ecosystem indicators of accelerating change were evidence to me of the limits being reached, they were not evidence to most people and wouldn't get much attention except from those already aligned.

It would require *economic* indicators that we were actually hitting the limits to really gain attention. The most obvious candidates for these were commodity prices, particularly food and oil.

Oil was a good candidate for convincing evidence because it had long been predicted that we would at some point reach "peak oil"—the point after which oil extraction can no longer be increased. There was a clear and established link between economic growth and oil consumption that made the "growth hitting its limits" logic simple for people to understand. This would also be a good test of the techno-optimist view—that markets self-correct because as resources run out, prices rise and alternatives come onstream. (While this is obviously correct in theory and over time, there are considerable challenges in the politics and economics of the transition and timing unless the price rises are steady and slow, which they rarely are.)

Peak oil is a good example of limits being reached because of the suddenness of the impact, comparable conceptually to the collapse of fisheries we discussed earlier. It's not that oil will soon run out; in fact nowhere close to it. Part of the way through global supplies, the rate of extraction of oil reaches a maximum as remaining reserves become increasingly difficult to extract. It's thus not the amount of oil that limits global supply, but rather the rate at which we can extract it. While production slows, demand continues to rise and in combination the price becomes volatile and increases rapidly. This is because oil is such a crucial part of our economy and is hard to replace quickly. The U.S. Department of Energy reported that the only way to avoid massive economic loss from a serious energy crisis would be to start preparing twenty to thirty years in advance. That was a good thought but would have been a more useful one thirty years ago!

So as oil prices hit new highs in 2008, it started to look like game on. However, while it's easy to explain resource limits being hit with a single commodity like oil, it's harder to communicate the linkages between systemwide resources and ecological limits and their economic impact. This is partly because of the incredible system complexity we have now built into the global economy. Food was therefore going to be an even more important example than oil because it brought this complex system of ecological, social, and economic drivers into a single indicator—global food prices. Food prices effectively measure all the issues we've been discussing around sustainability. Ecological drivers like soil quality, water supply, and extreme climate events mix in with social trends like increasing wealth-driving food choices and economic trends such as the shift of the corn crop into biofuels with government subsidies for corn-based ethanol.

From 2005 onward, we had seen increasing impacts of environmental and social pressures on food supplies. As argued by global experts like Lester Brown of the Earth Policy Institute, these pressures were coming together with great momentum after years of forecasts that they would do so. On the supply side, these included a challenging array of issues such as less unused arable land, loss of cropland to development and industry, overpumped aquifers, falling water tables, overallocated rivers limiting irrigation expansion, slowing growth in crop yields, increasing soil erosion, and deserts expanding due to overgrazing, overplowing, and deforestation. Many of these were assessed as ecosystem services in the *Millennium Ecosystem Assessment* we discussed earlier.

On the demand side, of course, we had an extra eighty million people to feed globally each year, along with increasing wealth leading to a desire to eat more grain-intensive livestock and the shift of corn in particular to use as a biofuel feedstock.

So as we moved toward 2008, alongside these underlying issues of supply and demand, we saw the impacts of climate change, with widespread droughts reducing harvests in many countries and floods destroying crops in others. Thus the conditions emerged for a perfect storm of economic growth hitting the system limits.

Sure enough, over the second half of 2007 and the first half of 2008, the logic of the sustainability argument found its way into the economy. For those who still think the environment is a place you visit on weekends, consider what actually happened over this period.

Food prices started to rise, driven by the array of system challenges referred to above, including climate-induced water shortages and degraded soil quality. As booming economic growth drove oil consumption, oil prices rose to historic highs, and as the techno-optimists argue, this drove investment in the alternatives. One of these was corn, which competes strongly for fuel with oil when oil prices increase. This caused U.S. farmers to switch from soybeans for food to corn for oil partly because of the subsidies for corn-based ethanol in the United States. Together these drove up both corn and soy prices globally.[3]

The gap in the soy market caused by the exit of U.S. farmers encouraged Brazilian ranchers to convert their ranches into soy farms, grabbing the opportunity presented by higher soy prices. This caused a gap in the meat market, which drove other ranchers to increase deforestation in the Brazilian rain forests to get new grazing land. There was also rain forest clearing for more soy farming. This deforestation is a huge driver of climate change. Climate change is blamed by many for the worst drought ever in Australia over this period, which saw wheat output decline, and for crop-destroying floods in America, both of which further drove up grain prices globally.

Food and oil prices soon soared to levels way above all historical highs. As Lester Brown points out, with people in poor countries spending 50 to 70 percent of their income on food, increasing food prices in 2007–2008 caused major political instability. Food riots and unrest spread across dozens of countries, and governments moved to ban food exports to protect their national supplies, further tightening global food supply and driving up prices. Even developed countries faced political unrest over spiking oil prices.

In another insight into the future, the food price rises in 2007 and 2008 drove those countries concerned about security of supply to invest in taking over agricultural land in other countries. While foreign investment in agriculture is not new, what is different this time around is an emphasis by some states on controlling land and growing food exclusively for export to the investing country, driven by concerns around food security. No one yet knows the full scale of land involved, in part because states are reluctant to publicize what has been called by some a "new colonialism."

One study by the UN's Food and Agriculture Organization and international NGOs found that in the five African countries of Ethiopia, Ghana, Madagascar, Mali, and Sudan, about 2.5 million hectares of agricultural land were acquired by foreign investors between 2004 and 2009.[4] This staggering figure represents almost half the arable land of the United Kingdom—but represents only a fraction of the land involved internationally. One estimate by the International Food Policy Research Institute put the total figure at 30 million hectares in 2009. Another estimate by the Oakland Institute puts the total at 50 million hectares (an area equivalent to half of all the arable land in China).[5] Prominent examples include an attempt by China to secure 3 million hectares for oil palm production in the Democratic Republic of the Congo, a signed deal for a South Korean company to grow wheat on 690,000 hectares in Sudan, and a large Saudi fund focused on buying up or long-term leasing foreign agricultural land.[6] When food runs low, it is the foreign power that has control over the land and the rights to its produce—media reports already indicate that Pakistan plans to deploy one hundred thousand troops to defend foreign-owned farms.[7]

It is inevitable there will in future be political unrest and geopolitical instability caused by poor countries losing their arable land to wealthier countries, especially when those countries bring in their own farmworkers to grow the food, displacing poor local farmers.

While on the one hand some would see all the above as the market at work, in reality it's more like a chaotic and risky scramble for resources in a world of diminishing availability. Lester Brown points out that unlike previous food price increases that were driven by a particular drought or monsoon failure and therefore returned to normal on the next harvest, these were unresolved long-term trends that were limiting food supply and increasing demand. It's harder for the market to respond with more supply if there is insufficient land and water.

This view has been reinforced by price movements since that time. While of course prices dropped with the global financial crisis hitting demand so strongly, even then they stayed well above historical levels, suggesting that we are now facing systemic shifts. As I am writing, wheat prices are spiking again, driven by floods and droughts across many countries, and Russia has just banned wheat exports to protect its food supplies. So these types of problems are rapidly becoming the new normal as we bounce around up against the system limits.

While in any particular crisis experts will argue as to the key causes, there always being many, 2008 certainly showed us what the Great Disruption will feel like. It presented a particularly good example of how resource constraints and ecosystem changes can create havoc in the human economy and do so in complex and unpredictable ways.

It is easy to forget in light of subsequent events that in early 2008 most market participants remained optimistic about the growth prospects for the global economy. Problems in the U.S. economy and rising global oil and food prices were seen as temporary blips that did not suggest anything other than business as usual.

And yet the signs were there, with these issues merely indicators of deeper structural problems in the global economy. When the banks started collapsing later in 2008, this became abundantly clear.

While I couldn't see the detail of what was to come, by early 2008, it was clear to me that the Crash was no longer a forecast but actually under way. As a result, I got to work on my follow-up letter to "Scream Crash Boom," this one called "The Great Disruption."

Although only a few thousand words, it took me over four months to write. I think in hindsight I was fearful of making the call in such a public way. Despite the oil and food price rises, we were at this stage still in boom times. I remember in the first month I was writing that the Dow soared from 11,800 back up to 13,000. Many saw this whole period as the triumph of globalized capitalism. The shakiness in the financial markets in 2007 and early 2008 was seen as a minor blip in an endless boom and an era of supercycles. Saying it was all over felt like exposing myself to serious ridicule.

Nevertheless, in July 2008 I sent the letter out far and wide. The first page read as follows:

> And so the moment arrives.
>
> In my first "Scream Crash Boom" letter of 2005 I forecast the inevitable crash of the global ecosystem. I said the resulting economic and social crises would then drive an investment boom in a new industrial revolution and economic transformation. I thought I was forecasting events a decade or two away. Now, just three years later, look around us. The global economy is trembling under its own weight. We see:
>
> - riots and political crises across Asia as surging food prices, driven by extreme climatic events and surging economic growth, put severe pressure on the daily lives of billions of people;
>
> - protests, strikes and political upheaval across the world as oil prices respond to the reality of limited supply, threatening recession, or worse;
>
> - global financial markets lurching from crisis to crisis as complexity, greed and interconnectedness drives the financial system to the edge;

- debate about external military intervention in countries that can't deal with the humanitarian consequences of extreme weather, such as Burma;

- scientists mystified by dramatic increases in melting at the Northern Polar and Antarctic icecaps, at rates way beyond their forecast models;

- and countless more impacts with floods and fires in the United States, droughts and dying rivers in Australia, melting glaciers all over the world, and on and on.

The ecosystem crash I thought was decades away is now underway and the resulting economic crash is not far behind, perhaps the slide has already begun.

It went on to talk about how this would all unfold over the years ahead and how the global financial markets were inevitably going to be hit by their own complexity:

We have built an incredibly complex, interlinked global society and economic system. While we're very proud of our creation, its very complexity makes it highly prone to shocks. The interconnectedness we marvel at could well be our downfall as parallel shocks bring the whole system down.

It was clear to me that whereas my friends in business would marvel at the incredible connectedness of the global marketplace, I like many others saw risk in bright red flashing lights.

The response to the letter was very strong. Unlike my 2005 letter, this was not being taken as a forecast of intellectual interest. This time people could feel something was wrong. There was a sense that the world was facing a serious, destabilizing period. While the financial and economic consequences were yet to unfold and the mainstream market had yet to feel any substantial effects, there was sufficient evidence—for those wanting to see it—that something was deeply wrong.

So the responses, even from corporate leaders, generally acknowledged the system was shaking, that there were now risks that could bring it all down. As a CEO of a major Australian company wrote to me, "This resonates very closely with how I'm feeling."

Another common response was to agree directionally but to be more optimistic about our ability to change. For instance, the CEO of a major company listed on the New York Stock Exchange said in an e-mail to me, "Directionally I feel you are right. I would debate the degree and how fast we will adjust when we see reality."

Of course, over the next year the economy went into its worst decline since the Great Depression. After the first flurry of blame on investment bank cowboys and weird financial products, people started to wonder if something deeper was going on. They started to question the system.

Thomas Friedman, long a passionate advocate for markets and globalization, wrote a *New York Times* column in March 2009 that asked:

> What if the crisis of 2008 represents something much more fundamental than a deep recession? What if it's telling us that the whole growth model we created over the last 50 years is simply unsustainable economically and ecologically and that 2008 was when we hit the wall—when Mother Nature and the market both said: "No more."

My view, firmly held at the time and since, is that 2008 was the year that growth stopped. It was the year, as Thomas Friedman said, "when Mother Nature and Father Greed hit the wall at once."

While I was naturally very focused on the environmental drivers of the Great Disruption, market advocates like Friedman were looking at the appalling behavior of the investment banks with horror. It was greed gone mad, bad enough in its own right but incredibly dangerous when it happens at the center of a complicated, interconnected system. Everyone had become addicted. When Iceland almost went broke, Friedman described the country as being like a "hedge fund with glaciers." But now the hedge fund had melted and the glaciers weren't far behind.

What brings these two drivers together is growth. The demand for growth drives investment bankers to take greater risks in order to deliver the profits and growth their CEOs and shareholders demand. Their cleverness in designing new products that no one else even understands ensures they deliver that growth and personally get their bonuses and promotions. They lend other people's money to people who can't afford to pay it back and offset the risk to themselves. The government dares not intervene because these bankers are driving the growth that keeps the masses happy and them elected. All growth is good, no questions asked.

In fact government actively supports the process and in doing so increases the risks further. They borrow to stimulate the economy, with the resulting massive debt putting the economy further at risk, while hoping growth will sufficiently increase government revenues to pay back the debt. Thus the system locks itself in to further addiction.

Of course no one will ever be able to prove what caused the particular crisis in 2008 because the system is too complex. We can't even forecast the oil price, a single commodity in a relatively simple market. So the idea that we can know in detail how the global economy and society behave in any particular year is not realistic.

What we can know, however, with a high level of certainty is how a system behaves when it reaches its physical limits. It is on that analysis I conclude we hit the limits in 2008. While the crisis may have manifested as food and oil prices spiking followed by a credit crisis, was that credit crisis caused by our addiction to growth and the need to provide cheap credit to drive it? Or did the doubling of oil and food prices take money out of the economy and reduce consumption of other goods on which growth depended?

We can't know. What we can know, because we can prove it with simple math and physics, is that the global economy is now bigger than the planet, and that means the economy at some point will stop growing. Whether that was 2008 or is still to come in 2012 or 2015 is of historical interest only. It is certainly going to come.

Furthermore, all the evidence to date says we're not going to have a smooth landing. It will be 2008 on steroids with volatility and a mad scramble for diminishing resources. We're going to drive growth up against the wall again and again, and it's going to hurt.

Then, when we get sick of the pain, we will change. But not yet.

CHAPTER 7

The Road Ahead—
Our Planetary Sat Nav

Before we take our story completely into the future, a few comments about that process are in order.

I have spent most of my life talking about the future; in fact, both as an activist and as a business strategy adviser, I could consider this to be my core trade. By its nature, forecasting is uncertain. Unlike the present, the future is hard to measure. The key to success is to be clear on what you can know and what you can't, and to focus on broad strategic direction. It is important to remember this is a game of probabilities, with the objective being to reduce risk and build the resilience required to cope with the range of most likely outcomes.

In the case of the questions we're covering here, this is an important and practical process, not one of intellectual entertainment. We face an unstable future, and our capacity to be ready for that, physically and psychologically, could well determine our success in navigating these troubled waters. Having a reasonably accurate view of what conditions we can expect is therefore a powerful tool.

The future is, after all, something we create, not something that just happens.

So what do we know? What roads are mapped and which ones are unexplored? The underpinning drivers of change here are unusually clear, compared with, say, business strategy for a technology company, where the myriad complexities of the market, technology, and consumer behavior are subject to many unpredictable, game-changing developments.

The situation with sustainability, particularly climate change, is much simpler. As we covered earlier in some detail, there will certainly be surprises in technology, politics, and events. But when it comes to thinking through strategy for business or society, the core drivers of change have negligible uncertainty. The underlying processes at work are simple, reliable, and entirely predictable. Blind hope for some surprisingly different outcome is just avoidance.

This is not to say these questions don't contain many uncertainties. They do, and we can divide them into two categories: natural and human. The natural ones are about how the environment behaves as a system, with interconnectedness, tipping points, and feedback loops. Examples are issues like the ocean's absorption of CO_2 emissions causing acidification, which can undermine marine life, then accelerating the collapse of fisheries.

The human ones include linkages between the ecosystem and the economy, as in our earlier example of the food system, where higher oil prices and subsidies for corn-based ethanol in the United States led to deforestation in Brazil, which worsens climate impacts, which drives up food prices. The other key human uncertainty is technology. There is always the possibility of some extraordinary technological breakthrough, for example, in very cheap renewable energy or in removing CO_2 from the atmosphere. The likelihood of these preventing the crisis is minuscule in my view because of the late start and the time it takes to get technology to mass global scale. However, such breakthroughs could have a major influence on the speed of our recovery.

These uncertainties remind us of the complexity we need to deal with. A valuable tool in analyzing complex systems is considering how other systems behave. While this has considerably less certainty than the physical processes referred to earlier, it still provides some useful lessons.

One of these is that when systems hit their physical limits, they tend not to do so smoothly but are volatile and chaotic. They bounce against them, falling back and then growing until they hit them again. These are periods of great activity and increasing intensity. The system keeps hitting up against the limits in different places, in different ways, trying to break through, until it gives up, recognizes the limits are immovable, and changes. Then there are two ways to go. The system can stop growing and stabilize, usually evolving to a higher state, or it can break down into a simpler system with less complexity (that is, collapse).

Another way of seeing the same issue of system behavior is through medical science. My friend Dr. John Collee, a medical doctor and Hollywood screenwriter (*Master and Commander, Happy Feet, Creation*), says the right comparison for the global ecosystem is the human body:

> Every patient with an incurable illness will ask how long they have to live. The answer goes something like this: "No one can say how long you may live, because every individual is different, but focus on the changes you observe and be guided by those. When things start changing for the worse, expect these changes to accelerate. So the changes that have occurred over a year may advance by the same degree in a few months, then in weeks. And that is how you can judge when the end is coming."
>
> Planet Earth, being a web of complex self-regulating systems, operates very much like a human body. Terminal illness gives us the template for most forms of ecological collapse. One set of changes initiates another, and so on in a downward cascade of negative feedback until the whole system falls apart.

As with all such theories, I approach this one through the screen of common sense. As argued earlier, it's not possible to analytically determine the precise path forward in a process with the level of complexity of human society within the ecosystem. What we can do instead is observe what we see and hear around us, consider the theories put forward, and make a judgment as to whether it makes sense. Using this approach both the comparison to other systems and the medical analogy are helpful. What they both say is that change will accelerate, that the impacts will get greater and closer together, and then the time for decision, to avoid collapse, will suddenly be upon us.

The simple conclusion is that we need to get ready for this point, which is the core reason for this book.

So how can we imagine this will unfold? How would these theories apply in the real world, and what are the types of actual impacts we can expect? What do we know from the science that can guide us? The "Great Disruption" letter I wrote in 2008 imagined that world and described it like this:

As our system hits its limits, the following pressures will combine, in varied and unpredictable ways, to trigger a system breakdown and a major economic crisis (or series of smaller crises) that will see us slide into a sustained economic downturn and a global emergency lasting decades.

- A series of ecological, social and economic shocks driven by climate change, particularly melting polar regions, extreme weather events and changes to agricultural output, will generate severe economic stresses, along with deep concern in the public and the global elites. This will lead to strong government intervention and generate a sense of global crisis.

- The combined pressures of increasing demand and lower agricultural output driven by climate change will lead to sustained increases in food prices—triggering economic and geopolitical instability and tension, with developing countries blaming the West for causing climate change.

- A deeply degraded global ecosystem will further reduce the capacity of key ecosystem services—water, fisheries and agricultural land. This will again impact food and water supply, political stability and global security.

- We will see even further sustained and rapid increases in oil prices as peak oil is breached. Yes, it will go up and down, but the trend will be clear. This will create enormous systemwide economic and political pressure, as well as a great conflict between expanding dirtier supply and cutting CO_2 emissions.

- As always in predicting the future, there will be surprises. These could be, for example, a serious global terrorist attack wiping out a major city or a pandemic shutting down global travel. Shocks upon shocks upon shocks.

- As this unfolds, our deeply intertwined and complex global financial market, prone to panic driven by fear and uncertainty, will suddenly wake up to the long-term implications of all of this. Perhaps driven by a series of major corporate collapses or national economic crises, they will then simply reprice risk in global share markets. This will lead to a dramatic drop in global share markets and a tightening of capital supply.

Over she goes.

The resulting series of economic and political crises will be massive in scale and decades long. They will last this long simply because fixing the causes while dealing with the consequences—a declining economy, political instability and accelerating climate change driven by earlier emissions—will take decades. With this level of crisis and change, the future becomes quite unpredictable and anything is possible, including some very exciting transformational shifts.

Why do I see this starting now? The system is too complex for analytically based certain predictions. We can't even predict the oil price, let alone the behaviour of the whole system. However, my intuition is screaming at me that now is the time, and the data I see confirms my intuition. If we go back to basics, the two key challenges we face—the availability of cheap resources to feed the economy and the ability of the earth's ecosystem to absorb our impacts—both have very clear indicators. So as the system hits the wall we should see a significant non-cyclical rise in commodity prices—especially food and energy—and significant evidence of accelerating ecosystem breakdown. These have for several years been my canaries in the "end of growth" coal-mine.

We see these indicators hitting hard now and the drivers behind them are profound, well embedded and have significant lags in them. So it's game on. From this point forward, the slide into crisis will define our political and economic world.

Is this all too pessimistic? I'm actually by nature a strongly optimistic person. I just look at the numbers and the science, and I see it coming.

I want to be clear, though, that this is not about the "end of the world" or an inevitable slide into collapse. It does, however, herald an unparalleled era of system stress, economic stagnation, and social tension—a global emergency during which we'll evolve a new economic model and then rebuild. I call it the Great Disruption because I believe it is far more likely to be a disruption in humanity's evolutionary process rather than the collapse of civilization.

This disruption will drive a transformation of extraordinary speed and scale. It will leave in the dust all other major global changes we've faced—those driven by war, technology, or globalizing markets. It will be an exciting and ultimately positive transformation, with great innovation and change in technology, business, and economic models alongside a parallel shift in human development. It could well be, in a nonbiological sense, a move to a higher stage of evolution and consciousness.

We're slow, but not stupid. I have no doubt we will respond—with intensity matching the crisis as it emerges—when we end our denial of the obvious logic we can all see if we choose to look.

Some who agree with my argument in general don't believe the economic crisis will be so severe. They argue, as the CEO I quoted earlier did, that we will respond more rapidly and avoid a full-scale economic and social crisis.

My response is that the economic challenge of leaving it so late to respond means we will get stuck for a while in a transition phase. There will certainly be a great push to build the new, but the old—the sheer scale of the old economy and the systemwide impacts of earlier pollution and environmental degradation—will drag us down and prevent us from transitioning quickly. This will bring us close to zero if not negative global economic growth for several decades as the old economy crashes and a new one is built. Volatility will see it rise and fall around that zero, and vary by country and region, but the general direction will be clear.

Why can't we respond faster? Why won't the boom of the new carry us through? The problem is in the pace and scale of change required. We will certainly see spectacular growth in many new industries, particularly energy technologies. But these start from a very low base, so even the large growth rates we can expect will take a while to have an impact on the whole economy. Until that happens, the great bulk of our current economy will be defined by a range of old technologies and industries, such as coal and oil. These will not be allowed to grow—because their growth would threaten the whole economy through worsening the ecological causes of the crisis. This in turn means many of these old industries will enter rapid decline, particularly in market valuation.

So while a rapid growth in solutions will certainly occur, this decline of the old, along with the considerable sunk capital such as functioning power stations that will need to be shut down, will create a significant deadweight on the economy while it's in transition.

Perhaps this by itself would be manageable with massive, warlike intervention by government and mass mobilization of the public. The challenge is that many companies and sectors depend directly on the ecosystem behaving in a certain way that can no longer be assumed. This will range from insurance companies that will struggle under the weight of climate disasters, risking insolvency, to tourism-based companies whose key attractions like snow or coral reefs will be gone or degraded, to food companies whose supply will be threatened or at least suffer enormous price volatility. And all the while people generally, including investors, will be feeling fearful and uncertain, undermining confidence and creating political and market volatility.

So without in any way ignoring the spectacular opportunities coming—in fact, we will go into them in some detail over the rest of the book—we should not be blind to the economic challenge of transition. I am confident we will get through this period successfully, but it will be hard work, it will not be smooth, and it will take time.

This reinforces the key conclusion all my work brings me to. This is a crisis we can no longer avoid. We've left it too late for that.

It is what it is. The sooner we accept it and the better we prepare, the less suffering there will be and the faster we will come out the other side.

CHAPTER 8

Are We Finished?

By now, there is a reasonable chance you've been having some fairly dark thoughts. You may be wondering if my view, that we will make it through this, is correct. You might be thinking those who argue we will just slowly slide into collapse may have a point.

Even if you haven't gone there, you may be having moments where you wonder: "What if this all goes horribly wrong?" Maybe moments of despair at the suffering to come, frustration that we've left it this late in the process, anger that it got to this stage, and confusion as to why. You may have considered what it all means for you personally—your family, your security, and the young people you know.

If none of these reactions apply to you, feel free to skip to the next chapter and get straight into what happens next. But I imagine most of you have had these moments. I certainly have. In that case, read on.

I have spent many years considering these questions. Whether this is a crisis we'll pass through or if we'll just face collapse. Whether a rational look at the science and politics warrants a response of despair or hope. I've also discussed these issues with corporate executives, activists, policy makers, and leading scientists over many years and considered their responses and approaches.

My conclusion is that over the next few years, the attitude we adopt—for simplicity let's call it hope versus despair—is perhaps the *most* profound issue we will face. I think it will be more influential on our future than technology, politics, or markets. This is a big claim, so it warrants some serious discussion.

The challenge we face with the Great Disruption is, in severity and scale, unprecedented in all of human history. The situation we will find ourselves in and the consequences that will unfold will be very severe. However, I have no doubt that we can survive and move through virtually any scenario imaginable if, and only if, we stay focused and determined and act together as a species. This conclusion is based on some important assumptions that are different from how many others see the world, so it's worth sharing them.

First, we have to accept that things are going to get ugly and prepare ourselves for this—physically, economically, and psychologically. This is not going to be inconvenient or unpleasant, this is going to be what James Kunstler described in *The Long Emergency*—a generations-long crisis that will need to be managed with focus and determination.

Second, we must drop the dominant assumption that has been held for decades, of how change will occur—steady, market focused, and by global consensus. We must rapidly get our heads around how it will actually occur—discontinuous, chaotic, and transformational change, driven by a war-footing type of response.

Third, we must now understand that the type of change we need will require a major evolution in human values, politics, and personal expectations. This is not a single technical problem like fixing climate change; this is a system design problem. We will therefore need profound shifts in how we behave personally and collectively.

Fourth and perhaps most important, we have to accept that this issue is now a human one. For decades people like me have advocated protecting the environment or preventing significant global changes to the ecosystem. We have to accept that it's too late for that. It is now inevitable that the whole planetary system will be profoundly changed by our actions, with implications for thousands and possibly millions of years.

This means we need to forget about "saving the planet." The planet will be just fine, it will recover very nicely, and it's not in a hurry. If it takes a million or a hundred million years to recover from our impact and get back on a new evolutionary path, this is no intrinsic problem from the planet's point of view. No, our issue is now *our* issue—do we want to "save" civilization and allow it to keep evolving and developing from the base we have built over the past ten thousand years? Or do we want to go back to a few hundred million people or fewer and start again? That is our choice, and it is the only choice we now need to make. It is a choice we *can* make, and getting through this is an outcome we can achieve, but only if we *decide* to do so. This is a future we get to make.

That's how I see it. You can make up your own mind as we explore these questions and our potential responses over the remainder of this book.

First, though, and within that context, I want to focus on the vexed issue of hope and despair. This is not an issue just of intellectual interest, though it certainly is very interesting. This is a determining issue. If we get this wrong and slip into collective despair and fear, we risk creating a self-fulfilling attitude. This is important at the collective level of broad society, but more urgently it is an issue for people actively engaged in these issues now. We cannot afford to have the most informed and engaged people withdraw, lose focus, or act even subconsciously in a half-hearted way. We have to believe we can succeed, and we have to believe it every day. As I said earlier, we can do this, but only with focus and determination.

I used to think despair about our potential in this area was a personality-driven response. That optimists were full of hope and pessimists went to despair. I think I was wrong. My view now is that despair is a completely rational and logical response to what we have learned about our situation. Confused? Read on.

This is not an intellectual question for me. It is deeply personal, and I have dived down into the depths of it. Let me tell you that part of my story. When I first started writing and presenting on "Scream Crash Boom" in 2005, I noticed I was much more engaged and passionate about the Crash than I was about the Boom, and partly as a result, so were my audiences. At first I thought this was just because I understood it better, with my background as an environmental campaigner and the amount of time I had spent examining the science of sustainability and climate change. It also had the drama of a crisis, making it an easier communications task.

To correct this, I spent more time exploring the extraordinary range of exciting activities around the world being undertaken by people preparing for the transition to a new economy. There are so many amazing stories, some of which we'll cover later, it is easy to get excited about what's possible. Despite learning a great deal and being inspired by the stories and people I came across, I found that my approach didn't fundamentally change. It was the Crash that got the attention and energy of both my audiences and me.

Then, when I was presenting to a Cambridge BSP seminar in New York in 2007, to a largely business audience, I was going through the Crash and was suddenly overwhelmed by a great sense of sadness, and I actually started to cry—not a good look for a big Aussie bloke!

Afterward I gave this a great deal of thought. Given that my purpose in doing this work is to motivate people to be inspired and active, projecting despair was not likely to be effective.

When I returned home, I was telling my wife, Michelle, the story of my tearful speech and we both started crying! We both felt the pain and the sadness but still didn't fully understand it. We were sitting in a café at the time, and I wondered what others would think if I said, "Oh, we're crying because the world is on the verge of a systemwide crash that will see massive global suffering and chaos for decades." If I did, they would look around at the lovely autumn day and probably call the mental health authorities to have us taken away.

Over the coming year, I noted my moods as I was presenting around the world and found I often went into a depression for several days after a big presentation, with the sense that the work I was doing was probably hopeless. I wondered if I was kidding myself that we had any hope of turning the situation around. An aspect of this was purely in the realm of personal psychology, and I put a lot of effort into looking at that. I wanted to know how much of this was about my response to the data rather than the data itself. However, this personal work, and the fact that there were plenty of data points around me, convinced me there was more to it than just personal psychology.

A new development in the issue had unfolded over the period 2004–2008. Some of the best-informed people in this area started to come over to the view, usually expressed in private, that we were just buying time and we wouldn't actually succeed. This development was not of the kind that is often dismissed as the "end of the world, survivalist" phenomena we have seen at other points in history. These were highly educated and experienced global experts who were analyzing the data and drawing the conclusion that it was simply, physically too late.

One of the more public and prominent of these experts is James Lovelock, a giant of a thinker in this area over many decades, who effectively founded the whole area of earth system sciences, the study of the earth as an integrated system. He was the founder of the Gaia theory—that the earth can be understood as a self-regulating organism. With a number of broad accomplishments under his belt, this is a serious scientist.

Now over ninety years old and still brilliant, Lovelock recently wrote what may be his final book, *The Vanishing Face of Gaia: A Final Warning*, in which he argued that the collapse of civilization was now inevitable. His primary reason for this conclusion is that as humans, we are just not smart enough to respond to a complex problem like climate change adequately. Like Collee's medical comparison earlier, it will overwhelm our response and bring us down. He believes we may end up with as little as a few hundred million people left on the planet, concentrated in the few areas still suitable for growing food.

He is far from alone in this view. Australian Clive Hamilton's most recent book, *Requiem for a Species*, takes a similar view, as evidenced by the title.

So feeling despair and a sense of futility is not just an emotional response driven by personality type. According to some seriously wise and highly informed people, it is a rational conclusion, drawing on human history and the scientific evidence. While I have absolutely been in that space, I have now come out of it, and I think they are wrong.

We will spend quite a bit of time on why they're wrong in a technical sense in the coming chapters, where we'll detail just how we can turn this around and why I think we will do so. Bear in mind that recent studies show that if we stopped emitting greenhouse gases tomorrow, temperatures would stop rising almost immediately.[1] We're not locked into climate disaster any more than we choose to be. Of course, stopping all emissions overnight would be politically impossible and inflict huge suffering. But avoiding any further warming is scientifically and technically possible, as we'll show. The principle challenge is finding the motivation to cut emissions with sufficient speed. For the moment, though, I want to focus on the attitude of despair and why we should be optimistic and believe that avoiding collapse is politically and humanly possible.

From my observations and discussions with others, I think despair is a stage we have to go through. It is in fact a positive sign and an indication of coming to the end of denial. On sustainability, most people start with denial—there is no serious problem. Then comes what we'll call "denial breaking down"—a more or less intellectual acknowledgment of the science up to a point, but without fully accepting the factual implications and emotional reactions that full acknowledgment would bring. Then comes full despair, sometimes with fear and anger on the way through.

My conclusion is that feeling despair at some point means you've genuinely and fully acknowledged the facts. This can perhaps be seen as a stage of grieving where, as in cases of personal loss, you recognize that your loved one is gone and isn't coming back. The reality has finally sunk in. So as a stage, it's actually healthy. Look at the facts we've been discussing and the full scale of their implications and then ask yourself, Wouldn't it be kind of weird not to feel despair and sadness in response? Anyone who doesn't feel this at some point is probably in denial—either denial of how bad it will be or denial that it's too late to prevent it, hoping some combination of political and technological sleight of hand will prevent it.

So ironically, if you're feeling despair, then feel good, you're almost there!

But while despair is a stage I think we all need to arrive at, individually and collectively, it's also one that we can and *must* move through. We face the same challenge when we deal with serious personal loss. We go from denial to despair. Then at some point we need to move on from despair—it's not a place in which people want to stay, even though it can be a difficult place to leave. This doesn't require us to forget the loss, or deny the sadness, but it does mean we have to re-find hope and empower ourselves through it. Otherwise we spiral into decay.

The easiest way to do that is to go forward. We act. We start doing things. This shouldn't be surprising—in other processes of dealing with grief and despair, we act as a way of reasserting control and direction over our lives. Of course, individual grieving isn't characterized by clear, distinct stages and progression. You might jump back as well as forward and feel conflicting emotions at various times. But generally, we accept the loss more fully as time goes on.

While all of the above can be considered at the personal level, it also needs to be considered at the collective, global society level. Without question, society is still in denial. Generally we are in the stage of "denial breaking down," in that we sort of accept the science but are in denial about its implications—the speed and scale of the threat. I'm not talking about climate deniers or antiscience skeptics. They can be ignored for two reasons. First, we can't help them, because as with an alcoholic in denial, no amount of data will change their minds—they simply don't want to face reality. Second, they don't matter. The physical science will overwhelm them in the end.

But collectively, we are in the "denial breaking down" stage, and this really matters a great deal because this is what's holding back change. This is an understandable stage, where people recognize the problem to some extent but hold back from full acknowledgment to prevent the emotional and practical impact true recognition would entail. So the views are things like "it's bad but not *that* bad"; "it's serious, but it's about the future so we have time"; "it's a global problem and we can't do anything about it locally." Another one is that yes, it's a serious problem, but it's caused by someone/something else (large companies, China, America, rich countries, population growth in poor countries—anyone but us). Denial is an amazing thing to watch and experience!

This collective stage will pass at some point relatively soon. Then we'll move through collective despair and fear and into full acceptance. Acceptance in our context becomes a source of empowerment. Big call? Not really. Let me explain why.

Let's look at climate change again as an example. The same principles apply to the whole of the Great Disruption, but climate brings the idea into sharp focus. I like to think of climate denial as a massive dam. Right now, there's some pretty big cracks in that dam. And before long they are going to rip right open. When a dam collapses, it happens suddenly and the water comes through thick and fast. This is how it will be with climate attitudes and, as a result, climate action. There's so much pressure built up that once the dam of denial breaks, the flood of acceptance will sweep away any remaining denial.

To understand this, it's important to recognize the *social* psychology of our response to climate. At the moment, the majority of people are in "denial breaking down"—they don't yet fully acknowledge the problem. This means that those who do get it are isolated and tend to talk to each other differently from the way they talk to those who aren't there yet. This is why as I sat in the café crying with my wife, I couldn't imagine explaining to those around me what I was thinking. This process reinforces the collective avoidance of full acceptance, because people feel strange talking about it for fear of ridicule. But once the change starts to kick in, this social phenomenon changes from being the biggest hindrance to the biggest accelerator. This reality, of group and social dynamics, is one reason change happens slowly at first and then incredibly fast.

So, yes, perhaps you're thinking, "I can see how it could happen in theory, but what would possibly trigger such a shift?"

When I discuss these issues with people who are in full despair, the response is usually along the lines of, "But you're telling me it's going to be really, really bad; how will we possibly cope?" I've been there myself frequently, so I know that feeling well!

Ironically, it's just this point—that the situation is going to be really, really bad—that gives me such confidence that it will turn, and the social dynamic referred to above, combined with the enormous back pressure behind the dam, means there's going to be a flood when it does.

I call what is coming the Great Awakening, a term I first heard used in this context by Professor Jorgen Randers.

Let me start explaining this from the point of the counterargument, generally referred to as "the boiling frog problem." This refers to the idea that a frog put into boiling water will jump out, whereas a frog put into cold water that is then slowly heated will stay there and boil to death.[2]

Some people argue that as humanity slowly slides toward disaster, we'll stay in ever more fanciful denial until it is too late and we are overwhelmed—that we will slowly boil to death.

There are three reasons this is wrong and why instead the Great Awakening will occur and we'll suddenly find ourselves in a completely new world, albeit a challenging world and one requiring a lot of work.

First, it will come upon us hard and fast when it does. The risk of collapse will soon be in our faces. This is incredibly clear from the science, and anyone who looks at it once out of denial draws that conclusion. While it's a much broader issue than climate change, the climate science gives it all a sharp focus. When it hits, it will hit economically, and then people at large will pay attention because it will affect them directly. Denial will then evaporate virtually overnight.

Second, we can respond quickly when we choose to, and this is fortunate because we consistently respond late. There are many indications in history and human behavior that this is actually standard operating procedure—late and fast. We wake up, then take whatever action is necessary to fix it. If an epitaph were to be written to characterize our generation, it might be: "They did it. They were slow, but not stupid."

Third, we will be capable physically and technically of turning the situation around at that point, because that point will be soon, and we are capable, when the alternative is collapse, of making an absolutely remarkable turnaround. This last point is key, because people won't end denial until they believe there is a solution.

Let me go through each of these in a little more detail.

First, we are not boiling frogs and will not stand by observing our decline. The reason I am so sure about this is that the momentum for change we have built into the earth's climate system is like a fast-moving heavy train hurtling toward us. We are standing on the train line, in heavy fog. The fog will lift, or the train will be so close we can see it and feel it, even in the fog. Then we will jump. We will most certainly not just stand there and watch it hit us.

The scientific evidence for the accelerating speed of the train is now all around us. Those with good senses can already feel its rumble. The critical recent shift in this evidence is that we can see the beginning of what John Collee argues with his medical analogy: The system will resist change and appear to be doing okay and then break down rapidly. The difference here, of course, is that we are not a "body" and as such cannot die. But we are now seeing rapid acceleration in the rate of change as the various uncertainties in climate and ecosystem science, like changes to the marine ecosystem, are all starting to tip the wrong way. There will be more examples in the coming years.

Clive Hamilton considers the question of denial deeply and concludes that the fog won't lift in time. He notes that accepting the personal loss of the death of an individual is harder when there is room for doubt about the death or where it can be blamed on someone else—both being present in the climate question. The question of blame is a vexed one, and I'll talk about how that might play out later. On the question of doubt, I agree that we won't wake up until we really feel it. Solid theory and science just aren't enough. But crucially, we're about to feel it like never before.

It is important to recognize that this will hit not just environmentally but economically. For all the reasons we discussed earlier, this will translate not just into local economic impacts, but into global ones as well, including the end of economic growth as we know it. People will then "feel" the issue in a new and directly personal way. Even those not personally affected will be able to relate to it. Terrorism was a powerful example of this. Even though few were directly affected by the 9/11 attacks, people around the world felt an emotional engagement with those who did. As a result, enormous political and economic changes were accepted from new airport security measures to changes to legal rights to two wars—because people could relate to the issues in a new way.

So the train hurtling toward us will become clear as the fog lifts, forcing us to jump rather than be hit. We will explore how this will unfold in the next few chapters.

Second, we need to remember that this type of response is normal for our species. We wait until the last minute and then we jump. We respond dramatically. You can argue this is stupid, but that doesn't change it. We wait until a crisis is imminent and then respond. This applies to our personal health, our business management, our economies, and our societies. It usually takes a heart attack, a financial crisis, or an invasion of Poland to get our serious attention. But then we respond dramatically. Slow, but not stupid.

This leads to the question I am most often asked on this matter: What will be climate change's "9/11"? What will trigger the shift? A hurricane hitting Wall Street? A typhoon in Tokyo? What is the climate equivalent of Hitler's invasion of Poland?

The answer is unsatisfying. While I am certain we will respond, it probably won't actually be triggered by a single event, although historians will probably agree on one after we've turned, to explain it. I'm sure of this because in reality we already have sufficient evidence, including unprecedented physical events, that if we wanted to believe, we would. The urge to deny unwelcome reality allows people to ignore any amount of data that challenges them—until they are ready to change. Then the evidence is obvious and accepted. So while facts are necessary, they are not sufficient. We will respond not when we accumulate an overwhelming amount of evidence—we already have that—but when we stop denying the significance of the evidence we already have.

Then there will be a tipping point when denial ends, and the reality that we face a global, civilization-threatening risk will become accepted wisdom, virtually overnight. At that point, we will respond dramatically and with extraordinary speed and focus. This moment, when it finally arrives, will be the Great Awakening. It won't be consistent or smooth, but this will be the overall direction.

But why is Lovelock wrong? Why will the crisis at that point not overwhelm our response? Why won't the risk of tipping points in the earth system drive us into the ground?

This is the third reason the Great Awakening will occur. When under great pressure, humanity is capable of extraordinary, imaginative transformation and political shifts that will in this case be capable of bringing us back from the brink and delivering a safe climate at the end of the crisis. This is very important to the end of denial. Unless we believe we can fix the problem, we will deny its existence.

Because little work has been done on dramatic CO_2 reduction strategies that actually fix the problem, this is a key area I have focused on for this book, with my colleague Professor Jorgen Randers. I detail our results in chapter 10. What it shows is that we are clearly capable of reducing atmospheric concentrations of damaging greenhouse gases at a scale and speed incomprehensible in the context of the debate today. Based on this, I am also confident that the same principle applies to other sustainability issues. This means whether the critical issues prove to be forests, peak oil, water, food supply, or pollution, we will still be capable, at a late stage, of physically and technically turning the situation around. We won't be able to prevent great damage or avert the crisis, but we will be able to prevent the collapse that Lovelock predicts.

The conclusion Jorgen Randers and I came to after doing this work was this: The change required to deliver a safe climate and sustainable economy is clearly not limited by our economic, physical, or technical capacity. In fact, taken in their relative contexts, the economic and technical difficulties of the actions we need to take to address our challenge pale in comparison with those faced and achieved in World War II.

So the only question is the willingness to act and the resulting decision to do so.

Making such a decision simply requires society to believe we face a crisis. Not just a normal crisis, but a serious crisis. This will be defined not by the arrival of the physical crisis, which has already happened, but by the moment when denial ends and we accept that the risk we face is not a less pleasant environment or dirty cities or the loss of some charismatic megafauna, but the loss of everything we have come to accept as "normal." It will be when we face head-on the risk of collapse.

Collapse is used a bit loosely in much of the discussion in this area, so we should consider what it means in some detail before we go on. I don't think we will actually see collapse but we need to understand the risk of doing so if we are to avoid it. The term has been popularized by the excellent work of Jared Diamond in his book *Collapse*, which looked at how environmental challenges have led to the collapse of past societies and civilizations. Collapse in the context we now face would not mean the end of humanity as a species. It would, however, mean the end of society as we know it. It would mean the breakdown of our political structures and the complete lack of coherent global governance, even by today's poor standards. It would mean the end of our current way of life and all the assumptions we make in the West, and in many parts of the developing world, about security and personal safety, food and energy supply, material quality of life, and advanced medical care. It would also mean a rapid decline in personal security, perhaps even a return to Thomas Hobbes's state of nature.

Diamond's work and that of others is enough to show that great civilizations can be brought to their knees by nature and that we must "choose" to survive. One of the societies analyzed by Diamond, the Maya of Central America, is also studied by Brian Fagan in his book *The Great Warming*. Fagan looked at the global effect on human societies of the medieval warm period between AD 800 and 1300. This period, when global temperatures were in some areas up to one degree warmer, brought down not only the mighty Mayan civilization and saw them abandon their temples on the Yucatán, but also the Cambodian civilization with its center at Angkor Wat and the largest preindustrial city in the world, and forced the relocation of the entire Puebloan or Anasazi cultures of the American Southwest.

One might suspect we are better resourced to deal with such challenges today. This is true, but it is worth remembering that the climate changes that brought down these people often resulted from just one degree of warming. Our challenge will be much greater and, more important, much faster than the natural processes that drove those shifts.

It is not hard to imagine what a serious collapse inducing global crisis would look like if you put together the trends we've been discussing. A global famine that sees a billion people or more starving to death; a series of wars raging in the Middle East and elsewhere over water; armed conflict between China, India, and Pakistan over millions of refugees from political breakdown and food shortages; the drowning of people and nations in low-lying islands in storm surges; the global insurance industry going into insolvency in the face of a series of climate disasters and the run-on effects in the banking industry with uninsured assets being used as debt collateral; the collapse of global share markets when the risks of all these things are priced into share portfolios.

Military planners, whose job is to rationally assess current and future threats to national security, are acutely aware of such risks, including the risk of collapse. In recent years, they have been closely examining how this might all unfold and what it means for the future of conflict and global security.

According to the former commander in chief of the U.S. Central Command, retired Marine Corps general Anthony Zinni, who participated in a high-level Military Advisory Board review on the subject, we either address climate change today or "we will pay the price later in military terms. And that will involve human lives. There will be a human toll." The 2007 report concluded that climate change would act as a threat multiplier by exacerbating conflict over resources, especially because of declining food production, border and mass migration tensions, and so on—increasing political instability and creating failed states—if no action was taken to reduce impacts.

The findings of this report agree with those of the confidential assessment of the security implications of climate change by the National Intelligence Council (NIC), the coordinating body of America's sixteen intelligence agencies. Former NIC chairman Thomas Fingar told Congress that unchecked, climate change has "wide-ranging implications for national security because it will aggravate existing problems," especially in already vulnerable areas such as sub-Saharan Africa and the Middle East. According to an NIC briefing document, by placing added stress on resources, climate change will "exacerbate internal state pressures, and generate interstate friction through competition for resources or disagreement over responses and responsibility for migration."

In 2010, the Pentagon's Quadrennial Defense Review acknowledged that climate change will act as "an accelerant of instability or conflict, placing a burden to respond on civilian institutions and militaries around the world." Frustrated with the lack of political response, thirty-three retired generals and admirals wrote to the Senate majority and minority leaders in April 2010, stating that "climate change is threatening America's security . . . it exacerbates existing problems by decreasing stability, increasing conflict, and incubating the socioeconomic conditions that foster terrorist recruitment. The State Department, the National Intelligence Council, and the CIA all agree, and all are planning for future climate-based threats."

Outside of the public eye, defense experts are blunt. "Disruption and conflict will be endemic features of life . . . once again, warfare would define human life," concluded a secret Pentagon report in 2004 on the impacts of climate change.[3]

The lesson of all these and other similar studies is clear. While there are many uncertainties in location, scale, and timing, there is now enough evidence that any rational review concludes we face the risk of worldwide collapse and the descent into chaos. The acceptance of this risk will be the tipping point for the Great Awakening.

Remember again, though, this is not about the data. The data clearly show we already face just that risk. The level of the risk can be debated, but even at the lower end it is at a level considerably greater than other risks we already respond to with massive military and security efforts and/or massive injections of public capital. That's why military planners around the world are now so focused on these issues. The evidence is in.

So the thing to look for is the end of denial.

Looking into future scenarios is helpful, but we can also look back to what we've actually done to find relevant comparisons. These comparisons provide lessons about likely tipping points, but also about how dramatically we can mobilize when we choose to act.

I often use the example of World War II as evidence of what we are capable of, both economically and physically and in terms of sudden political shifts. People tend to point out all the ways World War II was quite a different situation. The Allies faced a clear and personified threat in the form of Adolf Hitler. They faced a country they had fought only twenty years before and so were used to seeing it as the enemy. They were fighting something external, something foreign. This is significant— the best enemies have a face and are from somewhere else. In contrast, climate change is hard to personify and is something for which we ultimately have only ourselves to blame. There's no enemy to rally against, even though we try. And then they point to the invasion of Poland— that we haven't had an equivalent event on climate change or sustainability.

But on closer inspection, while there are some real differences, there are not as many as you might think, and there are many lessons and great encouragement in that experience. In fact, our response to Hitler is the classic example of slow, but not stupid; of late, but dramatic.

While everyone talks about the invasion of Poland as the trigger, the reality is that Hitler represented a severe and clear threat to other European powers much earlier. Hitler had launched a massive rearmament effort soon after installing himself as chancellor in 1933. He had violated the hated Versailles Treaty and remilitarized the Rhineland in 1936, a clear provocation to the French. He had annexed Austria in 1938 and launched a full-scale invasion of Czechoslovakia in March 1939. All this time, there was great debate and denial about the scale of the threat. It wasn't until the takeover of a third country, with the invasion of Poland on September 1, 1939, that war was declared. While the year before had seen increasingly serious mobilization efforts by Great Britain, appeasement continued for much longer than a rational response would have allowed.

In short, on the objective facts, Hitler represented a clear and undeniable threat long before action was taken to defeat him. Famously, Churchill and others had long warned of this threat and been largely ignored or even ridiculed. Society remained in denial, preferring not to recognize the threat. This was because denial avoided full acceptance and what that meant—war and a strong change to the status quo. Yet once they did, once denial ended, the response was swift and dramatic. Things changed almost overnight.

Without the benefit of a retrospective view, it would be much harder to predict when exactly the denial of Hitler's threat would end. So it's also hard to predict when the moment will come on climate, even though in hindsight, it will be "obvious."

It's the right comparison. We've had a rational and clear threat for a long time. We've had the Churchills arguing that case for twenty or more years and ignored them. We've had the false progress comparable to Neville Chamberlain's agreements for peace, such as the Kyoto and Copenhagen agreements. We have preferred to stay in denial. While this has been distressing for people in full acceptance, if we looked at history, it was predictable it would be this way. Looking at history, we can also conclude this, though: It will change. The dam will break, and then look out for the flood.

But a word of caution. Just as denial and pessimism can prevent action, ironically so can unstrategic optimism. If we sit back and passively wait for the dam to break, it will at the very least delay that day. Instead we have to choose active, engaged, and strategic hope.

I suspect that right about now you are looking forward to getting past this point in the book. You'd like to leave behind the endlessly detailed descriptions of the mess we are in and how much worse it's going to get. You don't want to read any more about the risk of collapse and the descent into chaos, and you'd like to take your mind off what all this means for you and your family.

Well, I have some very good news for you. You have just reached, right here in this sentence, the emotional low point of our story! From here on we shift into hope. Hope that is logical, uplifting, and a far superior place in which to live than that town called despair.

Hope is not a question of personal philosophy. In the face of uncertainty, operating from a stance of hope is a strategic and practical response. It is a way of approaching the world. As environmental writer Professor David Orr said of it, "Hope is a verb with its sleeves rolled up."

This could actually be one of the most important and strategic shifts the millions of advocates for action on sustainability now need to make. It could itself be the tipping point that brings on the Great Awakening.

This is a serious political strategy issue. Leaders and movements that painted a picture of hope, even in the face of deeply challenging circumstances, have driven all the great positive changes in history. Gandhi, Mandela, King, and Churchill all told a story of hope for the future despite the desperate conditions around them. Each held different levels of personal spiritual alignment with this position of hope, but they were all united in their strategic pragmatism. Hope works.

Martin Luther King's famous speech was not "I have a nightmare based on the evidence of racism all around me every day and the inability of people to change," it was "I have a dream." Nelson Mandela faced a country that was on the verge of collapse and chaos, with devastating violence between blacks and a ruthless white government that had been fighting change with military force for decades with the support of the white population. Despite having been imprisoned for decades, he drew on the best of humanity in himself and called on all the people of South Africa to aspire to a united country. By doing so, he achieved one of the most extraordinary transformations in history. With the slogan "Freedom in our lifetime," the African National Congress also projected this hope as practical, relevant, and worth fighting for.

I visit South Africa frequently, closing the circle on some of my earliest activism, and am always surprised how that country has changed since the end of apartheid. Whereas many argued change was impossible, the reality is that for all its challenges, a multiracial society is now the new normal—no one can imagine the world that was.

Perhaps an even more powerful example is Winston Churchill. A so-called realistic assessment of Great Britain's position at various stages during the war was that their position was hopeless and occupation by Germany inevitable. Churchill is of course famous for having suffered dreadful personal depression—indeed, some even argue that the practical situation he faced was so obviously hopeless that only a slightly unhinged man would hold out hope! In one analysis, psychiatrist Anthony Storr argued about Churchill:

> Had he been a stable and equable man, he could never have inspired the nation. In 1940, when all the odds were against Britain, a leader of sober judgment might well have concluded that we were finished.[4]

Despite the situation he faced and his personal challenges, Churchill led his country with a rallying cry of hope and certain victory while bombs fell around him. Of course, he is now seen as one of the great leaders of history.

On a practical, strategic level, navigating the crisis ahead while driving the economic and social transformation we need is going to require a great deal of such leadership. No one is likely to follow leaders or movements whose message is "the situation is hopeless and all is lost, but we may as well make a bit of effort on the way down"! Of course, not many campaigners are actually saying that, but if they feel it, even subconsciously, they risk projecting this into their work.

And let us remember that this is *not* like the situation Churchill faced, which was "realistically" hopeless. As we have outlined earlier and will return to in some detail, there is a rational argument that the future we wish for can be achieved—if we decide to pursue it. We know what we need to do, and we know how to do it. So we are completely capable of success.

So before we conclude this issue, I'd like to go back to my sadness at the state we are in and to the personal psychology of despair. It is very sad that we are going to wipe out 50 percent of global biodiversity that took billions of years to evolve. It is very sad that the changes that will now unfold in the global ecosystem means that billions of people will face painful, widespread, and long-lasting personal suffering. It is tragic that this will all occur without good reason and that we could have easily prevented it all.

I have even at various times felt a huge sense of personal failure as an environmental campaigner. Failure that my movement and my life's work has been unable to prevent this from occurring, despite the fact that millions of us could see it coming. I have felt anger in response and wanted to go back to campaigning so I could beat up on the companies like Exxon-Mobil that I think have done the most to derail efforts to address these issues. But in the end, I realize this is all just a projection of my sadness.

It is all very sad, and that was why I cried when presenting to that audience in New York. It was why Michelle and I cried when I recounted the story. However, it is what it is. Grieving is an appropriate response, but sustained despair is not.

One thing I have learned since understanding all this is that hope is self-reinforcing. If I focus on the Crash, I feel sad; if I focus on the opportunity, I feel good. If I live my days in hope, I am a happier person, and my wife tells me I'm a whole lot easier to live with! So it's a quality-of-life question as well as a good political strategy. And as I've argued, it's also a rational conclusion—the dam is about to break.

Given the challenges ahead, the choice to be optimistic is perhaps the most important and most political choice an individual can make. Once each of us has made that choice individually, it's up to all of us to go out and help others make that choice as well. The timing remains crucial on this issue. The sooner the shift comes, the more options we will have on the table and the less pain we will ultimately have to endure. So get out there, roll up your sleeves, and live in hope.

Be realistic, be a Churchill, and demand the impossible.

CHAPTER 9

When the Dam of Denial Breaks

When the Great Awakening occurs, the response of society is quite predictable based on previous major national and global crises. We consistently respond the same way.

It will be dramatic, high-profile, and expensive; it will engage most or all sectors of society; it will be framed by a shift into a "whatever it takes" approach to solving the problem at hand; and it will involve strong, direct intervention by government. Even though it is hard to imagine today, the global community will at this point—rapidly, though messily—develop a global emergency response to cut climate pollution and pursue a safe climate "whatever the cost." The transformation around sustainability more broadly will then follow rapidly.

The response will be framed by a single, critical idea. To quote my favorite climate change strategist, Winston Churchill: "It is no use saying, 'We are doing our best.' You have got to succeed in doing what is *necessary*."

Successfully averting the risks posed by climate change and other sustainability challenges will first require the elimination of the economy's net greenhouse gas emissions within a few decades. Such dramatic action will be dictated by the science of lags and the risk of tipping points we covered in earlier chapters; otherwise the risk of global collapse will be unacceptably high. Therefore, in the context of Churchill's comment, what will be "necessary" is an emergency response that will involve an extraordinary level of global cooperation and unity of purpose, well beyond anything we've ever seen and for which the only comparable, though still inadequate, example is the mobilization of most parts of the world during World War II. It will require a clear goal (a picture of "the enemy"), rapid change, considerable dislocation, and widespread sacrifice.

Humanity will then enter a multidecade response period, as described in forthcoming chapters, that will see us teeter on the brink of collapse but not fall over that cliff. Rather than the long-predicted war among civilizations, this will be a war *for* civilization. Fortunately, it is a war we can win. It is also a war with an extraordinary upside.

Before we describe how this dramatic shift will occur, we need to add one more piece to the jigsaw puzzle, without which this scale of shift in our political world is just too difficult to imagine.

In a real war, the objective is simply not to lose and, as a result, to keep things as they are. There are collateral benefits in technology, united societies, and so on, but the costs and suffering in a real war far outweigh the benefits. The "war" in our case is different. While losing is still catastrophic, as in a real war, thus eliminating the option of not acting, winning is not about keeping things as they are, but about making things immeasurably better from almost every angle.

Without in any way belittling the great suffering that will inevitably occur during this period, it is important to recognize early on just what an extraordinary opportunity this will be. While the initial response will focus on climate change, particularly energy, transport, and agriculture, it is clear as argued in earlier chapters that climate change is a symptom, not the problem. This means that to succeed we will have to rapidly expand our response to other sustainability issues, including addressing the consequences of a range of other environmental and resource constraints, creating a new model of economic development that doesn't involve consumerism or material growth, and eliminating poverty and extreme inequity. We will do this while building a more cohesive society both globally and locally. So the shifts we face will be deep and genuinely transformational and of great significance, even in the context of human evolution.

Even during the initial narrow focus on climate change, however, there will be countless social, economic, and quality-of-life benefits. These changes won't happen overnight, but they will happen much faster than most people think because of the urgency with which we will need to act globally.

An energy system, for example, based on solar, wind, and water power means that every country will have sufficient secure supplies of energy to be independent of the geopolitical and price risks of imports. The scale of investment in new technology required will be such that the costs of renewable energy will inevitably fall dramatically, providing even poorer countries with access to abundant, locally generated energy. This will certainly require funding from rich countries initially, but this is widely accepted in the international politics of climate change. As energy is so fundamental to improving the quality of life, this potential for energy independence has far-reaching consequences for economic development and poverty alleviation.

All economies will benefit greatly from having price and supply certainty on all energy supplies; after all, no one is going to be able to corner the market for sunshine and wind! Even at the individual consumer level, we can expect great savings through energy and fuel efficiency once this transformation is complete. The fuel cost, for example, for an electric vehicle is around 80 percent lower than the fuel cost for a gasoline vehicle. So even allowing for amortized battery costs, transport will become much cheaper and therefore more widely accessible.

Having cities with clean air because we eliminate the pollution from cars, trucks, and power stations will result in healthier children and lower health costs by, for example, greatly reducing asthma and other respiratory diseases. One study has shown that between 2005 and 2007 in California alone, failure to conform with federal clean air requirements created more than $193 million in hospital costs, with public taxpayer insurance schemes covering two thirds of that cost.[1] Designing our cities for walking, cycling, and smaller vehicles will result in stronger, safer, more cohesive communities and healthier people, delivering real enhancements to our quality of life.

On the broader global scale, the benefits to our geopolitical stability of eliminating conflict over oil and energy and being forced to address extreme inequity among nations and people will be considerable.

None of this takes away from the geopolitical, economic, and social challenges we will face during the Great Disruption, but these considerations provide us with important parameters that help frame the onset of the Great Awakening.

The political debates on climate change and sustainability have been framed around the idea of acting voluntarily and with great social and economic cost and risk. The arguments against action are therefore framed in loss to quality of life and risk to economic activity and jobs (ignoring the actual huge economic upside in building a new energy system). In that context, when even mild action such as putting a price on carbon pollution or encouraging a multidecade transition to clean energy is strongly resisted, the sort of shift I'm describing appears incomprehensible, perhaps even impossible. So let me be really clear—this is not the context in which the Great Awakening will occur. Instead it will be like this:

As we discussed in the last chapter, when denial ends, the dam holding back public opinion and climate action will collapse. At this point, our leaders will be forced to act urgently and comprehensively. We saw how strongly they responded to the comparatively minor hiccup of the global financial crisis. Who would have expected the world's governments to suddenly spend trillions or a U.S. president to take draconian action like nationalizing banks and auto companies? When the alternative is catastrophic, the inconceivable rapidly becomes normal. So imagine how they will act when they realize the very existence of civilization is at stake and economic growth is immediately threatened, not for a few quarters or years, but indefinitely.

This is where the importance of the upside described earlier is key and will frame the response. Unlike war, where it is solely the fear of loss that motivates action, in this case we will have fear of loss *and* great benefit to acting. So it will become a no-lose decision point. Don't act, and the economic and social suffering will be immeasurable. Act strongly, and the benefits will be historic, motivating, and future shaping in addition to clearly reducing the suffering otherwise faced.

It is easy to imagine the political speeches we will hear when this moment arrives. Our leaders will be using the rhetoric they use in war, calling on us to act at a moment of extraordinary historical significance, to make sacrifices in order to avoid catastrophe and instead build a more prosperous and safer world for our children.

As argued earlier, when I described how the responses to my presentations changed when I shifted focus to the personal economic risk, it is important when imagining this awakening to remember the nature of the risk and the way it will be portrayed. It is true we have an appalling record of responding to environmental threats, and this will continue.

We will not respond to climate change or sustainability even when it's clear we risk wiping out 50 percent of the diversity of life on earth. We will respond when the threat is to our economy and lifestyle. Our record of responding to these kinds of threats, whether war, economic calamity, or natural disasters, is impressive. And so it will be in this case.

So what will this feel like in the politics of the day? How will historians view this dramatic shift in humanity's direction?

There will be two types of responses that will unfold in parallel but at different speeds. I see these two responses shaping the next forty years or so, and we will explore them over the remainder of the book.

First will be the old economy and system trying to fix itself with existing assumptions and mechanisms. This response will assume we can continue to have economic growth, but that it needs to be more efficient and with lower carbon intensity.

Second will be the push to build a new economy with transformational thinking. This will include a shift from consumerism and a physically defined quality of life along with strong moves to more localized economies and stronger global cooperation.

Both the old economy and new economy approaches are critical in different phases; it is not a battle between them. However, it is the new economy response that will ultimately become dominant for the reason outlined in earlier chapters—the physical impossibility of continued material economic growth.

The old economy response will be about leveraging existing economic and political models, systems, and beliefs to mobilize society's emergency response plan. This will be a genuine emergency, a warlike mobilization of resources and people to apply the brakes before we hurtle off the cliff. It will need strong, dominating government, systemwide intervention, technological fixes, and market mobilization. These are things we're very good at. I will describe what this approach might look like in some detail in the next chapter, "The One-Degree War."

Many "new economy" thinkers will resist this response, using arguments like the often used quote from Albert Einstein that you can't solve a problem with the same thinking that created it. They will be partly right and partly wrong. They will be right in the sense that if we don't challenge the fundamental design problems in the global economy, including our beliefs and values, we cannot solve the underlying cause of the climate and sustainability problem—our economic and social model of progress. They will be wrong, however, in the sense that when we wake up to this crisis, we will have very little time left to avoid catastrophic collapse. We will have neither the time nor the political capacity to undertake a genuine system transformation *and* deal with the immediate crisis. Doing so would create too great a risk of going into economic breakdown and political chaos.

The new economy response will occur in parallel and will be equally critical. It will have a slower start but in the end be more powerful. It will be focused on sustainability in its full implications rather than just climate change. This will involve questioning fundamental assumptions and accepted wisdoms about the global economy. It will challenge the obsession with growth and explore models of steady-state economics, as argued by the former World Bank economist Professor Herman Daly and other eminent economists and commentators. Those advocating this response will argue for a redesign of the global economy to become a closed-loop system with no waste, aligned with biology and the ecosystem, as argued by two of the great thinkers in this area, Janine Benyus in *Biomimicry* and William McDonough in *Cradle to Cradle*. Many of these ideas are already being put into practice by entrepreneurial companies and by global corporations, but they will need to be taken to scale and supported with government regulation and pricing.

The deeper ideas behind this new economy are already well established, with growing numbers of people rejecting consumerism and the inherent obsession with material wealth. These people are instead focusing on building stronger communities with greater resilience and on enhancing our quality of life rather than our quantity of stuff. These ideas are focused on making us happier, a worthy cause indeed. This type of response will grow steadily and will have a strong consciousness or spiritual component, arguing for a deeper examination of our values and beliefs. It will put forward an aspiration for a growth in consciousness and for living a life not in fear, but in love and hope.

Many old economy thinkers will resist this, using arguments of market economics and the belief that people are naturally greedy and self-interested. They will argue that material wealth is something we have aspired to for thousands of years; that we are genetically encoded to compete and have conflict; and that all this higher-purpose stuff is for the birds, or at least the monks. They will make the case that we haven't got time for all that soft stuff, we've got a war to fight!

They too will be partly right and partly wrong. They will be right in the sense that the fundamental transformation required to properly address this problem will take too long to attack the needs of the immediate crisis, where solutions must be found in years, not decades. They will also be right that our genetic coding does drive a whole range of behavior and that is a major challenge for us to overcome, as argued brilliantly by Jared Diamond in one of the books that has most influenced my life's thinking, *The Rise and Fall of the Third Chimpanzee.*

They will, however, be wrong in that simply applying technology and the power of markets and capital to this problem, while essential, will only buy us time, it will not solve the problem. Even if we stabilize the climate by eliminating greenhouse gas emissions, endless economic growth is still not possible on a finite planet when that economic growth involves material consumption. Decoupling economic growth from material growth is only a "slow it down" strategy. It simply reduces our speed as we head for the cliff. The numbers just don't stack up, as we covered in chapter 4.

The old economy thinkers referred to above are wrong in another respect as well: Not only are humans *capable* of fundamental change and overcoming our genetic urges, but such capacity *defines* our development and growth as a species. It is true that we were only recently apes, but we have come a long way and we still have a ways to go.

To argue we are naturally greedy and competitive and can't change is like arguing that we engage naturally in murder and infanticide as our forebears the chimps do and therefore as we did. We have certain tendencies in our genes, but unlike other creatures we have the proven capacity to make conscious decisions to overcome them and also the proven ability to build a society with laws and values to enshrine and, critically, to enforce such changes when these tendencies come to the surface.

So don't underestimate how profoundly we can change. We are still capable of evolution, including conscious evolution. This coming crisis is perhaps the greatest opportunity in millennia for a step change in human society.

While both approaches just described will inevitably be pursued, there will be great debate on which one is right, using the arguments covered above. I believe putting energy into these arguments will not be of great benefit and shouldn't get much attention. It is inevitable that those in power now, who run the "old economy," will do their utmost to preserve the existing system and will argue strongly that it can be saved with a new model of economic growth. Many will rail against this, but to little effect. An existing system is powerful and doesn't give up its power lightly.

Besides, we need them to run the war, something they're very good at! Indeed, if they don't run a successful war, we will be building a new economy from the village up with just a few hundred million people and a whole lot less technology and knowledge, making that job far harder and slower. Not to mention the suffering of billions of people on the way to that new starting point.

The efforts of those who seek to build a new economy should instead be focused on doing just that: working on building new economic models and ownership structures, developing successful purpose-driven businesses, and driving the transformation in culture and values we will need. The laws of physics dictate that the old economy approach will fail because continued material economic growth is impossible. So we need to be well advanced on the solutions when that is accepted.

What all this means is that to get past the Great Disruption and to the better world on the other side, we need *both* approaches to be unleashed with full fury. This will be messy and confusing, but that is just the way many things are going to be over the coming decades.

We will now address the first of these approaches, the inevitable, exciting, emergency response to climate change. This is where the fun really begins.

CHAPTER 10

The One-Degree War

Like most advocates for action on sustainability, I've had days when I find it hard to imagine the world waking up as comprehensively as it must to address these issues effectively. Indeed, while I've been writing this book, some argue the tide is going firmly the other way. The Copenhagen Conference failed to deliver tangible progress, the science has been under attack again, opinion polls are going the wrong way, and there is little evidence that governments will translate widespread and genuine concern and understanding into real action. The boiling frog is indeed getting hot!

So why am I so confident the world will respond and that when it does, it won't be too late? I answered the first question in the last chapter, but the second question needs a more detailed response—will it then be too late? This question has been the focus of a great deal of my research over recent years. However, not only do I describe here a technical answer to the question "Will it be too late?" but I have become convinced in the process of investigation that this is more or less how the future will unfold. It is how we will both survive the impending sustainability and climate crisis and begin the process of building a new economy and society. This is where we come into our own.

This research led me to a new understanding of what's possible. Up until this point, like most advocates for action in this area, I shared the assumption that society was capable of letting the situation reach a point where it would be "too late," a point where we would not be capable of stopping a runaway process of ecological collapse. This risk of a runaway breakdown is perhaps the most important issue in this whole area. It is of great concern to scientific experts seeking to understand whether there are tipping points where the global ecosystem takes over and acts on such a scale that nothing we do can have any influence.

I am pretty confident such points exist, but I am also now firmly convinced we will act before we reach them. I wasn't always so sure. It was only when I understood what a true crisis response could achieve that I realized just how dramatically we can, and I believe will, respond when we do. It is not a pretty picture, but it is a realistic one.

In doing this research, I was joined by my friend and colleague Professor Jorgen Randers, professor of climate strategy at the BI Norwegian School of Management. I mentioned Jorgen in chapter 2 as one of the original authors of the Club of Rome report *The Limits to Growth*. He has been a tireless advocate for action on sustainability since that book was published in 1972 and became the bestselling environmental book of all time. He is deeply experienced in these issues and from many points of view. Along with his MIT PhD and his current professorial role, he has been a company director, a business school president, deputy head of the World Wildlife Fund (a global NGO), and an investment manager.

Jorgen and I are on the core faculty of the Prince of Wales's Business and Sustainability Program, an in-depth seminar for corporate executives run by the Cambridge University Programme for Sustainability Leadership. After one of these seminars in 2007, Jorgen and I, joined by my wife, Michelle, took some time out and went mountain bike riding in the Barrington Tops National Park in Hunter Valley north of Sydney. Over dinner one evening, the three of us were discussing how we saw the global response unfolding as the economy moved beyond the limits to growth. We had first discussed this issue a year earlier with the team at my advisory business, Ecos Corporation, brainstorming what a global crisis response might look like.

With thirty-five years of focus on that very topic, Jorgen had a great deal of wisdom to share. Indeed, in 2004 he had published, with his colleagues from 1972, the thirty-year update to *The Limits to Growth* titled *Limits to Growth: The 30 Year Update*, where they explored this very question.

Around the time of our discussion, there had been greatly renewed public attention on climate change and sustainability. Governments and the corporate sector were engaged deeply on these issues, and the public, driven by major climatic events and high-profile campaigners like Al Gore and Tim Flannery, had put the issue at the forefront of public and political debate. So many experts argued we'd turned the corner and would now start to see serious political action.

Jorgen was skeptical of that view. He had seen the issue ebb and flow over many decades, from the 1970s oil shock through various peaks of attention in the 1980s and 1990s to the then emerging global financial crisis. He was convinced the world still wasn't ready for the type of transformational action required to shift the global economy. He mounted a convincing argument, so our conversation moved to when we thought real action was likely to occur and what the science told us about the implications of acting at that stage. Would it be too late? If not, what type of response would then be necessary to prevent societal collapse?

Our first conclusion was that the world was probably still a decade or so away from really engaging with a comprehensive response. We knew what this meant, given the lags in the global ecosystem and what the latest scientific research was saying about accelerating impacts. Any response that hoped, at that late stage, to stabilize the global ecosystem would have to be breathtaking in scale, certainly compared with any proposal on the table in 2007. Otherwise it would indeed be "too late" because the lagging impacts would overcome anything less. So we knew immediately we were talking about an economic and social mobilization comparable to that in a world war.

Two things occurred to us as we explored this idea further over the coming days, while cycling and walking through the mountains. First, there would have to be a major global crisis before such a response would be implemented, because nothing else would drive the dramatic shift in the political context that would be necessary. Second, we knew of no mainstream global research under way to define the response that would then be needed to be effective. All the work being done was based on what Churchill called "doing our best" rather than "what was necessary." The science was clear on what was necessary, and we knew even the most dramatic proposals on the table in 2007 didn't come close.

These conclusions gave us some important insights into how the future would unfold and also set us a clear task to take on.

The fact that a crisis would be needed before society responded actually meant such a crisis was inevitable. As we covered in the last chapter, the momentum of change in the physical system will inevitably cause the Great Awakening, which will in turn trigger a societywide crisis response. This meant the scale of response we foresaw, impossible to imagine in 2007, was not just possible but actually highly likely. History suggested as well that when it emerged, it would do so apparently suddenly, with most people caught by surprise.

That in turn meant the world at this time would urgently need a well-considered crisis response plan but wouldn't have one. So we decided to start the process by writing our version of such a plan and putting it into the public domain. Over the following two years, we did so.

Our prime objective was to encourage other experts to engage on the approach, ideally motivating government policy makers to dedicate adequate resources to a comprehensive version of such a plan, even if just as a contingency. Our other objectives were to alert climate advocates, businesspeople, and the community in general that such a warlike mobilization was at least likely, and therefore we all needed to prepare for it.

We concluded our work and after peer review put it into circulation in 2010 via the academic publication *The Journal of Global Responsibility*.[1] This paper provides the foundation for what I present here.

As we covered in the last chapter, there will be two types of responses when the Great Disruption gets into full swing. First the old economy, recognizing the scale of the threat, will try to right itself. This will be a fight for the survival of that system and its associated power structures. Systems fight hard to protect themselves. What I describe here is the centerpiece of how I believe the response of that system will unfold.

Remember that at this time, the world will have woken up to the fact that we are at risk of collapse. There will be acceptance that action can no longer be delayed, because if it is, key tipping points could be passed that would put survival at risk. There will be sufficient present impacts to eliminate any serious political debate about the causes or the risks—in fact, at this point there will be powerful political forces, in business, the military, and the community more broadly, demanding urgent and dramatic action. This demand will be sufficient to overcome the vested interests' fight for protection of their economic wealth.

There are parallels in this to the context in which World War II was declared both in the United Kingdom and in the United States. Therefore, World War II contains many lessons for us here, above and beyond great Churchill quotes.

When this situation emerges, the first question to be answered will be Churchill's "what is necessary." While it is obvious that the challenge we face is much broader than climate change and goes to the essence of our socioeconomic model, climate change will be the prime focus. There are two reasons for this. First, the system will correctly judge that climate change is the most immediate, clear, and present danger and that if it is not effectively addressed, economic and social collapse will prevent anything else from being dealt with. Second, the system will incorrectly believe that we can continue with our present economic model if we decouple growth from CO_2 emissions and make our economy greatly more efficient in material consumption. As we've discussed the data indicates this is not true, but the system will not be able to cope with that reality, because it will threaten power structures and philosophies too completely; so denial of this will continue for a while longer.

Given that the first point is true, however, there will be great benefit in having society focus sharply on greenhouse gases and climate change. It will, after all, as we will see, require an extraordinary level of focus and effort to be effective.

So with this in mind, what will be *necessary*?

To the objective observer, the climate science is clear on what is necessary. The framework for this science generally translates into how many degrees centigrade we can allow the average global annual temperature to rise above the level it was before the Industrial Revolution. This then translates into a maximum allowable level of greenhouse gas concentrations in the atmosphere to keep below that given temperature target. This concentration level is generally measured as CO_2e (all the main greenhouse gases converted into their equivalents in impact to CO_2, the key greenhouse gas of concern). While this science is imprecise because of uncertain feedbacks, it is currently assumed that to have a reasonable chance of achieving two degrees of warming, the greenhouse gas concentration in the atmosphere must be kept to less than 450 ppm CO_2e.

Using these measures, allowing even two degrees centigrade of warming is too dangerous. Although broadly accepted as an important goal by policy makers, including the 2009 Copenhagen Conference and hundreds of global corporations, few mainstream science groups actually argue that this is a "safe" level. Rather, it is assumed to be "the best we can do" based on the analysis of what is politically "realistic." Two degrees will in fact lead to widespread environmental, social, and economic disruption, including widespread threats to food supplies, dramatic increases in extreme weather, and a significant rise in sea level. Most important, we would still face the risk of runaway warming threatening the stability of civilization. So two degrees of warming is an inadequate goal and a plan for failure.

The logical, science-based response is to set a target that gives society a "safe" outcome. Based on currently available science, bringing global warming back to below one degree centigrade above preindustrial levels can be considered reasonably "safe" for humanity on a crowded planet. Returning below one degree of warming, in other words, is the *solution to the problem*. It is "what is necessary."

Therefore, Jorgen and I concluded that when the crisis hits and the scale of the threat is understood, society will demand a plan to achieve no more than one degree of long-term warming. It was interesting that in our research we concluded that the CO_2e concentration required to achieve this was around 350 ppm. This is the same level being called for by scientists such as James Hansen of NASA and also endorsed as the likely end target by many others. It is also the focus of many in the global climate movement, particularly around Bill McKibben's 350.org. Many scientists in the heavily politicized arena of climate understandably prefer not to enter the public debate on what is a safe target, given that even two degrees creates such resistance. However, I've now had enough private conversations with world-class scientists to be confident that the scientific community will before long settle on this as the upper end of the right target range.

It is interesting to consider the context of risk here. The nature of emissions reduction curves (how an end target translates into annual reductions to get there) means it's very hard to strengthen targets later. So the logical approach to uncertainty, given what's at stake, is to have a tighter target and then lift it later if the science firms up. So from every rational view, one degree is the right place to start at this stage.

Some respond to such a target as unachievable, believing we are inevitably on our way to two degrees or more. In considering this view, it is critical to differentiate between what people believe is politically "realistic," which is a subjective judgement, from what would be technically possible if we decided to address the issue with our full capacity.

In a 2010 issue of *Nature Geosciences*, two Canadian scientists used existing models to demonstrate that if we stopped all emissions tomorrow, temperatures would stop increasing almost immediately and decrease over time.[2] In summary, the only warming that is truly "locked in" is that we choose to create by continuing to emit. A separate study in *Science* in September 2010 found that if all existing energy and transport infrastructure was used for its natural lifetime, but no new infrastructure emitting greenhouse gasses was created, warming would peak at 1.3 degrees and then start declining.[3] Again, the conclusion is that we can physically do this—we just have to want to do it bad enough.

So if one degree is what is *necessary* and more than this is defined as the "enemy" for our "one-degree war," what action is required to win the war, and would the required action be possible to achieve? In other words:

1. Is an agreement to achieve such a plan politically conceivable?
2. If it were, is it technically and economically possible to reduce global greenhouse gas concentrations to a level that will bring warming back below one degree?

Clearly, agreement to a one-degree war plan is hard to imagine in today's world. However, in both World War II and the recent financial crisis, there are clear examples of how fast things can change and how apparently intractable opposition and resistance can quickly evaporate. In the case of World War II, the speed of response by the United States was extraordinary. For example, whereas in 1940 U.S. defense spending was just 1.6 percent of the economy (measured as GDP), within three years it had increased to 32 percent, and by 1945 it was 37 percent. But the GDP increased itself by 75 percent in that time, making the observed increases even more extraordinary.[4] Similarly extraordinary political decisions were made to direct the economy. For example, just four days after the bombing of Pearl Harbor, the auto industry was ordered to cease production of civilian vehicles.[5]

Gasoline and tires were rationed, campaigns were run to reduce meat consumption, and public recycling drives were held to obtain metals for the war effort. Yes, there was still plenty of resistance, but the political leadership of the day, with public and business support, simply overrode it for the greater public good—because the consequence of failure was unacceptable.

So it *can* be done. But *how* would it be done? It is unlikely that the one-degree war would result from a universal global agreement. The process around the Kyoto Protocol and the Copenhagen meeting shows how difficult global agreements are. This difficulty in reaching consensus is often put to me as evidence that we will fail to act on climate change. My response is to ask, "Can you think of other examples where a major military action or economic transformation was driven by a consensus global agreement?" On what basis did we ever believe such an approach would be possible with climate change, especially when many participants have actively sought to undermine it?

We didn't seek a single global agreement to free trade before any action was taken, for example. If we had done so, we would probably still be negotiating on the preamble fifty years later! Instead we started with consultative bodies like the General Agreement on Tariffs and Trade (GATT); we negotiated agreements between individual countries and then expanded them to regions. Meanwhile, very, very slowly, we built the global infrastructure for governance of trade, taking from 1947 with the formation of GATT until 1995 to form a body with enforcement power, the World Trade Organization (WTO). More than sixty years after GATT, even the WTO is still not global in impact, with even China joining only in 2001—that alone took fifteen years of negotiations.

So on climate change, an even more complex economic issue and with significant business opposition to change, it is hard to imagine we would jump straight to a single, legally enforceable, global agreement even in a crisis.

When we do decide to launch a rapid response, it is far more likely that a small number of powerful countries, a kind of "Coalition of the

Cooling," will decide to act and then others will follow. Some will follow in order to align with the major powers, and some will be under military, economic, and diplomatic pressure to join.

In a technical sense, this process is easy. A full 50 percent of global greenhouse gas emissions will be covered if three "countries" (China, the United States, and the EU-27) agree to act. If we add another four countries (Russia, India, Japan, and Brazil), the coalition will control 67 percent of global emissions.[6] Add a few friends and we soon move to more than sufficient impact to tackle the problem. We saw this start to emerge in Copenhagen, and while it will be messy and will ebb and flow over coming years, there is no doubt in my mind that this is the primary way progress will emerge.

The answer to the first question is therefore clearly yes. When we accept the crisis, we are capable of taking the political decisions required to get to work on the action plan. So is there an action plan that would work?

What our work showed is that based on current knowledge and technology, a one-degree target is completely achievable and at an acceptable cost compared with the price of failure. It would be very disruptive to parts of the economy and to many people, and it would require considerable short-term sacrifice, but it certainly "solves the problem."

So from both questions, our political decision-making capacity and our technical/economic capacity, the issue is not humanity's *capacity* to act, but the conditions being such that humanity *decides* to act. Identifying this point is simple: When the dominant view becomes that climate change threatens the viability of civilization and the collapse of the global economy, a crisis response will rapidly follow. Then society's framework will change from "what is politically possible" to Churchill's "what is necessary." Until then, little of real substance will happen except getting ready for that moment.

What would such a "war plan" look like? Can we forecast the likely response that will be implemented when the moment comes? Jorgen and I thought so. In designing our draft plan, we estimated a start date of around 2018, not as a precise prediction, but we needed a start date to model our response and its impact, and 2018 was our best judgment on when this would emerge. Post-Copenhagen, it still seems like a reasonable forecast.

We concluded that at that late stage, four types of actions would be required to take control of the crisis:

1. A massive industrial and economic shift that would see the elimination of net CO_2e emissions from the economy within twenty years, with a 50 percent reduction in the first five years.

2. Low-risk and reversible geoengineering actions to directly slow temperature increase, to safely overcome the lag between emissions reduction and temperature impact.

3. The ongoing removal of around 6 gigatons of CO_2 from the atmosphere per year for around one hundred years and the long-term storage of this CO_2 in underground basins, in soils and in biomass.

4. Adaptation measures to reduce hardship and geopolitical instability caused by then unavoidable physical changes to the climate, including food shortages, forced migration, and military conflict over resources.

It is a symptom of the magnitude of the task that even with the dramatic action proposed in our one-degree war plan, warming would continue above one degree until the middle of this century, before falling back to plus one degree centigrade by 2100.

We suggest fighting the one-degree war in three phases:

1. **Climate War. Years 1–5**. Modeled on the action following the entry of the United States into World War II, this would be the launch of a world war level of mobilization to achieve a global reduction of 50 percent in greenhouse gas emissions within five years. This crisis response would shock the system into change and get half the job done.

2. **Climate Neutrality. Years 5–20.** This would be a fifteen-year-long push to lock in the 50 percent emergency reductions and move the world to net zero climate emissions by year 20 (that is, in 2038 if we start in 2018). This will be a major global un-

dertaking, requiring full utilization of all technological opportunities, supported by behavior and culture change.

3. **Climate Recovery. Years 20–100.** This would be the long-haul effort toward global climate control—the effort to create a stable global climate and a sustainable global economy. Achieving this will require a long period of negative emissions (i.e., removing CO_2 from the atmosphere) to move the climate back toward the preindustrial "normal." For instance, some refreezing of the arctic ice cap will require removing CO_2 from the atmosphere through geoengineering actions, like burning plantation wood in power stations and storing the emissions underground using carbon capture and storage (CCS). We believe humanity can complete the stabilization job in the first decades after 2100.

We tested our suggested emission cuts in the C-ROADS global climate model developed by Climate Interactive, an initiative of Ventana Systems, Sustainability Institute and MIT's Sloan School of Management.[7] This confirmed that implementation would deliver broadly the following results:

- The CO_2e concentration falls below 350 ppm by the end of the century, after peaking at around 440 ppm.

- Global temperature does temporarily rise above plus one degree centigrade in midcentury, then falls below plus one degree centigrade around the end of this century.

- Average sea level rises by 0.5 meters around 2100 and continues rising to a peak of 1.25 meters around 2300. This is still very disruptive and might trigger a tighter target, but 1.25 meters over three hundred years is at least more manageable than current forecasts with good preparation given the longer time frames.

In broad terms, what this all means is that the climate would be stabilized and manageable for global society. There would still be substantial changes to the climate, disruption to the economy and food supplies, and great loss of biodiversity. However, it would be manageable and it would reduce the risk of the collapse to a tolerable level. It would also allow stronger action if the science indicates the situation is worse than expected.

So it seems it is possible to design a plan that would achieve the required reductions. Of course this is just indicative. What is needed is a multiyear detailed modeling and planning exercise on a scale only governments could afford to devise. Our point was simply to show what is possible. So what types of real-world actions does our plan indicate would be required?

We proposed a dramatic and forceful start of the one-degree war, for two reasons:

1. There is disproportionate value in early actions.[8] As the impact of emissions is cumulative, cuts taken earlier in a program save much larger and more disruptive reductions later.

2. History indicates that successful responses to crises tend to involve urgent, dramatic actions rather than slower, steady ones. This engages the public and breaks the tyranny of tradition.

The one-degree war plan therefore proposes a series of global measures to achieve a rapid halving of CO_2 emissions during the initial five-year C-war, through linear reductions of 10 percent per year. The C-ROADS model indicated that it takes cuts of 50 percent by 2023 to reach our goal. Even then, this cut must be followed by reductions to zero net emissions by 2038 and net absorption, each year for the rest of the century, of 6 $GtCO_2e$/year (gigatons of CO_2 equivalents per year). While the initial 50 percent in five years is very challenging, it is certainly doable. Critically, a slower start would make it challenging to achieve the one-degree goal.

The good news is that cutting by 50 percent by 2023 can be achieved with the types of initiatives that studies like those by international management consultancy McKinsey & Co indicate will cost society less than €60/tCO_2e.[9] (ton of CO_2e). The bad news is that making these cuts at a faster speed will, by conventional wisdom, increase the cost. This is based on infrastructure having to be scrapped before the end of its useful life and because technologies will have to be implemented before they are commercially mature. If this is accurate, it is the unfortunate consequence of acting late, as we will be. Delaying action would, however, just make that worse.

There is a counterargument that was not possible for us to model, but we were inclined to support, that a warlike mobilization of the global economy to transform our energy and transport infrastructure will not only be affordable, but may in fact trigger so much innovation and economic activity that it ends up being positive economically. This is argued by many analysts in this area, who see renewable energies as so immature that they will inevitably become not just cheaper than today, but cheaper than fossil fuels even without a carbon price. I cover this further in coming chapters.

Certainly the types of approaches proposed in the one-degree war plan would unleash massive innovation and scale, so this would rapidly be proven either way. It is the case in previous wars that innovation drove new industries and great efficiencies because the determination to achieve an outcome forced major breakthroughs in technology and overcame normal commercial development impediments.

This debate is largely of academic interest only, as the crisis then present will dictate that the approach has to occur, largely regardless of the cost. I don't imagine there was much of a cost-benefit analysis done on the Manhattan Project when the U.S. government decided it needed to produce an atomic bomb. So we can safely leave to history the judgment of relative costs of CO_2 reduction.

To provide a flavor of what we can expect to see when the type of response we are forecasting occurs, I will list some edited excerpts from our plan. They indicate the types of actions that would be required in the first five-year period to get the global economy on the path required to ultimately bring global temperature increase below plus one degree centigrade.

Cut deforestation and other logging by 50 percent

Reduce by one half the ongoing net forest removal and land clearing across the world, including tropical deforestation. At the same time, concentrate commercial forestry operations into plantations managed to maximize carbon uptake. This will require significant payments to developing countries, for the climate services provided by their intact forests, but is surprisingly cost-effective and doable.[10]

Close one thousand dirty coal power plants within five years

Close down a sufficient number of the world's dirtiest coal-fired power plants to cut the greenhouse gas emissions from power production by one third. We estimate this implies closing down one thousand plants,[11] resulting in a parallel reduction in power production of one sixth. (Power production would fall proportionally less than emissions, because the dirtiest plants emit more CO_2 per unit of energy.)

Ration electricity, get dressed for the war, and rapidly drive efficiency

In response to lower power supply, launch an urgent efficiency campaign matched with power rationing. Include a global campaign to change the temperature by one to two degrees centigrade in all temperature-controlled buildings (increase/decrease according to season). Make this part of the "war effort" as a public engagement technique, with large immediate power savings. On the back of this, launch an urgent mass retrofit program, including insulating walls and ceilings, installing efficient lighting and appliances, solar hot water, and so on across both residential and commercial buildings. This would have significant short-term job creation impacts.

Retrofit one thousand coal power plants with carbon capture and storage

Install CCS[12] capacity on one thousand of the remaining power plants. This huge investment would be much simpler through international standardization. The CCS technology will also be needed for removal of CO_2 from the atmosphere later in the one-degree war (generating power using biomass and sequestrating the CO_2). CCS is not yet commercially viable and will require heavy government intervention. However, Jorgen strongly believes CCS will be mandated because it is a simple, albeit expensive, way of reducing greenhouse gas emissions, whereas I'm more skeptical, as I will cover in chapter 12. It's not important at this stage, as all technologies will develop and actions taken will adapt accordingly.

Erect a wind turbine or solar plant in every town

Build in every town of one thousand inhabitants or more at least one wind turbine. If there is no meaningful wind, build a solar thermal or solar photovoltaic (PV) plant instead. Beyond the CO_2 and renewable technology acceleration benefits, this would have the powerful impact of giving most people in the world a tangible physical connection to the "war effort."

Create huge wind and solar farms in suitable locations

Launch a massive renewable energy program focused primarily on concentrated solar thermal, solar PV, and wind power—on land and offshore. Given the urgency, the initial focus will need to be on those areas with most short-term potential for mass rollout, with finance supported by global agreement. The DESERTEC initiative for large scale renewable energy generation in north Africa connected to the European grid provides an interesting concept of what would be possible with a multilateral focus.[13] On a global scale, various studies have shown how we could move to a 100 percent renewable energy system relatively rapidly. A recent global study showed how this could be achieved by 2030 with full baseload coverage. Of particular interest is that it concluded it would actually be cheaper than fossil fuels and nuclear power, due to the considerable efficiencies inherent in an energy system based on renewable generation and electricity use.[14] All such modeling exercises are problematic and subject to controversy, but there is certainly massive potential in renewables with a war effort–type approach.

Let no waste go to waste

Ensure that all used materials are recycled and reused, at the very least to recover the embedded energy. To force this, limit production of virgin aluminum, cement, iron, plastics, and forest products—possibly through international agreements to restrict their use through higher prices or a special global emissions tax on virgin materials. Drive public recycling as part of the war effort (there are good examples here also from World War II, where mass public recycling drives focused on key materials).

Ration use of dirty cars to cut transport emissions by 50 percent

Launch large-scale replacement of fossil-fuel cars with chargeable electric vehicles—running on climate-neutral power—along with a massive boost in fuel-efficiency standards, bans on gas guzzlers, and greater use of hybrid cars. Public repurchase and destruction of the most inefficient vehicles ("cash for clunkers" schemes) may help speed the transition and help address equity issues. Given the time it will take to scale up production, there will need to be rationing of the purchase of gasoline and diesel and other restrictions on their use such as special speed limits on fossil-fuel cars. Such restrictive measures would help drive acceptance of electric and efficient vehicles that would be free of such controls—the fast electric car can wave as it passes the old gas guzzler on the freeway!

In World War II, fuel in the United States was rationed at four gallons (per vehicle per week), then reduced to three gallons, and finally reduced in 1944 to two gallons. Alongside this, a national 35 mph speed limit was imposed, and anyone breaking the limit risked losing his fuel and tire rations. The government ran marketing campaigns to support these measures, such as advertisements asking, "Is this trip necessary?" and education campaigns on "how to spend a weekend without a car."[15] It seems there were early-day environmentalists at the U.S. Defense Department!

Prepare for biopower with CCS

Interestingly, the C-war may not see a large increase in the use of biofuels for land transport (not even second-generation fuels made from cellulose). It seems better for the climate to grow the cellulose and burn it in power stations with CCS, thereby removing CO_2 from the atmosphere while making power and heat. For this reason, boosting cellulose production (in plantations and elsewhere) will be key.

Strand half of the world's aircraft

Reduce airplane capacity by a linear 10 percent per year through regulatory intervention and pricing to achieve a 50 percent reduction in airline emissions by the end of year 5. This will force the rapid development of biofuels for aircraft because of the commercial imperative to do so and force a cultural shift to electronic communication and away from frivolous air travel.

Capture or burn methane

Put in place a global program to ensure that a significant proportion of the methane from agricultural production and landfills are either captured for energy purposes or at least burned to reduce the warming effect of that methane by a factor of 23.

Move away from climate-unfriendly protein

Move society toward a diet with much less climate-unfriendly meat—through public education backed by legislation and pricing. This should be not against particular meat, but against the associated emissions, so that preference is given to protein produced with lower emissions. There are large differences among protein types—emissions differ from soy, chicken, pork, and beef (and within beef, from grass vs. grain fed, particularly noting the emerging science that cattle grazed in certain ways can dramatically increase soil carbon). Therefore science-based policy should be established to encourage the most impactful behavior change and for meat to be rated CO_2e/kg and priced accordingly. We note that the U.S. government ran an effective "meat-free Tuesday" campaign during World War II. There is now already a community-based Meatless Monday campaign.

Bind 1 gigaton of CO_2 in the soil

Develop and introduce agricultural methods that reduce greenhouse gas emissions from agriculture and maximize soil carbon. This will require significant changes in farm technology and farmer psychology, and we are unlikely to get far during C-war. But the effort should be started immediately in preparation for the large-scale binding of carbon in forestry and agriculture that will be necessary from year 5 onward in order to remove CO_2 from the atmosphere over the rest of the century. In both cases, the object will be to grow as much plant material as possible and ensure that the bound carbon ends in the soil or in subsurface storage, not back in the atmosphere. Currently, global forests bind some 3 $GtCO_2$e/yr. Hopefully—through the use of fast-growing tropical plantations, supplemented with industrial growth of algae—we could achieve the binding (and safe storage) of some 6 $GtCO_2$e/yr from forestry and agriculture combined in future decades.

Launch a government- and community-led "shop less, live more" campaign

In order to free up finance, manufacturing capacity, and resources for critical war effort activities, a large-scale campaign to reduce carbon-intensive consumption, or at least stabilize it, would be of great help. This will align well with the general need to shift the economy away from carbon-intensive activities toward climate-friendly experiences. We would propose a bottom-up and top-down campaign to highlight the quality-of-life benefits of low-carbon lives with less stuff.

While all these actions may seem draconian or unrealistic by the standards of today's debate, they will seem far less so when society moves to a war footing and a focus on "what is necessary." Once more, World War II demonstrated that seemingly unachievable actions quickly became normal when delivered in the context of a war effort. They ranged across dramatic increases in the level of taxation, the direction by government of manufacturing, and engagement campaigns to drive public behavior shifts. So once more, the plan asserts that the challenge is not to find appropriate actions, but to make the decision to move on the problem.

The full plan, available from the Journal for Global Responsibility Web site,[16] provides further details on these and other actions that would be required. These include how we could raise $2.5 trillion per year by year 5 via a global carbon tax and how this could be used to finance the measures required to compensate the poor, reduce disruption, and create the new industries and employment required. We also cover the types of multinational decision-making bodies that would be required, including a Climate War Command, and more detail on the actions required after the first five-year war, including major reversible global geoengineering projects to reflect sunlight and remove CO_2 from the atmosphere and stabilize the global climate.

The point is not to say that Professor Randers and I have the right plan or have defined all the right actions. What we sought to establish, and the point I'm making here, is that a study of history indicates that we will, in the end, embark upon a crisis response to climate change, and when we do, we can see through our plan that quite extraordinary reductions and management measures are practical and achievable. The plan also indicates the economic cost will be considerably less than unchecked climate change.

Of course, there will be significant disruption as old industries are closed and dislocation as people are moved on to new economic activity. But in a real war, such losses are caused by the decision to go to war. In our case, losses would occur anyway, because climate change would inevitably drive the collapse of the economy if strong action wasn't taken.

The exciting thing about such a plan is that, unlike in a real war, deciding to launch the one-degree war doesn't cost any lives. Instead it saves millions of them. It doesn't shift economic resources onto wasteful though necessary activities, it redirects them to build exciting new industries that will enhance the quality of life for the people of all countries involved. It doesn't waste a generation of youth and leave the survivors traumatized, it educates a generation in the technologies of the future and drives productive innovation that builds new companies and industries.

It is a war we have no choice but to fight and great benefit to gain from declaring.

CHAPTER 11

How an Austrian Economist Could Save the World

People respond to the one-degree war plan in one of two ways. One is that everything we're doing now in this area is pointless and irrelevant, so we might as well just sit back and wait for the world to wake up. I understand this response emotionally, because when measured against what will be required, all of today's actions and proposals can hardly even be advocated as effective training exercises, let alone a serious contribution to the task at hand.

Other people have a more positive response that goes something like this: First there is great relief that we can actually fix this. That despite the decades of delay, a point will arrive when we'll wake up and get down to the serious work of fixing the problem. Phew, we're not going down after all!

They also see that the decades of planning and talking means we have all the answers to get on with the job—we know what we need to do. Then they realize the scale of the response coming and the light-bulb goes on—we better get ready, in fact we better just get to work and do it! They see that now is the time to prepare our companies, our communities, and our lives for what's coming and start to make things happen. They see a world of enormous possibility open up before them, to think large and act at scale.

They're right. We've got a lot of work to do, and we need to get on with the job, *right now*. That's why sitting back and waiting is definitely the wrong reaction.

So how and when will this unfold? And what do we need to do now?

We'll answer these questions for individuals and communities later, but in the next few chapters I want to focus on the economic implications and how the future will unfold for business, including the role of government in driving that. I do so partly because many readers will be working in business and will be wondering what it means for them. I also do so because I have believed for many years that we are going to need business and markets fully mobilized if we are to achieve the historic task ahead of us.

This is where my favorite economist comes in. Both as an activist and as an entrepreneur, I have always been particularly fond of the Austrian economist Joseph Schumpeter and his theories of creative destruction. He pointed out that markets are basically "a process of industrial mutation that incessantly revolutionizes the economic structure from within, incessantly destroying the old one, incessantly creating a new one."

When I first read these words, I realized they could be describing an ecosystem like a rain forest. It is, after all, a stable overall system, but within it there is a process of constant and dynamic change as old things die or are destroyed and new life is created. Like the market, an ecosystem is at once beautiful and brutal. While we look at the rain forest as a magnificent, peaceful place, if you're an animal being torn apart by a predator, you may have a different view.

Markets are not an entity or a sector of society, but a system and process that we are all part of. This is what led me to advocate while I was at Greenpeace in the 1990s that markets could be a powerful delivery mechanism for social change. In the context of the scale of change we are discussing with the Great Disruption, we will be seeing Schumpeter's creative destruction on steroids.

First, though, a few comments on business and markets in general. Some people see the behavior of many of our current companies and their executives and respond with a generalized view that companies are bad and markets are inherently destructive because of their single-minded and at times brutal pursuit of financial wealth.

As will be clear from my comments earlier in the book, I agree with the many justified criticisms of our current economic model and of many companies and business leaders. The mess we're in was delivered by this model, and our companies and their leaders have played a significant role in that process. However, I also see many attributes of business and markets that are positive and effective, especially when you want to build a new economy quickly and globally.

After decades in both the nonprofit and corporate sectors, pondering these issues deeply, I have come to the view that this is not primarily about organizational form (that is, the organizational ownership structure). It is about people, values, and the design of the system.

For example, it's not that people who work for companies are bad whereas those who work for NGOs are good. Indeed, some of the most genuine and compassionate people I know have spent their whole lives working in the corporate sector, and some of the most destructive people I know work in the not-for-profit community. And of course vice versa. Different types of institutions are simply ways of organizing people to achieve a given outcome. People make them what they are and determine what they do.

Whether an organization is for-profit or not, it is certainly the case that its culture and purpose are critical issues, I think perhaps the most important ones. I am dismissive of the idea that companies can exist with a central goal of generating wealth for shareholders. This to me is a shallow and wholly ineffective way to organize people, which is what companies do—organize people to deliver an outcome. Even though this runs counter to the dominant thinking in most companies, it is not actually a radical idea and is well discussed in the business literature. Even the so-called father of shareholder value, former GE CEO Jack Welch, came out after his CEO tenure and said, "On the face of it, shareholder value is the dumbest idea in the world. . . . Shareholder value is a result, not a strategy. . . ."

It is also the case that markets and business work well only when adequately guided and controlled by society as a whole, through regulation and goal setting by government and by active consumers and community groups holding companies to account. As free market advocate Tom Friedman said, "I don't want to kill the animal spirits that necessarily drive capitalism—but I don't want to be eaten by them either."[1]

One of the realizations I had when we were running campaigns at Greenpeace against corporations was that we were part of the market, that campaigns attacking company brands based on their performance on environmental or social issues could be seen as market forces. Another way of characterizing this was as community regulation.

In the public debate, we often hear questions like "Are you in favor of free markets or regulation?" This is a false dichotomy and dangerously simplifies the issues. Markets work only because of regulation. At its most basic level, for example, business could not function without contract law, which is simply regulation to put structure and rules around social expectations of trust. Regulation makes business function, and good regulation makes business function better. On environmental regulation, many, such as Harvard Professor Michael Porter, have long argued that tighter environmental regulation is a key source of competitive advantage for nations, and benefits rather than inhibits business success—a concept known as the Porter Hypothesis.

As argued by Jared Diamond in *The Third Chimpanzee*, in genetic terms we were quite recently apes, and it is our conscious choice to control our negative genetic tendencies. Regulation is the manifestation of this conscious choice to be a civilized society, with the definition of "civilized" developing and changing over time.

Within climate change, what we now need is for society to set clear and precise guidelines as to how the economy as a whole and each business within it is going to have to behave with respect to greenhouse gases. Likewise more broadly on sustainability. If government does so, I am convinced that business and markets are a key and effective delivery mechanism for the change we need.

First, though, back to the economist whose concepts best describe why markets are a good vehicle for the transition through the Great Disruption.

Schumpeter describes the process we need perfectly when he refers to incessantly revolutionizing the economy from within, destroying the old one and creating a new one. Despite being a fan of well-regulated business and markets, I can see clearly that we need to destroy large parts of the old economy and create new parts. This requires Schumpeter's "destruction" of many existing companies, some of which desperately deserve it. We all have candidates we'd like to put on that list; at the top of mine is ExxonMobil.

We need to do all this, however, while keeping the system as a whole as stable and productive as we can, delivering jobs, goods, and services to the people this economy serves. This is where we need to clearly separate the system—the global economy and society—from the components of the system—individual companies, technologies, and products.

Businesses and markets work inside such a system. A system where NGOs can campaign to hold companies accountable for poor behavior. A system where consumers can reject products and employment from a company that is damaging to society. A system where governments, acting in the interests of the people, can change the rules as needs demand and in doing so put some companies out of business and create the conditions for new ones to emerge. Of course, these things don't always happen, but they all sometimes do. This is what the system design allows, so it shows what's possible for us to create within it.

Where we've gone wrong in managing this system is that we've put the economy on a pedestal as a god that must be protected, with economic growth the metric and our current companies as the foundation of that pedestal. The assumption has been that if government focuses on driving economic growth, all other things will follow.

What we need now is for the conditions to be right for brave government to recognize that the economy serves the people and their quality of life and then acts to deliver this outcome. I accept that individual components of the system, companies, workers, and investors, will naturally and often legitimately argue against change. No one likes to give up what they have, so we all resist. We need government to say: "Yes, I hear your concern, but the greater good demands that change occurs, so let's talk about how to manage that change fairly and equitably. But change *is* going to occur."

Of course, in detail this becomes a matter of degree. During the public controversy that raged on climate change legislation in Australia in 2009, I had a private conversation with a CEO that summed up the challenge well. He was telling me how they should be compensated for the "completely unexpected" shift in regulation to control CO_2 emissions. I thought to myself, "If this is unexpected to you at this stage, after twenty years of public debate, then you are clearly incompetent as a business leader. If you couldn't see this coming as a key risk, then you simply weren't doing your job." Mind you, I didn't say it to him quite like that!

One of the reasons Schumpeter's market works is that individual companies and investors take risks and manage these risks based on their likely return for doing so. If they get it wrong, they fail and pay the price. Government's job is to ensure that the overall economic system functions effectively, not to protect all the component parts from change.

So in the case of the CEO above, yes, there is a legitimate role for government in helping the transition occur as smoothly as possible, particularly when change wasn't forecast. But companies must bear the loss for making bad risk decisions, and on climate change, the risks have been clear for a long time. Going forward they are even clearer, so losses should and will be borne. That's how markets should work.

This raises the question of what role business can and should play in sustainability more broadly. While some people judge business and markets too harshly, risking throwing out the baby with the bathwater, others have unrealistic expectations of what business is able to do voluntarily. I had both these views reinforced by spending a large part of my working life inside the corporate sector as an adviser to CEOs and senior executives at major corporations across the United States, Europe, Asia, and Australia.

I formed Ecos Corporation in 1995 after leaving Greenpeace. I was keen to pursue the idea that business could be mobilized to drive change on sustainability and so formed Ecos to test the idea. Some of my friends who were experts in this field argued that 1995 was too early for there to be a viable commercial business in this area and I should consider forming a nonprofit foundation to work with companies.

I realized, though, that coming out of twenty years in activism, I would need to be in business myself to earn the trust of business leaders. I also wanted to understand business properly, and that meant knowing what it felt like to be an entrepreneur, to have your family's income and security depend upon the performance of your business. As I soon learned, whereas in a well-funded nonprofit organization you can have the wrong idea for years, the market is far more ruthless with mistaken views of what the world needs. This meant being in business kept us focused on what was real for market participants and kept us from getting too far off track with respect to business relevance.

The business ended up being very successful and operated for thirteen years until it was sold in 2008. We built a team of twenty incredibly committed and skilled professionals working around the world advising companies on how to see sustainability issues as market forces and integrating them into business strategy. Our clients cut across all sectors and many countries, with companies like DuPont, Ford, Diageo, BHP Billiton, WMC, ANZ Bank, Insurance Australia Group, China Light and Power, Zurich Financial Services, Placer Dome, KPMG, and Anglo American.

I mention this to point out that my views on business weren't formed just from being an observer. They were developed through my experiences as a business owner and entrepreneur working for over a decade at the top levels of companies around the world, seeing what's possible and what's not for companies that seek to lead in this area.

We always advocated to our clients that business strategy should be centered around a clear social purpose, for the reasons previously discussed. However, we recognized that our clients' bills had to be paid, along with a reasonable return on capital. This wasn't a casual afterthought, an "oh yes, you need to make money"; it was central to our work. Around this time, the focus in corporate responsibility was on the "triple bottom line," a phrase coined by my good friend and one of the world's outstanding corporate sustainability pioneers John Elkington, founder of the U.K. firm SustainAbility. It meant that companies should deliver and report on social and environmental performance as well as profits.

In contrast, we centered our strategic advice on what we called "single bottom line sustainability," meaning that the pursuit of profit, without which no company can succeed, and the pursuit of sustainability should be a single mission, not separate, parallel efforts.

In 2002, Don Reed and Murray Hogarth, two of our most experienced advisers, and I released a major report with the title *Single Bottom Line Sustainability*. It caused quite a stir in the corporate sustainability community around the world because we argued that companies should take *only* those actions in sustainability that delivered definable financial benefit to the company.

It wasn't that we believed in shareholder value as an end in its own right. Ecos followed its own advice and was clearly purpose focused. We were transparent about being in business to drive change toward sustainability, not to do whatever our clients wanted to pay us for. However, we recognized that unless we gave advice to clients that delivered value, they wouldn't keep following it. If we wanted to drive sustained action on sustainability, that action had to deliver measurable financial reward for the companies involved.

Perhaps the most significant thing I learned over more than a decade doing this work was that companies' capacity on issues like sustainability is limited in material impact until the market and regulatory context are in place to reward or punish them for their performance. While we had success in getting our clients focused on the right activities, even the best of them soon came across limits to what they could achieve as leadership companies in front of market trends.

One of our major relationships was with Ford Motor Company, where we worked with many executives, but particularly Jacques Nasser as CEO and to some extent with Bill Ford as chairman. We were joined in this work by Geoff Lye and his team from SustainAbility in the United Kingdom.

Ford faced a classic sustainable business dilemma. At this time they were making most of their profit from selling SUVs and pickup trucks. This had been a very successful strategy, but after a few years it became clear that while sales and profits were holding up, increasing public and regulatory concern about safety and fuel economy meant there was a conflict between the short-term financial strategy and the longer-term business strategy. There was a significant risk that either through regulatory action or customer sentiment change, the market could shift suddenly, leaving Ford vulnerable. Bill Ford even had the courage to raise this dilemma and challenge in public forums.

We worked with a group of up-and-coming executives and Ford's scientists to review the climate science and what it meant for Ford's product strategy. What became clear to them was that the market was inevitably going to shift at some point, and because of the long lead times in new products, Ford needed to shift focus onto fuel economy and climate change as a central part of their business strategy, so they would be prepared. Nasser understood the strategic imperative in these issues and brought us into the full executive on a number of occasions to explain the strategy as it was developing and to develop the executive team's understanding of climate change and other sustainability business drivers.

He understood that having a strategy dependent on cheap oil, a price-sensitive, nonrenewable resource with global climate impact, was a risky strategy, and shifting the fundamental direction of a company of Ford's size was not going to happen quickly.

Many Ford people were passionate about these issues, particularly the up-and-coming executives who saw this as the company's future, and they worked hard to make change happen. Unfortunately, during this period Ford had a major safety crisis erupt with the Firestone tire recall and the recession of 2001, which distracted the leadership from the longer-term sustainability issue.

Nasser got the issues and was a powerful and entrepreneurial force for change in this very old company—the media even referred to him as the "hard-charging Aussie." Bill Ford had great personal belief in environmental issues, even advocating a gasoline tax, as well as having the cultural magic of being from the Ford family. But because they couldn't forge an effective working partnership, Nasser left.

The company floundered for some years following. Ford did some great work after that point, including releasing the world's first hybrid SUV and developing some excellent small-car models like the Focus that were great successes.

However, Ford faced serious challenges when some years later customer sentiment suddenly turned with rising oil prices and Ford's key sales strength, SUV and truck sales, plummeted—just in time to be magnified by the global recession. Having launched some more efficient models earlier, they were in much better shape than GM when the crisis hit and didn't take government funds to keep them afloat. But they never reached their full potential to be an American powerhouse in environmentally advanced cars and were still too reliant on larger, heavier vehicles. They got no encouragement to change from the U.S. government, which kept gasoline prices low and fuel-efficiency standards that were not competitive with the rest of the world's markets.

This whole experience was an important lesson in the leverage of culture and leadership in driving change. These factors are enormous influences on what companies will and won't do in this great transition. Ford of course has survived and prospered to date, but whether the company will continue to do so when the Great Disruption takes full hold, only time will tell. And who knows what more could have happened if Nasser the driven change agent and Bill Ford the environmentalist could have forged an effective team.

At least Nasser will be able to put his experience on climate change to good use now that he's chairman of BHP Billiton. This is the world's biggest natural resources company with investments across a broad range of commodities, including coal and uranium, thus being on both sides of the climate debate.

Another of our key relationships at Ecos was with the DuPont Company. We worked there with Dr. Paul Tebo, who drove their activities around sustainability and was the most effective corporate change agent I've ever known. The CEO during most of my time with DuPont was Chad Holliday, who still stands out as one of the most committed and thoughtful CEOs I have worked with anywhere in the world. Chad was responsible for leading DuPont's transformation toward sustainability from 1998 to 2008.

My favorite story involving Chad is a fine example of my earlier point about the importance of organizing a company around social purpose, with shareholder value being a measure of success rather than an organizing principle.

I was giving a talk with Chad to DuPont's global safety and sustainability leaders. I raised the issue of DuPont as an institution and who really cared about it. DuPont is a proud company with a two-hundred-year history that lives and breathes its culture; you can't spend time there without getting a sense of it. I provocatively said to Chad and the other leaders: "So why does it matter if DuPont exists? You just produce products and create jobs, so if you cease to exist, we can just replace you with another company that produces similar products and creates jobs."

The discussion was dynamic, and I could see the lights switching on in people's eyes around the room. If the company didn't stand for anything, if it didn't exist as something more than a machine that produces things and jobs, then it actually had no inherent value to society as an institution. Of course creating shareholder value matters, but it's not a reason for existence. No one lies on his or her deathbed with the regret "Gee, if only I'd generated more value for shareholders, my life would have been more worthwhile"!

Chad pulled me aside afterward and said, "I now understand what you're trying to achieve here; keep it up." He understood that purpose was central to culture and therefore to financial performance. For years after that, we worked with the company on many issues, connecting them to diverse external stakeholders, aligning their portfolio of businesses to sustainability, identifying new business areas to invest in, and helping them focus on changing the regulatory environment in ways that would reward them for being cleaner than their competitors.

One of these projects was a manifestation of this purpose focus. DuPont is world famous for their workplace safety performance, which is truly outstanding. Dr. Paul Tebo, nicknamed "the Hero of Zero" for his relentless pursuit of the idea of zero workplace injuries, had led the programs in this area, building on a two-hundred-year-old company focus on it.

At this time Paul was expanding the company's focus into sustainability and had been working with Chad and his executives to shift the company's strategic focus to one of delivering societal value, helping society meet its needs through the use of science. The objective was to deliver social needs with minimal environmental impact and align this strongly with the creation of shareholder value for DuPont—what they called "sustainable growth." This was a major shift for a chemical company Greenpeace had targeted as the "world's biggest polluter" when the company topped the United States' toxic release inventory!

Chad and his team decided that with safety being core to DuPont's culture it would be the ideal test platform for their new strategy. Under the leadership of Ellen Kullman, they brought their various safety-related businesses, products like Nomex (fire-protective clothing for firefighters) and Kevlar (for cuts and bullet protection), with their safety consulting business, DuPont Safety Resources, led by Jim Forsman, to form a division focused on saving lives. Of course they sought to generate value for shareholders in doing so, but the language of Ellen and Jim's team clearly showed they took saving lives very seriously, with targets for lives saved by country and region. It was in their language every day. The division grew successfully, and its leader, Ellen Kullman, became the global chair and CEO of DuPont when Chad retired from the role.

In all our work at Ecos with dozens of companies, DuPont was perhaps our most successful because the company fundamentally changed its business model from a shareholder-value-focused chemical and fossil fuel company to a purpose-driven science company that had worked out how to make money by doing good. It was still sharply focused on generating financial value, but it did so under the umbrella of a clear social purpose.

When I recently checked in with DuPont to see how they had progressed since our work there, I was pleased with what I heard. When Paul Tebo retired in 2003 he was replaced by Linda Fisher. Linda's title was expanded to include chief sustainability officer, reflecting Tebo's success in helping DuPont see sustainability as a mission, vision, and growth agenda rather than a compliance role. CEO Ellen Kullman has now targeted DuPont's growth around four megatrends that align well with a response to the Great Disruption—working toward the development of abundant food, reducing dependence on fossil fuels, protecting people and the environment, and growing businesses in emerging markets. DuPont now allocates 75 percent of their research and development dollars in these four areas. Linda's role is to help business units see such sustainability trends as shaping forces for their business strategies. She tells me they are also now seeing, just in the past few years, more pull from customers about the sustainability of their offerings.

But even DuPont bumps up against the limits of leadership. They have more products and solutions to customers' environmental and social needs than the market is yet ready for. With no cost to pollution, their solutions of lighter cars, smarter building materials, and a range of other clever uses of science and technology find a good market but not one that has yet rewarded them strongly for their leadership. Recognizing this, they focus on shifting government policy to tighten standards, with Chad having played a strong and vocal role on issues where many in the business community were not yet with him, such as advocating caps on CO_2 pollution. Ellen continues this approach but still finds other companies opposing such measures.

This is not to understate DuPont's substantial achievements and excellence as an example of what can be achieved by corporate leadership.[2] Far from perfect and with many legacy pollution issues, they are nevertheless at the top of their class, and their contribution to society and to the public debates on these issues has been substantial and deservedly recognized. I point to it as an example that even DuPont, one of the most progressive old companies in the world, with sixty thousand employees and a $30 billion turnover, with passionate and committed leadership, can have little impact on the overall market when the framing conditions of the market aren't in place to reward them for leadership.

That brings us back to the role of government.

With fifteen years working as a business adviser and business owner, I have learned how markets can and can't contribute to the task at hand. Markets are a powerful delivery mechanism, but companies cannot and will not pursue activities that are not profitable. When companies can pollute for free, they will do so. The best companies in the world can resist this tide, but in the end the tide will wash over them.

The solution is stronger government action, and despite public debate arguing this is bad for business, the opposite is in fact the case. As Harvard professor Michael Porter famously proved, government regulation for tougher standards can make countries and companies *more* competitive, not less.[3] So if the U.S. government had enforced fuel economy standards similar to those in Europe and Japan, Ford and GM might never have faced the crisis they did when oil prices spiked, and DuPont would have sold more lightweight materials to them, creating more American jobs in the process.

Companies will rarely ask for such change by themselves; indeed, the U.S. auto industry fought furiously against tighter fuel economy standards in the mistaken belief they were bad for business. Government needs to apply some tough love to such irresponsible adolescents and put in place the boundaries that will make them better grown-ups.

So the major transformation we are about to embark upon will be initiated and driven primarily by government, when forced to do so by the people. However, when government acts, the change will be delivered by business and markets, and at that point the companies that are best prepared, like DuPont, will win the competitive game. In the meantime, many leading companies, who see this as the right thing to do and in their self-interest, are actively supporting tighter regulation. But government will in the end drive it. That is government's role—to cage the market tiger.

How will this unfold in practice? When the awakening occurs, governments will, under pressure from citizens and progressive companies, look to the science for advice on what is needed. The science is already clear on this and will be even stronger by then. It will be, for example, to slash CO2e emissions urgently and dramatically, and such advice will frame government policy.

The one-degree war plan outlined earlier gives one scenario of how this might unfold, as well as an indication of what response will be necessary. While the actual program put in place will vary from this, the science suggests the scale and timing are not likely to.

This will then unleash a torrent of investment by old companies and entrepreneurial start-ups that will reshape whole industries. The new companies will pose a serious threat to the incumbents, as we are already seeing in the auto industry, where both global giants and scrappy start-ups are racing to bring electric cars to the mass market. This is just one example of the game-changing transformations we will see that will reshape industries.

Schumpeter's creative destruction means that many of our current companies simply won't make it, though many will. It also means that a good proportion of the world's top one hundred companies in twenty years' time are names you haven't heard of yet but exist today and are champing at the bit for the race to start and the opportunity to knock over some of the old players. This is exactly what markets are good at.

What the final shape of all this will be, with what technologies, what companies, and which countries end up winners and losers, is full of uncertainty, but the outcome is not. When we act, we will eliminate net CO_2e emissions from the economy in an amazingly fast transformation and then move on to the rest of sustainability.

Slow, but not stupid.

CHAPTER 12

Creative Destruction on Steroids— Out with the Old, In with the New

Whenever I give a presentation to a business audience about how dramatic the change is going to be, there are always some who respond, "Yes, I can see *why* it should be like that, but I can't see *how* it's going to happen, so I just don't think it's going to."

When I say it's inevitable because the science says these kinds of reductions are essential for economic and social stability, they respond, "Perhaps, but I can't see *how*," and they go into the limits of known technology, markets, incentives, government regulation, public support, and so on. Then I ask, "So how do you think it will unfold? Will we just slide into collapse?" There is rarely a cogent answer, just a repeat of the reasons they think it won't happen.

I now understand this common response but didn't until a conversation I had a few years ago with the CEO of a large global coal company. We were having a private conversation about the scale and pace of change on climate policy. I was saying how, based on the scientific assessment of required emission reduction pathways, the change would have to come fast and furious when it did because of our continued delays—delays they were advocating. Therefore, short of some remarkable progress on carbon capture, coal would then go into rapid decline. His response was he couldn't see *how* this could happen. He said there was simply too much coal and too much momentum in the economy to stop it from being burned. Society needed the energy, and coal was plentiful and cheap. It suddenly occurred to me just how different our worldviews were in framing business strategy.

He saw the world as an engineer. He had to see *how* it would happen to believe it *could* happen. This is a good attribute in engineers, by the way, who work with the laws of physics, which are constant. But in this case, as the CEO, his "how" was considered only in the context of his present market framework, where price determined success and political support was high. So from his worldview, although he was a rational person and saw what the science demanded, he just couldn't see the world acting to achieve that outcome. He didn't think about the implications of that deeply because it wasn't a changeable outcome for him—the shift simply wasn't going to happen. Of course, his self-interest and that of his company made having this view easier for him, but that wasn't the only driver.

My worldview was as a systems thinker and environmentalist. I saw what *needed* to happen, based on what the science was telling us were the consequences if we didn't act. I knew society would, in its own interest, have to make that result happen to suit those immovable needs.

From my worldview, I saw his strategy, which was to assume decades of further growth in coal consumption, and *knew* it couldn't happen. For me, the mechanism that would prevent it from happening was a secondary issue—we would find a way to get it done—whereas for him, it was the primary issue. To me, either we would cut CO_2 emissions and he would lose his market or the world economy would collapse under the weight of climate and sustainability impacts and he would lose his market. He looked around and saw energy demand rising, coal being cheap, and many major countries having strong policies in support of coal. This made the science, while important, just one consideration. We agreed to differ.

Science is absolutely central to business strategy in this area. Science is also the reason I am so confident in how these issues will unfold. The world is a system that includes the ecosystem, the market, and human society. This means that even though we can't pin down precise forecasts of individual events and the behavior of individual system components, we can safely assume, with sufficient certainty for planning, that the system as a whole is going to behave in certain broad ways, according to the laws of science and the history of how humans respond to threats.

I recognize, of course, that there is always some inherent uncertainty, but for the purposes of planning business strategy or our lives, there are some things we can pretty much rely on. So when I say "near certainty," this is what I mean—a likelihood so high that it should be central to planning for the future.

Many such near certainties are currently being ignored by major global companies and investors. As a result, they face catastrophic financial risk that hasn't yet been priced into the market.

One of these certainties is that the only future a business should plan for is dramatic, discontinuous change. Remembering that our economy operates inside our environment, this is what the science says is inevitable, so this is what will happen. If I am wrong about a one-degree war kind of response and we don't act, then the economy will collapse under the weight of climate and sustainability impacts. That will also result in dramatic, discontinuous change. Mind you, there is little point in planning for that scenario, because a collapsing global economy would be so chaotic that any business strategy made today wouldn't be of any relevance!

To further explore how this all translates into the market and business strategy, including how investors should see these issues, I will focus on climate and energy. There is much more to how this will unfold than energy, including, for example, huge changes in food and agriculture, transport and city design, materials flow, manufacturing, and packaging. But a focus on climate and energy provides us with a critical insight into the process as well as the most important short-term economywide impacts on both markets and emissions.

I will start with the things we know, the things I'm calling near certainties. One of these is that there is no significant future for coal or oil, short of some surprising breakthrough in technology. I realize I'm making a big call here, one that means pretty much every coal mining and oil company in this multitrillion-dollar market is more or less finished. This will be a surprise to most of them, so I had better explain.

We discussed earlier the need to reduce CO_2e (greenhouse gas) concentrations to 350 ppm and aim for one degree of warming above preindustrial levels. While I'm confident this is close to the target we'll end up with, for now we'll explain what's coming using the much less stringent target already accepted by most of the world's governments and major corporations. This target is for us to limit warming so it does not exceed the very dangerous two degrees. Even this "plan for failure," as I referred to it earlier, means we face discontinuous and dramatic change in the market—change that few investors and companies are considering, even though it is clear for all to see.

To examine these implications, let's take a look at the science. A useful starting point is a study conducted by the highly respected German government–funded Potsdam Institute for Climate Impact Research (PIK), led by Professor Hans Joachim Schellnhuber, whom I've worked with on various Cambridge programs. The PIK conducted a study that calculated what a two-degree target meant for the total amount of CO_2 that could be emitted—in other words, what was our total fossil-fuel budget? Remember in this context that a significant proportion of CO_2 stays in the atmosphere for a long time after it is emitted, some for over one thousand years. This means what counts is the total amount we put up there, rather than when we put it there. That gives us a budget— the total amount we can burn to achieve a given outcome in CO_2 concentrations in the atmosphere and resulting temperature. The answer provided by PIK is that we can emit around 890 billion tons of CO_2 between 2000 and 2050, if we want to reduce the risk of exceeding two degrees to below 20 percent. (Some would argue a one in five chance of catastrophic warming is still too high, but let's accept this for now as the minimum sensible target.)

The PIK then calculated, if we carried on with business as usual, when would the budget be used up—when would *all* the fossil fuels we can afford to burn be gone, requiring a complete stop in their use? Assuming we chose to reduce the risk of going past two degrees to about 20 percent, the answer would be that it will all be gone by 2024. This would still leave around 75 percent of proven economically recoverable reserves in the ground and an even greater proportion of total reserves never to be used. As the famous quote goes, "The stone age didn't end because we ran out of stones."

Remember, these are scientific, business, and economic assertions, not moral or ideological ones. This is good old-fashioned rational analysis.

So again, staying rational, there are only two paths we can go down. We act dramatically, within a decade, to slow down and then eliminate the burning of coal, oil, and gas, or we race past two degrees, racing toward the cliff of climate change spiraling out of control, not being sure where that cliff is or how big the fall will be. Not really a hard choice.

Now let's consider this simple scientific analysis of the available fossil fuels in the context of business and markets. By definition, here we move from science and certainty to markets and assertion.

What about CCS? Can't capturing the CO_2 and burying it in the ground save at least the coal industry? There is little doubt in my mind that CCS can work in a technical and environmental sense. It seems it will be possible to capture CO_2 from power plants and bury it safely. It will be complex and may take longer than we'd like, but it seems achievable. That is not the problem.

The challenge is economics. The question is, will the cost of burning coal added to the cost of capturing the CO_2 *and* transporting it *and* burying it safely be able to compete with the cost of renewables? (Noting as well that using CCS dramatically reduces the efficiency of power generation from coal.) By contrast, renewables are proven technologies, are already being invested in at scale, are falling in price rapidly, and are not burdened by the capital risk and time delays of the massive new infrastructure required for CCS.

The time frames involved and the immaturity of CCS compared with the large commercial investment and research under way in renewables make it hard to see how coal with CCS can win the market battle.

I support government investment in CCS, and I hope it becomes a viable technology because we'll need it for purposes other than coal, such as removing CO_2 from the atmosphere. One way of doing so would be burning biomass like trees in power plants and then capturing the resulting CO_2 and burying it, thereby generating electricity with negative CO_2 emissions. So it should be supported.

Many otherwise rational people analyzing the coal issue fall into what I call the economic inertia trap—we have an enormous amount of coal, the industry is large, therefore it will keep going. Markets are far more brutal than that. If coal can't compete, including maintaining government and community support, it will die a market death. While its inertia will slow that death it will not prevent it.

I am skeptical of CCS's viability as a commercially competitive option when used with coal. Consider this: Despite decades of talk, at the time of writing there is not one commercial-scale demonstration project capturing and sequestering large amounts of CO_2 from a coal-fired power station. Not one. All the various technologies needed are being used somewhere, but that doesn't mean they are commercial in combination, especially given the time challenge of mass deployment by 2020. So the market's view is clear. Despite coal-mining companies having their whole existence at stake, that a successful CCS industry would be worth trillions, and that there is enormous government political support for CCS, including funding, no company in the world has committed to building a full commercial-scale power plant with CCS.

Meanwhile we are already seeing spectacular growth in renewables, with investment approaching $200 billion per year even in the context of difficult economic conditions. Unlike politics, markets are ultimately rational, that's why we see so little commercial money going into CCS. Or as we say in Australia: Talk is cheap, it takes money to buy beer.

I should be clear I'm certainly not against society investing in CCS and matching commercial money to do so. As we'll discuss shortly, I think the market should be let rip on finding solutions, and we should not dictate technologies that are in or out. We should only dictate outcomes in terms of clean and safe. I'm just expressing my opinion on this particular one, as a business strategy risk question.

So is CCS technically possible? Yes. Would I recommend an investment fund relying on it to save their investments in coal? That would be a big call.

So back to our 2024 deadline and the investment implications of all this. Given that a sudden stop to all coal, oil, and gas consumption is not realistic and that CCS is at best a risky strategy, action will have to be taken, and urgently, to slow down growth in the use of fossil fuels, to allow our budget to last longer. Since no serious action is on the table yet, it will still be some years away. Yet we know the longer the delay, the harder the brakes will then be put on because the cliff can't be moved. It's those damn laws of physics again.

What this means is that, as of today, there is a huge risk in the valuation of all coal and oil reserves and therefore of all coal and oil companies. The market hasn't yet priced in that around 75 percent of known economic reserves may never be extracted *and* sometime in the next decade, government will have to dramatically curtail the consumption of coal, oil, and gas.

This means that within this decade, and I think earlier rather than later, whatever government actually does, the market will wake up to the political and commercial risk and dramatically mark down those companies' value. Every year that passes the risk gets higher and the fall becomes harder. When it happens, lower share price equals lower capital for investment, and the terminal decline of those industries will begin. Money will then move into clean forms of energy, making the perception shift self-fulfilling. When it happens, it will occur virtually overnight, as markets tend to shift sentiment in that way. Governments will then abandon support for coal and oil and go with the market toward renewables.

So in summary on this topic, it is clear government has to take action, so they will. That action must result in dramatic reductions in CO_2 emissions, and the science says that must result in the decline of coal and oil, followed soon after by gas. There are no realistic scenarios where this can be achieved if we wait past 2015–2020, unless we decide to go past two degrees of warming. Given that all the world's major governments and most major companies have agreed not to, the logic of the economic risk flows pretty easily.

So if you lose your shirt on your coal and oil investments, don't say you weren't warned!

This is just one example of the market implications of our "near certainties." Now we move into the great unknowns. Without coal, oil, and gas, we're going to need a whole lot of new technology and infrastructure. This is going to be the mother of all economic booms.

What will be the result of this transformation? Which technologies will succeed and in what time scales? For investors reading this, where's the money going to be made?

Two notes of caution before I give my opinion on these questions.

First, we are now moving firmly into an area of major uncertainty, and we should be comfortable with that. We don't need to know *how* we're going to achieve it because we have a strong history of achieving what we set out to achieve as a society. If we were relying on one technology or even one class of energy generation, I would not be so comfortable asserting this, but we have a plethora of different possibilities for achieving our desired outcome, and we can be certain a number of them will succeed in achieving our objective of CO_2-free energy supplies across the world at a manageable price.

What technologies we have available certainly matters, and that's why I'm going to cover it here. We need to understand the range of potential ways forward so we can make a broad assessment of the realistic potential. We also need this so policy can be made and investments placed. However—and this is really important going back to my coal company CEO—it is not a question of *how* we will do it that will determine *what* happens to initiate it.

When Great Britain went to war in World War II, do you think they had clarity on all the details of transitioning into a war economy *before* they made the decision to act? Of course they considered it, as we must, but it wasn't a determining issue because there was no choice. Do you think President Roosevelt calculated the United States could win the war by increasing military spending to 37 percent of U.S. GDP and producing a nuclear bomb before he decided to enter the war? Of course not; he just knew they had to succeed and so they would. He had confidence in human ingenuity delivering under pressure, when it's given defined parameters and political support, and so must we.

So the countless analyses that have been done on technology and how we can transition to them are useful and worthwhile, for a whole range of reasons. But they are not what will determine whether we act, Mr. Coal CEO; we will act because we have to.

The second note of caution is on ideology and technology.

People focused on this area become fascinated by the technologies involved in the required energy transformation. Of course, our fascination with technology is not limited to energy and climate change. People love technology and love talking about it. There is nothing inherently risky with this until we turn it into an area of emotional belief. It is still relatively harmless if the issue is Apple vs. Microsoft, Ford vs. GM, or PlayStation vs. Xbox. But it matters a lot when applied to energy technology.

This has become a dangerous and destructive tendency on *all* sides of the climate debate, because it turns technologies into questions of belief, where you are asked to take sides. Are you pro or anti coal, nuclear, solar, and so on? This undermines rational thought. I've had many conversations inside companies where I hear completely ridiculous things from otherwise rational people. Another coal company CEO took me aside one day and told me about all the downsides of wind and why its potential is so exaggerated. He explained that the life cycle CO_2 cost of wind makes it worse for climate change than coal. Only when questions become ideological do science and facts go out the window like that. (In case you're wondering, wind power's full life cycle CO_2 emissions are lower than coal's by about 99 percent!)[1]

Both sides are guilty, with some environmentalists being opposed to carbon capture and storage because it would be used to keep the coal industry alive, as though the objective were to kill the coal industry rather than to stop CO_2 emissions.

Nuclear power is the most fascinating in this regard because for decades it has defined an almost religious belief. The broadly defined liberal or left-leaning side of society was avowedly antinuclear, and the broadly defined conservative, pro-market, right-leaning side of society was pro-nuclear. In recent years with this "right-wing" technology being a beneficiary of the focus on the "left-wing" issue of climate change, nuclear power has cut a swath through this ideological divide. Some environmentalists, like James Lovelock and James Hansen, now actively support nuclear power. On the other side, various right-wing ideologues have had to come out in support of action on climate change.

A great example of this was Hugh Morgan, a mining company CEO, archconservative commentator, and unarguably Australia's most effective and powerful climate denier and opponent of action over many decades. (His company, WMC, was a major Australian mining company, and my company consulted to them when they produced an environmental report in the late 1990s.) After he'd left his CEO role, Hugh was still active in the public debate. I heard him do an interview where he argued that he didn't believe in climate change or the need to act. Then he advocated that people should definitely support nuclear power as the best solution to climate change (he was involved in a new nuclear venture). Such bizarre inconsistencies are inevitable when you lose the ability to think rationally by burying yourself in ideology.

There are many arguments against coal and nuclear power and many arguments for caution in taking various renewables to scale. That is not my point. I'm simply advocating a careful, rational discussion about the opportunities open to us and an intelligent debate about the alternatives, in the context that a failure to change will have consequences.

That's why this matters, because it has consequences. Of course we need to have opinions about technology, particularly in business and investment strategy. However, when people *campaign* against technologies, as questions of ideology and belief, then argue we shouldn't invest in them, we act more slowly because uncertainty is sown on our ability to move forward. This makes government less inclined to act.

So with these two notes of caution, where do I think we will go with technology? I certainly believe technology will play a critical role in the way forward. However, I'm not a techno-optimist who believes technology will fix it all. As we covered earlier, climate change is just one issue in sustainability, and there is no way we can address all our challenges with technology and keep growing the economy. This is made even stronger by the rebound effect, where technology drives efficiency and efficiency drives more technology use. This means behavior change and shifts in how we organize our lives will in the end be essential. But technology will be an important enabler.

To avoid the techno-ideology trap, it is helpful to have some criteria to consider technologies against. For energy, mine are simple. They have to deliver close to zero CO_2 emissions, they should be as safe as we can afford, they should be able to be rolled out at scale quickly, and they should be considered in a systems context. The latter means we should consider factors like our quality of life, our geopolitical security, and our future prosperity and economic stability. In other words, remember we are designing a society, not a gadget.

With these criteria in mind, I know I cannot avoid the question "What about nuclear?" so I should cover it first.

I don't see how nuclear can even be a good partial solution given the complications of waste, terrorism, and supply limits. I'm certainly open to being persuaded why I might be wrong, but I haven't been yet. When I'm asked about nuclear power in public forums, which I frequently am, my answer is this: If you're asking me would I rather have nuclear power or climate change, the answer is straightforward. Nuclear power is preferable, but it's the wrong question. The question should be what is the cheapest safe form of available energy that emits zero CO_2.

If that is the question, I suspect neither coal with carbon capture, for the reasons I outlined earlier, nor nuclear power will give us the answer. But we should let the process unfold and allow the market, which will incorporate the price of risk and public acceptance, find the best solution. I would be delighted if CCS became sufficiently competitive to retrofit every coal plant in the world in a decade, and I would be very happy to hear of a proven way to use nuclear power without radioactive waste, risk of meltdown, or producing materials that were dangerous in the hands of terrorists or rogue states.

However, against the criteria listed above, and on what we know today, renewable energy and geothermal together provide an intrinsically more elegant and intelligent solution to our energy needs than anything else. If we have the opportunity to move to a safe, clean, widely available energy source with zero fuel price and very low geopolitical supply risk, then we should try our best to make it work. Even if it costs more in the short term, surely the benefits of setting ourselves up for a more prosperous, stable society make that effort worthwhile.

Apart from the lack of CO_2, the extraordinary amount of solar energy arriving on the planet means renewables make intuitive sense. Consider this: Every hour an amount of energy equivalent to what all of humanity uses in a year hits the earth's surface from the sun. Even after allowing for the limits in accessibility and converting this into useful energy, a year's supply arrives every week.[2]

Another "annual supply" of energy is available from the wind every month and another one *again* each month from geothermal. Then there is the hydro from rivers and energy in the waves and tides. So there is just *so much* energy available, it is implausible that we cannot access it effectively and at a reasonable price if we put our minds to the task.

Energy has been fundamentally important to humanity's progress throughout history as it is today. This is one of the reasons action on climate change is controversial—because energy supply and availability is so critically integrated into our lives and our economy. That's why recognizing the enormous amount of clean and safe energy we have available to us is such an important mental shift. We think we live in scarcity and as a result often act from a place of fear. The truth is very different. We live on an abundant planet and our future progress is now only constrained by our thinking.

There is further reinforcing logic at a system design level for solar and wind power. The fuel cost for generation is zero and the energy is available all over the planet, meaning all those imports and impacts on balance of payments are gone. This global energy security also largely eliminates a whole range of related geopolitical risks and the resulting military threats and instability, not to mention the enormous costs involved. The savings on offer are tangible and we don't have to look hard to find real numbers. A fascinating peer reviewed study reported in the journal *Foreign Policy* pointed out that keeping aircraft carriers in the Persian Gulf from 1976 to 2007 cost over $7 trillion. This was a direct subsidy as the explicit mission was to secure oil shipments.[3] Such missions will not be required to keep the sun shining or the wind blowing.

Another advantage of renewable energy is having zero fuel cost meaning no price uncertainty once plants are built. This allows business to guarantee their energy price and contract it for decades into the future, greatly reducing the energy price risk for long-term investments for energy-intensive industries. This makes national economies more resilient as well.

This is also interesting at the consumer level—imagine buying a car with a five-year contract to lock in your fuel supply at a given price because the energy provider had in turn locked in their price with a solar power plant.

Another powerful argument at the system level is that everything we've learned about technology indicates renewable energy will get cheaper and cheaper. Unlike fossil fuels, which we know will increase in price because of supply constraints and extraction complexity, renewables will get cheaper as they go to scale and keep doing so for decades to come. They don't leak into the ocean, they don't involve blowing up mountaintops, and there is no risk of peak sun, not for a few billion years, at least!

Of course, there are issues to overcome in going to scale like the supply of some rare metals used, water access, matching supply-and-demand timing, and connecting to the grid. But these are all being worked on today in the real world of the energy market and can be solved. My personal view is that the result will be energy cheaper than today, available in all countries within a few decades. With a war effort dedicated to the task, we can expect that even sooner.

This widely available, steady-price electricity is likely to transform the car industry as well. With electric cars already on the verge of widespread availability, we can expect dramatic change in our cities and our power systems. Having millions of battery-powered cars means that the auto fleet can also become a giant distributed storage system and each car can become a personally owned power utility. So when your car is parked and there is a peak demand for power on a hot day, you can sell the electricity in your car batteries back into the grid at a profit!

These are some of my conclusions on technology. We'll return to more examples of such new business opportunities in later chapters on building a new economy. If you want to investigate the energy issues more deeply, there are many high-quality analyses available. In particular for the whole picture of climate solutions, I would recommend Al Gore's book *Our Choice*. For a brief overview of how we could shift to 100 percent renewable energy in twenty years, I would recommend the Stanford University study summarized in *Scientific American* that I referred to earlier.[4] For those who want a deep dive into energy, I'd recommend the free downloadable book from David MacKay at http://www.withouthotair.com.

The key investor point is that we have many, many options for clean energy; they are not laboratory experiments but serious full-scale commercial enterprises today. If you have any remaining doubts this is a short-term commercial issue, consider that in 2008 and again 2009, more capital was invested in new renewable power generation than in new fossil-fuel and nuclear power generation.[5] The game is now firmly on.

As the market sorts this out, something else will come into play that I am convinced will kill off nuclear power and coal with CCS. That is the speed of change.

There is an understanding in the long cycles of technology penetration, one which holds that people usually underestimate how long it takes for a technology to reach critical mass and then overestimate how long it will take to go through exponential growth. We see this play out in many areas on a regular basis, like digital music being around a long time with little impact, then suddenly booming. Likewise digital cameras, e-book readers, and so on.

This is how it has been and will be with clean energy technologies. People say solar has been twenty years away from being competitive for forty years! True, but now we're actually seeing the price fall dramatically and, perhaps even more critical, the amount of investment in the area growing exponentially. While the percentage of installed energy from renewables is small today because of the long capital cycles, growth rates of 25 to 40 percent per annum will soon overcome that. And again, that's before government gets serious about driving change.

What are the business and investment implications of all this?

Much has been said about the economic transformation to a low-carbon economy. None of this compares with the real scale of the opportunity or the commensurate level of risk to those companies that aren't ready. As outlined in previous chapters, government will have to act ruthlessly and firmly when they act. They will not tolerate the prevarication and debate we have seen around us in recent years. Government attitudes will resemble those in war, with a level of determination and focus that will see change occur messily and inefficiently but quickly and reliably. Government will ensure the public is deeply engaged and supportive, as they will need this support to implement the required actions.

The scale of change needed has been compared to a transformation like the Industrial Revolution. Even this doesn't adequately frame it, because that happened relatively slowly. I think of the coming transformation being like a twenty-year dot-com boom on steroids with military support. Schumpeter's creative destruction will move through the economy like a wild fire through a dry forest.

To implement this change quickly, government will have to direct the market to achieve a given level of emissions reduction in a certain time frame. The economic shift will be much faster than most commentators believe, because most analyses assume normal market conditions and investment cycles, not government mobilizing on a war footing with associated market intervention.

So we can assume humanity will respond late, with a plan something like what Jorgen and I developed in the one-degree war. This is not a pretty story for most companies, many of which will be replaced by smarter, faster, new companies.

Change on this scale will create some big winners among disruptive companies with new technologies and business models that address what will then be urgent social needs. It will also create some big losers among companies that are slow to respond or make the wrong call on the direction of change, such as backing the wrong renewable technology or staying with fossil fuels too long.

Consider some of the changes that have been associated with the move toward digital technology—minor in scale compared with those we face in dealing with our current challenges, but interesting examples of industry shifts. Kodak, one of the giants of the photographic industry until the 1990s, proved unable to cope with the shift to digital, even though they knew it was coming, and had to sack 60 percent of their workforce of sixty thousand. One of the successes of digital technology is the U.S. company Netflix, started as a DVD-by-mail company but now increasingly focused on unlimited streaming movies online. By taking advantage of the smaller size of a DVD and now streaming technology, Netflix was able to essentially destroy the giants of the video rental market in just a few years. Blockbuster shares, trading at $30 in 2002, now fetch less than $0.20. At one movie a day, the Netflix service costs just $0.30 a movie—a price that the old Blockbuster model simply can't match.

Unlike the boom in the dot-com industry, when the new economy was hard to touch, making it at times difficult to differentiate talk from reality, the transition to a low-carbon economy is more nuts and bolts. I heard recently about a green investment fund that bought stocks in a ball-bearing company because they expected dramatic growth in sales to wind power companies for their turbines.

Also different from the dot-com boom is that many of these new businesses will have real-world income, selling electricity to utilities obligated by law to buy an increasing percentage of their power from renewable or other low-carbon sources. The numbers quickly become substantial. In 2008, about 125 million households in the United States spent an average of about $104 a month on electricity bills. That's over $150 billion a year (and growing), just in residential consumer spending, just on electricity, just in the United States. When you include commercial and industrial electricity bills, total U.S. end user spending in 2008 amounted to a staggering $363.7 billion.[6] This is just what end users pay for what they consume each year, so behind that is trillions invested in the capital equipment and infrastructure required to generate and deliver that output. Given that is just for electricity, not counting the much larger value in oil for transport being converted to renewable power in a few decades, this is a breathtaking opportunity.

There's certainly massive numbers involved. The 2009 *World Energy Outlook* by the International Energy Agency forecast that $10.5 trillion in *additional* capital spending would be required for energy infrastructure under a proactive response to climate change just between now and

2030. Many analyses focus on the cost of all this change and wonder how we can afford it, especially if the economy is struggling at the time we choose to act. What they're not taking into account is the similarly breathtaking opportunities to save money through energy efficiency, perhaps one of the most exciting areas of short-term opportunity for investors in this whole space.

The IEA's current estimates suggest that the economic benefits of energy efficiency will be significantly greater than all the costs of the investments required to start decarbonizing the energy system. Their assessment suggests that from now to 2050, the incremental investment required to reduce emissions by 50 percent is around $46 trillion, with a major focus on energy efficiency. It sounds like a lot until you consider that resulting fuel cost savings of $112 trillion delivers a net economic benefit of around $66 trillion. Even discounted at 10 percent, this means a net savings today of $8 trillion.[7] So again we see that the actual action required isn't hard or expensive, it's the decision to get on with the job that seems to be challenging.

As a result of the delays to date, we can be sure the coming market-driven change will not be smooth. But then markets rarely are. This poses particular challenges for investors who have to make decisions on timing. If you're still thinking this is decades away, though, think again. HSBC estimates the global market for low carbon technologies will exceed $2 trillion per annum by 2020, with capital investment of around $10 trillion during the current decade.[8] It also forecasts that China will overtake the United States in share of the global low carbon market while India will overtake Japan, cementing the geopolitical power shifts I will cover shortly. With the transformation thus in full swing by the end of this decade, anyone guiding a company or investment fund needs to pay careful attention now. While it will start with a focus on energy and water it will soon spread to all aspects of the high-carbon economy and then to sustainability more broadly.

Some of you are thinking, "Haven't we heard all this before, several times? Wasn't the energy revolution going to start in the 1970s with the oil shock and the beginning of the solar revolution? Then oil prices went down and it all went away? Haven't people been saying ever since that the boom is 'just around the corner'?"

Yes, all true, but this is fundamentally different for a simple reason.

Each previous time, the transformation has been driven by economics; fossil-fuel prices went up so alternatives became competitive. We have let the market determine the pace of change, yet put no price into that market for the damage caused by climate change. So before, the argument that the alternatives were uncertain, or more expensive, was a really significant commercial impediment to change and a barrier to new policy to support that change.

This time, it's driven by science. It doesn't matter if oil and coal completely collapse in price, which I think they may well do at some point as clean energy takes off. We simply won't be able to burn them because of the CO_2 impact. Through markets, taxes, or straight-out regulation, the science dictates that government stops us from burning fossil fuels that emit CO_2. (Unless, of course, the much lower price for coal then makes coal with CCS economically competitive! That would be a good example of the unpredictability for investors in this area, but either way energy generation that emits CO_2 is finished.)

All this means that, unlike the past forty years, it doesn't matter if clean energy is more expensive anymore. In many cases it's not anyway, and it will all get cheaper from here on, but that is now irrelevant. When you accept what we face, price no longer matters.

I know this seems like a ridiculous argument when so much of the impediment to change has been price, but think about it. When we wake up to the issue, do you really think we'll do the assessment "Can we afford to save civilization, or would we rather keep our energy costs down while we hurtle off the cliff into collapse"? Of course we won't.

I've used power generation as my prime example of the business opportunity and of technology options. This, however, is just the opening shot in a business sense. Yes, we have to produce power differently, but we also have to retrofit every house in the world to make it far more efficient, with insulation, draft proofing, double- or triple-glazed windows, and the like. We have to replace the auto fleet and build new infrastructure to support electric cars or whatever technology wins that race. We have to recycle and reuse 100 percent of all materials, including all drink containers, computers, and cars, by offering incentives to do so, like having container deposits on the one hundred billion or so plastic bottles and aluminum cans used in the United States each year.

And then we move into changes in agriculture to maximize the uptake of carbon in soil and to prevent the nitrification of our waterways. We'll also need infrastructure and systems to manage and deliver water differently with changes in rainfall patterns. And on and on it goes, all the way through the economy.

This has all been argued before, in fact for many decades. This entire time people have advocated the need, to investors, governments, and corporations, that we should drive these changes—and by the way, it would be a great commercial opportunity if we did so. It was just that, though: advocacy that people *should* pursue it.

Now it's different. I am not advocating the change; I'm saying it's here and it's unstoppable. The only question for business and investors is who gets on the boat and who drowns, because the tide has clearly turned.

CHAPTER 13

Shifting Sands—From Middle Eastern Oil to Chinese Sun

History has many examples of powerful companies, countries, and empires that have fallen because of complacency. They think they are protected by their size and momentum, forgetting the lessons of the world's oldest surviving "civilization"—the global ecosystem: Survival in a system is not about size or strength, it's about capacity to adapt to changing circumstances. Consider the dinosaurs.

Being responsive to change requires us to understand what might be coming and to be as ready as we can be for surprises—to consciously and deliberately develop resilience.

The reason resilience is now so important is that we have unleashed massive change on every level. Change that is physical—the impacts of shifting climate zones, refugees, weather disasters, and rising sea levels—but also geopolitical and economic. In this new world, which resources are valuable in economic and geopolitical terms changes dramatically, including the end of oil, shifts in economic competitiveness, and conflicts over resources, including water.

To get ready for these new system conditions, we have to consider both practical preparedness—investing in the right technologies—and psychological readiness—can we cope with uncertainty and rapid change? Will we seize the opportunities or get stuck lamenting and resisting the pace and scale of change?

In this context, all participants need to keep their eye on the prize on the other side and ask: Is my family, company, community, or country ready for what's coming?

As we covered in the first half of this book, system shocks are now unavoidable. What *is* avoidable is failing to respond effectively to stabilize the system in response. The more we think through the possibilities and the better we prepare and respond, the greater our chances of both dealing with situations that arise and leveraging them for maximum benefit.

This brings me to the geopolitical implications of what this all means for countries and national competitiveness. In this context, there are four issues I'd like to cover:

- The security and economic consequences of the *physical* impacts of climate change, coming as they are on top of existing sustainability challenges.
- The global and national shifts in economic competitiveness caused by both the shifting value of resources and the shift to new technologies.
- Challenges to the moral authority of different cultures and economic systems, driven by their ability to respond to the coming crises.
- The process of retribution and accountability for creating the problem.

The physical, security, and economic consequences will now be significant regardless of our response. Even with a response as dramatic as the one-degree war, the climate will continue to change physically and many other sustainability issues will have significant social and economic impact. We are already seeing this with water availability shifting, increased extreme weather, sea level rising, food supplies being threatened by climate, and other sustainability limits being breached. All these trends will now accelerate. While this is well understood at the scientific level, we are just beginning to think about planning for the economic, security, and social implications.

A prime example of this is food shortages, supply shocks, and price volatility. Given that we experienced shortages and price spikes in 2008 and again in 2010, the pressure now piling up on the food supply system makes it inevitable that more of this will come. On top of the already stressed supply situation, we face a 33 percent population increase and greater per capita demand driven by more wealth and associated expectations for more complex diets. While agricultural production has increased dramatically over recent decades, it has stopped increasing on a per capita basis. There is also a price to pay for the industrialized farming techniques that have delivered this, such as the nitrogen overload that has yet to fully work its way through the system.

We see food as a natural healthy industry. In reality, the nitrogen fixation on which it relies is highly carbon intensive, and industrial agriculture (in stark contrast with traditional agriculture) is a nonrenewable industry (that is, dependent upon things that run out). This makes it unstable in the coming world.

The industrialization of food is not just about the physical impacts on the environment, however. We now have an integrated global food supply system that is highly specialized and commoditized. While these types of systems deliver great efficiency and low costs, they are particularly prone to shocks and change. As the New Economics Foundation (NEF) pointed out in its report *96 Hours to Anarchy*, Western countries have now created such a finely tuned, just-in-time food supply system that the loss of transport, for example, would see supermarket shelves in some countries empty in just four days. All it would take would be a terrorist attack on fuel depots, a peak oil price panic, or a pandemic keeping drivers at home, and chaos could erupt very quickly, with enormous social and political consequences.

This system is already tightly wound and highly stressed. Climate change is only increasing the pressure, making the global geopolitical risks even greater. We can expect major issues in India and China because, already struggling under the impacts of environmental degradation, the water supplies that feed their agriculture are being threatened by over use, magnified by climate-related shifts. Serious food shortages affecting this region of two billion people could soon lead to widespread geopolitical, economic, and social consequences, with resulting refugees and social and security instability.

There are many other such examples around the world. With so many of the world's people living in coastal regions, sea level rise will have major impacts on security and stability, particularly in poor countries, with the potential for millions of refugees well documented.

The conflicts that will inevitably arise and the shift in power among countries that will result are impossible to accurately predict. However we certainly need to get our militaries, security think tanks, and development and aid bodies to ramp up their planning for these developments. We can't now avoid such impacts, but we can certainly get ready to manage them by building the requirement for resilience into our planning.

These are the negative geopolitical impacts, but there will also be some significant impacts for the relative competitiveness of nations in the transformation to a low-carbon economy. For some, these will be positive, for others much less so.

Countries that depend on oil income, for example, could find this income virtually disappear over a few short decades. The security implications of resulting failed or conflict-ridden states across the Middle East and elsewhere could be dramatic.

While not significant on a global scale, my own country, Australia, is an interesting illustration of the global trends. We will lose our significant historical competitive advantage of cheap energy and export income from plentiful coal. With one of the highest per capita CO_2e emissions in the world, Australia quickly finds itself at a competitive disadvantage when a high-carbon price is applied. We are already suffering the physical impacts of climate change disproportionately, with severe drought and water shortages wreaking havoc both on our agriculture and on city water supplies. We have had tragic wildfires in recent years that have been so far out of historical experience, they have necessitated the design of new ratings systems for severity of fire conditions. With the likely loss of coral reefs, we also face severe impacts on one of our key income earners, tourism. Some would say all this was karmic retribution!

On the other side, however, we have many advantages and opportunities. Our large land area means we have the potential for significant scale impact with soil carbon. If the science confirms that cattle can be grazed in ways that lock up soil carbon and thus make grazing cattle a net carbon sink, then our vast areas of country become an exciting opportunity with potential global impact.

Our hot, dry continent is blessed with lots of high-intensity sunshine, making our country particularly well suited to solar power. This applies both at the domestic level with distributed power and solar hot water and at the utility level with solar intensity, meaning we can produce energy at a lower cost than many other places in the world. We also have a long coastline for wave power, plentiful agricultural land for wind, and some excellent geothermal areas.

These issues play out differently in each country, but it is already clear they will lead to major shifts in relative economic power around the world.

At the global scale, the most interesting competitive battle is likely to be China vs. the United States. While the United States has considerable advantage with its history of success in innovation and technology, its lack of responsiveness to date is causing this advantage to move steadily to China.

There is great irony in this. For decades, many Western companies have argued against stronger environmental policies on the grounds of loss of competitiveness to China and the developing world. The argument has been that if Western countries made their companies behave more cleanly, Chinese companies would be able to outcompete them because they could pollute freely and therefore have lower costs.

What's been happening while the West has been delaying action, partly in response to this argument, is that China has caught up and is now seriously pursuing a low-carbon economy. Do they want to save the world? No, they want to own it. As Tom Friedman argued:

> Yes, China's leaders have decided to go green—out of necessity because too many of their people can't breathe, can't swim, can't fish, can't farm and can't drink thanks to pollution from its coal- and oil-based manufacturing growth engine. And, therefore, unless China powers its development with cleaner energy systems, and more knowledge-intensive businesses without smokestacks, China will die of its own development.

So China has become an example of the Great Disruption and perhaps provides an important insight into our future. They are being forced to act, with rapidly increasing intensity, because they are hitting the physical limits of their economic growth model. They are not quite in an emergency response phase, but they are seeing clear economic consequences of environmental system impacts and are taking stronger action in response, including major interventions in the market such as closing down dirty industries and strongly supporting the growth of new cleaner ones.

Whatever the motivation, China has the potential to dominate the technologies of the future with the advantages of both scale and the capacity for rapid change. I wouldn't be surprised if China puts in place a national system for pricing carbon pollution before the United States and Australia can get it through their respective political processes.

China already boasts the world's richest solar entrepreneur, Dr. Zhengrong Shi, who spoke to me passionately about the need to address climate change when I addressed an event launching his business in Australia. An accomplished solar scientist, he is determined to make solar cost competitive with coal. Chinese born Dr. Shi was educated in Australia but saw the urgent need and great business opportunity to apply his skills in his home country so went home and founded Suntech Power. In a move laced with irony, Suntech is now opening a plant in Arizona, making it the first Chinese clean tech company to bring manufacturing jobs to the United States. China also has a world-scale electric car and battery company, BYD, that has significantly boosted Warren Buffett's wealth. Buffett bought 10 percent of BYD in 2008. BYD beat GM and Toyota to market with the first plug in hybrid vehicle and proposes to sell all electric cars in the United States by 2011. Unusually, the United States is looking like a laggard in this technology race. Indeed, in lists of the top ten companies in various new energy technologies compiled by investment bank Lazard,[1] the United States lags behind Japan, Europe, *and* China, an uncomfortable place for a country that has prided itself on technology and entrepreneurial leadership.

China is not alone. India already has in place a carbon tax on coal to raise money to invest in promoting renewables. Brazil is emerging as a bioenergy superpower. According to the bankers at HSBC, South Korea committed 78 percent of its recent economic stimulus packages to environmental measures, while the United States focused just 11 percent in this area.

The point of all these examples is not to prescribe an approach, but to argue that all countries now need to see this issue for what it is—a *current* driver of change in what makes a country competitive. Countries that assume their current strength will protect them are likely wrong. Remember, strength counts for little against a more responsive competitor.

In the longer term, some deeper issues will emerge as we see who succeeds in adapting to the emerging world. The Western model of market-based democracy clearly dominated the twentieth century. Indeed, without China's success late in the century, it would have been indisputable. While people express various levels of discomfort with the political, social, and cultural approach of the United States, the world's people have largely tried to emulate much of what the country represents. Reinforcing this has been the dominance of U.S. power in most areas of competition and conflict; whether it was World War II, the cold war, the technology revolution, music and film, or overall wealth creation, the United States represents the success many aspire to.

As the twenty-first century gathers momentum, however, it is not at all clear that the United States will be able to maintain its dominance and critically whether it will still represent the most effective political and economic model that others will want to follow. China in recent years has been taking increasingly dramatic decisions to force environmentally driven change in its economy while market-based democracies have floundered. While many are skeptical of China's capacity to carry through, there is plenty of evidence to suggest its market is accelerating ahead of the United States already. China is already the world's largest solar PV manufacturer and the largest market for wind power.

What if the United States, saddled by debt and military costs and well behind in the race to new energy technologies, continues to drift as emerging countries like Brazil, India, and South Korea forge ahead? What if China can maintain stability and lead the way on the environmental and technology transformation now under way? Will China's very different approach to decision making, democratic freedoms, and open society be a hindrance, as many commentators argue? Or will it be an advantage, enabling them to leapfrog in technology and drive change without the pesky limitations of Western democracies' corporate lobbying and populist politics slowing down change?

If China succeeds and the United States fails, the implications could go well beyond the shift in economic competitiveness and wealth. It could undermine the moral authority of democracy and lead to a shift in global geopolitics back toward autocratic regimes. The worse the crisis of the Great Disruption becomes, the greater the risk this will occur. What's at stake here is more than economic success.

Such a result is certainly not inevitable; after all, the United States and United Kingdom led the victory in World War II against nondemocratic enemies. And there are many powerful and proven economic benefits to democracy and freedom, with the U.S. success in technology and innovation often being put forward as an example. Likewise many argue that China's restrictions on freedom will lead that country to political instability and possible breakdown.

Nonetheless, however many of us view democracy as a superior system, we should not lose sight of the inherent risk to it in the period we are entering. This is now a high-stakes game.

Whichever way all these issues unfold—and it is probably the most unpredictable area of all—what is very clear is this: The social, security, and economic implications of climate change and sustainability will force a major realignment in world geopolitics. In this process, responsiveness to change will determine the winners and losers, not a preexisting power or authority.

On a smaller stage, one of the more interesting developments will be the response of "victim" countries, those nations that have contributed little to the problem but face catastrophic impacts. Alongside this will be the legal and economic conflicts in rich countries over the relative contribution and impacts on different sectors, companies, and individuals. As the world enters a full-scale physical and economic crisis, people will be looking for revenge on the perpetrators. This will be messy and complex but will certainly occur.

It's not hard to imagine how this might unfold. When low-lying countries like Tuvalu, Kiribati, or the Maldives cease to exist because they're under water, their citizens are going to be pretty cranky. In all likelihood they're going to want to blame someone and seek retribution. Also in all likelihood the world will (sadly) largely ignore them no matter how just their cause, because these countries are small and not very powerful.

However, when great swaths of countries like Bangladesh, China, India, and the United States become affected, when we have hundreds of millions of refugees, geopolitical conflict, and trillions of dollars of real estate devalued by risk of sea level rise or extreme weather, we will no longer be able to ignore the question of cause and accountability.

Some of this will play out in the geopolitical realm, where poor countries demand compensation from those rich countries whose pollution largely caused the problem. These poor countries will expect military and food aid to deal with the consequences. Some of it will play out in the courts as individuals, countries, and companies sue those they consider responsible, first for the pollution and second for the decades of prevarication and delay, particularly by deliberate cover-ups or misrepresentation of the science. Some of the world's biggest corporations will be on the firing line. Will today's coal and oil companies become tomorrow's asbestos or tobacco companies?

As well as legal actions and campaigns attacking reputation, some of this will be simple economic transfer within the economy as governments force the costs of pollution onto the companies that create it. A 2010 study[2] suggested the economic costs of the environmental damage caused by the top three thousand companies in the world were around $2.2 trillion for the year 2008. This represented about one third of all their profits. At some point, governments and others will be coming after these profits that have been "taken from the environment."

Sadly, it is also seems inevitable that some of this will play out in acts of terrorism against countries and companies. Whether or not you believe terrorism is caused by injustice, it is certainly fueled by it. Many long conflicts throughout history have been created by the loss of land or the sense of injustice at damage done to a culture or group of people.

There is surely no greater injustice than the elimination of your country's existence or the death of many of its people—especially when it's done for the sake of more cup holders in your car or a larger television for the spare room.

CHAPTER 14

The Elephant in the Room— Growth Doesn't Work

This century is going to be a wild and exhilarating ride. The pace of change will be breathtaking and the twists and turns unpredictable. We will face the real and present danger of falling off the cliff and plunging to our demise. Assuming we make it as I think we will, the year 2100 will be met with a huge planetary sigh of relief: Phew, that was intense!

But in telling that whole story, we have a ways to go yet. It may seem like a fair bit to cope with—the economic crisis of the Great Disruption, followed by the one-degree war and the complete transformation of the global economy to zero net carbon, all happening in parallel to a global realignment of geopolitical power, accompanied by widespread military and social conflict from ecosystem breakdown. All that, however, is just act one.

Now we come to the most exciting and most significant part of our journey.

Despite achieving all of the above, we will still have one more obstacle to clear before we move to the next stage of humanity's development. We can be sure of this because of where we started, with the physical limits of the planet.

Exploring this is the subject for the remainder of the book, so before we do so, let's take a moment to remind ourselves of the story so far.

We started with the acceptance that, despite fifty-odd years of investigation, science, and talk about the limits to growth, little has changed. With the global economy now hitting the limits of both the planet's finite physical resources and its capacity to absorb our impact, this economy is grinding to a halt. It is doing so messily and unevenly, but the effect will be the same. This will unleash a crisis that will be recognized in two successive phases.

The first phase of recognition will be the failure of growth, which will be a massive economic and political crisis because our global system is based on the assumption that economic growth is the foundational source of our society's prosperity and success. It is the way we are supposed to consistently and indefinitely improve the quality of life for all, including bringing the poor out of poverty. It is also how we are supposed to amass the resources and technology needed to address all our other social and environmental challenges. So the failure of growth will be correctly seen as the failure of the underpinning idea behind our progress. The cultural, political, and values consequences of this will be profound. Therefore we will resist acceptance for some time while we desperately try to restart growth.

The second phase will be the recognition that the end of growth is being caused by hitting the planet's physical limits. This, as we detailed earlier, will have consequences across the global system, including reinforcing the end-of-growth crisis by convincing people it is not a temporary problem. With widespread humanitarian, social, political, and physical impacts, there will then be enormous pressure on our global political, security, and economic system.

We then covered that once we woke up, the response of this system would be swift and dramatic. The established power elites will see climate change as the cause of the crisis and as a threat to their ongoing power and influence because it puts the whole model of progress into question. They will then act swiftly to address that problem, along the lines outlined in the one-degree war plan Jorgen Randers and I drew up. They will be successful in addressing climate change because, as we covered earlier, human ingenuity combined with a global warlike mobilization by governments will be able to achieve extraordinary things and do so remarkably quickly, even with the predicted late start.

Initially this will be seen as the solution to the failure of growth, because the extraordinary level of economic activity that will be required to achieve the elimination of net CO_2 emissions from the economy will create exciting new companies and industries and cause a realignment of national competitiveness. In the short term, this will appear to put growth back on track. Indeed, on the surface it will have all the hallmarks of a breakthrough that proves the power of markets and economic growth.

This creative destruction on steroids will be a sight to see, and we all look forward to watching the failure of some old economy dinosaurs and the birth of tomorrow's giants in renewable energy and other climate-friendly solutions. We will see amazing breakthroughs in technology that significantly enhance our lives and show just how good we are when we get focused on fixing things. Our cities will be cleaner, our transport cheaper, and our agriculture transformed. These will be exciting developments and will bring great benefit to humanity, not least of all by averting global economic and social collapse.

This phase of transition, however, will inevitably be messy, with chaos and volatility at the social, economic, and political levels in various countries at various times.

Despite the challenges involved and the decades of what will effectively be a war mobilization, we will get through all this. We will then be very pleased that we dodged the climate bullet that threatened to bring us down. We will be able to celebrate our resilience and our ingenuity, the brilliance of the human mind, and the power of innovation and markets to drive rapid global change when government puts in place the rules to guide it.

However, it will not be enough.

This is because, as we covered in the first half of the book, the problem is not climate change. That is just a symptom. The problem is the delusion that we can have infinite quantitative economic growth, that we can keep having more and more stuff, on a finite planet. We cannot, and that is just a fact.

We can and will perform what today feels like economic miracles, like eliminating the coal, oil, and gas industries and replacing them with new ones. We can use our extraordinary ingenuity to find ways to transform agriculture, cities, and transport systems. We can do all this while keeping the global economy and society within some general sense of order.

We can do all that, but we can't change the laws of physics and biology. For as long as we have a society that defines progress through material wealth, we will just keep hitting the wall defined by those laws again and again until we wake up.

At this stage, we can't know which particular physical limit beyond climate will force this issue. However, with nine billion people aspiring to a Western standard of material living, we can be sure the limits will be hit.

The *Planetary Boundaries* report released by the Stockholm Resilience Centre suggested there were nine boundaries we cannot cross and maintain a sustainable economy. They are climate change, stratospheric ozone, land use change, freshwater use, biological diversity, ocean acidification, nitrogen and phosphorous inputs to the biosphere and oceans, aerosol loading, and chemical pollution. Of course, such individual boundaries are useful to define the challenge and measure progress, but as the report points out, the system is all connected and crossing one boundary will increase the likelihood we will cross others. So it is likely we will face several of the boundaries at once.

While that list adequately defines the physical ecosystem limits, there are many other limits as well, including good old-fashioned resource limits. Where do we think we'll get the iron ore and other materials to build the cars we will need if all nine billion people achieve their aspiration by 2050 to live like Americans? Even if they all emit no CO_2, building and maintaining six billion cars, ten times the current number globally, would still require an extraordinary amount of materials that can come only from nature.

Some would argue we will develop new, natural biomaterials to build our cars—plastics that come from plants. On what part of our already shrinking arable land supply, then further stressed by rapidly shifting climatic zones, do they think we will grow the food and graze the cattle to feed us the advanced diet nine billion people aspire to, if we have to *also* grow the trees and plants to make plastics for six billion cars and the rest of our products? Not to mention the land needed to grow the trees and plants we will need to make the paper and timber for nine billion people *and* grow the trees and crops we will need to absorb the already emitted CO_2 and also create the biofuels for our cars and planes (noting that the corn required to fill one twenty-five-gallon SUV tank can feed one person for a full year). Altogether, this makes a lot more land than we've got. When you look at the system as a whole, you realize many otherwise appealing solutions can't *all* happen.

The list can go on. Into the metals for electronics, the fish for our protein, the building materials to house nine billion people, the water for our water-intensive manufacturing, agriculture, and lifestyles. And on and on. . . . We can replace coal with solar power, but we can't build houses, cars, and phones out of air.

Will there be extraordinary innovation and changes in materials and agriculture? Absolutely. There will be breakthroughs in technology that will take our breath away with their simplicity and brilliance. We will all wonder why we didn't do it much earlier. However, despite those breakthroughs, which I am very excited about, it is delusional to believe we can keep growing a materially based economy without hitting the physical limits of the planet. You can debate the precise timing, but not the basic principle. An infinite growth economy on a finite planet just doesn't add up. This is the way it is, and we have to accept that, along with its implications. As Senator Daniel Patrick Moynihan said: "Everyone is entitled to his own opinion, but not to his own facts."

So despite our herculean efforts on climate change, we will not have solved the underlying problem. The growth economy cannot and will not continue to grow.

So this is where we are in our story. The now emerging failure of growth means our current model of social and economic progress is now in the messy and painful process of dying.

The *only* choices we get to make are how and when we change, not whether. We *have* to redesign the economy, and with it much of our politics, personal expectations, and market, to fit in with the immovable physical reality of a finite planet. As one of the leading economists in this area, Professor Herman Daly, described it:

> The closer the economy approaches the scale of the whole Earth the more it will have to conform to the physical behavior mode of the Earth. That behavior mode is a steady state—a system that permits qualitative development but not aggregate quantitative growth.[1]

While the end of growth is inevitable, there are many choices to make in how we respond. Choices about when we begin the process and what we change to. We need a steady-state economy, one that doesn't grow or rely on growth for its stability and functioning. Don't confuse steady state as in "still and not developing," though. We have to design an economy that is rich in progress and increasing prosperity, but not destructive in physical impact. This means we will replace it with a much deeper and thoughtful approach to human development, one that will improve the quality of life for all.

This is the topic for the remaining chapters: to put forward some ideas about what choices we need to make, at the personal, corporate, national, and global levels.

While this change is inevitable and ultimately positive, there will still be a great deal of angst. Remember how people attacked *The Limits to Growth* in 1972. Leaving behind growth is going to be challenging for many people, and they will defend the old approach. This requires us to be clear on what we have to leave behind. What do we have to lose? How well has the growth economy been working for us?

The basic premise of growth, the promise made by its advocates, is that we will all be better off if the economy grows. Yes, the rich get richer, but the poor get richer as well. So as long as we're all becoming better off, the system is working and we're all happy; that's the claim. The marketing of this model of organizing society has been extraordinarily successful. All around the world, regardless of political system, people have aspired with few exceptions to apply some form of the Western model of market economy to their lives in the belief they would be better off. So has it delivered?

Let's look at the answer from two perspectives, the global capacity of the system—is the economy strong and able to keep delivering?—and the personal human level—is it making our lives better?

At the system capacity, the answer is certainly, on balance, no. What we have achieved is what Professor Herman Daly called "uneconomic growth." In economist-speak this means "the quantitative expansion of the economic subsystem increases environmental and social costs faster than production benefits, making us poorer not richer, at least in high-consumption countries."

In other words, while we appear to be getting richer because we have more stuff, we are spending all sorts of hidden capital to get that stuff, so our actual real net wealth is going down, not up. This is like maxing out your credit cards and buying holidays, new clothes, and TVs. You feel rich for a month, then the credit card bill comes in and you can't pay it, so you have to sell your house to do so. Numerous economic analyses, such as the *Millennium Ecosystem Assessment*, show that the net wealth (total capital stock) of the human economy is degrading faster than we are creating new wealth. So while the amount of money in the system increases and the measures of economic activity rise in volume, value is in fact being destroyed, not created. That means economic growth is failing to deliver greater wealth—it is in fact uneconomic.

Of course, it doesn't feel like that on the ground. In the West, we've never had it so good with regard to our material lifestyle. And if you're one of the hundreds of millions of people in China, India, and elsewhere who have come out of grinding poverty over recent decades and are now living better lives, it also feels great. All that, however, is just like the lifestyle funded by credit cards. It does feel good . . . until the bill comes in and you lose your house. My argument is that this is the decade when the bill arrives, and if we're not careful, we'll lose the big house.

So how about at the personal level? In the West, we have had spectacular success in growing our economies since the middle of the last century. As we discussed in chapter 1, we have lives our grandparents would look at in awe. The life of the average middle-class family in the West would seem to them like the lives of emperors and kings of yesterday. So despite being uneconomic at the macro level, it *has* delivered at the personal level. But is it still doing so?

Surprisingly, the answer is also no.

For readers who want the theory, Professor Herman Daly argues the point as follows:

> The logic of the SSE (steady-state economy) is reinforced by the recent finding of economists and psychologists that the correlation between absolute income and happiness extends only up to some threshold of "sufficiency," and beyond that point only relative income influences self-evaluated happiness. This result seems to hold both for cross-section data (comparing rich to poor countries at a given date), and for time series (comparing a single country before and after significant growth in income).[2]

What that means is we get richer, but once out of poverty, we don't get any happier. We can observe what Daly argues in our personal lives.

Sure, on the surface we love our gadgets, our houses, our cars, and our holidays. We certainly wouldn't give them up lightly if we were asked to. But we also know that the fleeting satisfaction these things bring doesn't last. That's why we keep buying more of them. Every study into relative life satisfaction and happiness suggests we don't gain any significant advance in collective quality of life through further economic growth after our basic needs have been met. The data is consistent across cultures, countries, and time.

The only source of gain is that when one person does better than a peer, that person feels better. So getting more money and stuff than whomever you compare yourself to does bring a level of satisfaction because it increases your self-worth. But the net gain for society remains at zero, with all of us just switching places around inside the system in a pointless game. All this happens while the planetary credit card gets maxed out.

Surely we can do better than that.

One of the arguments most used in favor of continued economic growth is something along the lines of, "Yes, but the poor of the world aspire to our standard of living and they're entitled to it. How dare you apply your middle-class Western concern for the planet to deny them that right?"

My initial reaction when I heard this was irritation, because the argument is usually made by right-leaning, free market businesspeople or commentators. My experience is that these people have rarely showed any great concern for the poor previously. In fact they usually blame the poor for their poverty, arguing it's their lack of personal effort to succeed in a free market world. Of course now that concern for the poor serves their self-interest of defending growth, they've changed their view. It reminds me of a quote favored by my late father-in-law, Max Grosvenor: "Hell hath no fury like a vested interest masquerading as a moral principle."[3]

That aside, though, my more considered response is to go back to the core argument as to what's wrong with our current economic system. Quantitative economic growth is, let's be clear, very effective at improving the quality of life and life satisfaction of the poor. Countless studies have shown that, using a measure of purchasing power parity, going from an income per annum of $0 per capita up to around $10,000 to $15,000 per capita delivers a dramatic and sustained improvement in quality of life. This means it works up to a family income of around $60,000, then any further average improvement stops.

So I am not arguing that quantitative economic growth doesn't work for the poor; it most certainly does. The problem is that the system that currently delivers this assumes, and in fact depends on, the rich getting richer in order for the poor to be less poor. The math of economic growth means the rich getting richer also increases inequity—this is both the logical result and the evidence of the past forty years. This means the system design requires increasing inequity for the poor to be less poor.

So morality aside, what's wrong with inequity and the rich getting richer? The problem is the research now shows that increasing inequity within nations *degrades* the quality of life for *all* its citizens, including the rich ones. We'll return to this later. So the net result of all this is that using economic growth to address poverty means the rich getting richer with the resulting inequity ultimately degrading the quality of life of all in that society. Okay, so the rich don't get any happier, but the poor do; so can't the rich suffer a little for the poor's benefit?

This leads me to my second considered argument as to why alleviating poverty is not an argument for economic growth. If economic growth is uneconomic—that is, it destroys our capital base, thus destroying wealth—then it is not generating net wealth for anyone, including the poor. Yes, for a short time, a fleeting moment in the history of humanity, some of the poor will see an improvement in their quality of life. This will work until the whole economic system collapses once the capital stock is depleted (the point we are now approaching rapidly), after which everyone will become poor. That will certainly deal with the problem of inequity, but it doesn't seem like an intelligent way to run a society.

If you find yourself in an argument with someone on this issue and the logic offered here isn't working, try this fact from the New Economics Foundation. For every $100 of economic growth between 1990 and 2001, only $0.60 went toward poverty reduction for those on less than $1 a day. So the vested interests are defending their $99.40 of gain on the grounds of the $0.60 going to the poor.[4] Sounds like heartfelt concern indeed!

So as an approach for dealing with poverty, our current model of economic growth is certainly not going to work. We will return later to what will.

Of course, all the data is just reinforcing what common sense and instinct are telling us anyway. I have conversations with people all around the world who aren't experts but are questioning the current model at a personal and observational level. They look at their own lives, and despite being told their increased material wealth over recent decades has made them and their society better off, they aren't sure their quality of life has improved. They are working hard yet find themselves deeper in debt. They look around and see communities that are less connected and less safe. They see their children growing up in a world that is fearful and uncertain of its future. They read the science about the emerging crisis in the global ecosystem, and they are starting to wonder whether we are on the right track. Some are downshifting their lifestyles and finding that less money, more time, and less stuff are actually making them feel better and their lives happier.

Of course, here I am focusing on the big picture of humanity's progress—how are we going and where do we need to go next. I am certainly not simply dismissing the past fifty years of human progress, and I recognize the many significant gains made in medicine, technology, and our understanding of how the global ecosystem operates. My key argument is a simple one. Whatever its past successes, the system is no longer delivering the outcomes we designed it for, and if we don't respond to the signals around us, we face serious risk that those advances we have made in the past fifty years will be squandered and we will take a great leap backward.

So it is time for a change, pure and simple.

CHAPTER 15

The Happiness Economy

We now have two reasons to change.

First, we have no choice, and that's always a good reason! The impossibility of continued quantitative economic growth means we'll be forced to shift to a new model of human development to avoid collapse.

Second, the old model has passed its use-by date anyway; it *has* delivered, but it can't any longer. It's not enhancing the quality of life for those whose basic needs have been met, it's globally uneconomic because it is destroying our capital base, and it can't even deliver for the billions of poor because doing so will bring down the whole system, hitting the poor the hardest.

But what will we change to? What is the radical new way to organize society and the economy? How could it work, and how can we transition to it?

The really interesting thing you discover when you look into these questions is that the way forward is neither radical nor new. This moment in time, the end of growth, was in fact foreseen by the founding fathers of economic theory and market capitalism as a natural point we would *inevitably* reach. As expressed by John Maynard Keynes, arguably the most influential economist of the twentieth century:

> The day is not far off when the economic problem will take the back seat where it belongs, and the arena of the heart and the head will be occupied or reoccupied, by our real problems—

the problems of life and of human relations, of creation and behavior and religion.

Even further back, in 1848, one of the pioneers of economics, John
Stuart Mill, anticipated the transition from economic growth to a "stationary state." In his *Principles of Political Economy*, he wrote:

> The increase of wealth is not boundless. The end of growth
> leads to a stationary state. The stationary state of capital and
> wealth . . . would be a very considerable improvement on our
> present condition.

And preempting critics over 150 years later, who today argue that
economic growth is essential for human progress, he wrote:

> It is scarcely necessary to remark that a stationary condition of
> capital and population implies no stationary state of human
> improvement. There would be as much scope as ever for all kinds
> of mental culture, and moral and social progress; as much room
> for improving the Art of Living and much more likelihood of
> its being improved, when minds cease to be engrossed by the
> art of getting on.

Scarcely necessary indeed. We can go still further back, virtually to
the beginning of economics as a field of study, to Adam Smith, whose
famous 1776 book, *An Inquiry into the Nature and Causes of the Wealth of
Nations*, was described as "the effective birth of economics as a separate
discipline." Adam Smith assumed and indeed forecast the end of economic growth and the transition to a stable-state economy, for various
reasons—including what he saw as the obvious limits of natural resources.
Smith reasoned that all economies would eventually reach a "stationary
state" when they had "acquired that full complement of riches which
the nature of its soil and climate, and its situation with respect to other
societies allowed it to acquire; which could, therefore advance not further and which was not going backwards."[1] So over two hundred years
ago, the founder of modern liberal economies recognized what we have

since forgotten—that any economy remains constrained by its "soil and climate" or its natural resource base.

Thus it seems the arguments against growth are *not* the territory of radicals seeking to question the capitalist model but have in fact been long understood by capitalism's founding fathers as a logical point we would inevitably arrive at.

Now that we have arrived, our task is to define what this steady-state economy will look like and how to transition toward it. We have to transition to it rather more abruptly than was perhaps expected or risk undoing the hundreds of years of progress that got us to this point.

There is more good news in this history. Because the logic has always been so clear, a great deal of work has been done to define our task and many guidebooks have been written.

One of the organizations most active in this area is the New Economics Foundation. When I met with the NEF's executive director, Stewart Wallis, he raised an interesting issue that struck me as perhaps our most urgent task. The design of a steady-state economy is in fact not that difficult. The challenge, he argued, is this: There is a significant difference between a steady-state economy—one designed to operate that way—and a failed growth economy, which would be the absence of growth from our current economy. His concern is that a failed growth economy, with rising unemployment and many other social and economic challenges, poses a serious threat to social and political stability and could lead to considerable suffering. He pointed out that a steady-state economy can be designed to avoid this, but it must be just that—designed to do so, including the transition to it.

The challenge Wallis gives us is to act before this point is reached, so we can actively move to a new model rather than letting the old one fail, which would then make transition much harder. The NEF has focused on how the transition could work and what concrete policies could be put in place now, with immediate benefit. Many others have also proposed actions governments and individuals can take now that start to move us in the right direction.

Such transition measures also give us insights into what a steady-state economy would be like. These are not all new ideas. In fact, many of them are already in existence in mainstream policy. Others could easily be applied now within current economic structures.

One example is cap-and-trade systems on key resources. These are being applied to both resource supply (such as fisheries, water) and pollution amounts (CO_2, SO_2). Another major one already on the agenda and in progress in some countries is to start moving taxes from things we want more of (for instance, labor) to things we want less of (pollution/resources). This encourages employment (addressing one of the key risks of a failed growth economy) and discourages material use and waste (reducing the risks of economic shocks that a sudden change like peak oil pose). Such a shift in the tax approach would also reward those who choose to work less and consume less, an idea we'll explore further shortly.

Some proposals include setting limits on inequity, a major challenge we'll come to in the following chapters.

We can also put in place systems, in addition to tax changes, that actively encourage the workforce to choose to work and spend less, by providing more flexible working hours, including more part-time work. This starts to slow the economy without increasing unemployment as a result. It also generates a cultural understanding and live examples of people living happily in new ways—less work, less debt, less stuff, more fun, more community, and more security.

What the work of all these pioneers, from Adam Smith to Herman Daly, and the work of groups like Center for the Advancement of the Steady State Economy (CASSE)[2] and NEF tell us is clear. The task before us, while not simple, is also far from impossible. Given such change is the only option we have before us, short of allowing society to collapse, this is a welcome relief!

Getting to work on this transition will bring a substantial upside. While, as covered earlier, our response to climate change will deliver many immediate improvements in our quality of life, it is in designing a steady-state economy that the benefits really flow. This is where we start to reinvent the way we organize our economy, society, and lives to unleash our full human potential and creativity. In doing so, we will get to steadily improve life satisfaction and eliminate many persistent problems that have long dogged us, some throughout our existence—problems like extreme poverty and inequity, like unsafe communities and unhealthy cities, like our overworked and time-poor lives and resulting strained families. We'll return to this, including what we can do now to start the process by acting at the personal level.

While personal action will be important, especially at this early stage, urgency will require us to apply the enormous power of government to the task. We need policy that is designed around improving quality of life rather than economic growth for its own sake. It is frankly ridiculous that for many decades, the key measure by which we have judged governments' performance on social progress has been GDP, the total amount of economic activity in a nation. It is as though any economic activity is good, and therefore the more the better. This obsessive focus on economic growth as an end rather than a means has led to a very unhealthy system of measurement of progress. Despite the lack of evidence to support the current approach, it is a system that few mainstream political leaders have questioned in recent times. Consider though Robert Kennedy, who said in 1965:

> Too much and for too long, we seem to have surrendered personal excellence and community value in the mere accumulation of material things. Our Gross National Product . . . counts air pollution and cigarette advertising and ambulances to clear our highways of carnage. It counts special locks for our doors and the jails for the people who break them. It counts the destruction of the redwoods and the loss of our natural wonder in chaotic sprawl. It counts napalm and it counts nuclear warheads, and armored cars for the police to fight riots in our cities.
>
> Yet the Gross National Product does not allow for the health of our children, the quality of their education, or the joy of their play. It does not include the beauty of our poetry or the strength of our marriages, the intelligence of our public debate or the integrity of our public officials. It measures neither our wit nor our courage, neither our wisdom nor our learning, neither our compassion nor our devotion to our country; it measures everything, in short, except that which makes life worthwhile.

There was clearly some serious reflection going on at this time following a period of such prosperity. Republicans were on the job as well, as indicated by President Nixon's comments in his State of the Union address of 1970:

As we move into the decade of the seventies, we have the greatest opportunity for progress at home of any people in world history. Our gross national product will increase by $500 billion in the next 10 years. This increase alone is greater than the entire growth of the American economy from 1790 to 1950. . . . In the next 10 years we shall increase our wealth by 50 percent. The profound question is: Does this mean we will be 50 percent richer in a real sense, 50 percent better off, 50 percent happier?

As Robert Kennedy suggested forty-five years ago, we need to stop measuring our progress by *quantity* of activity and instead start to measure *quality* of life. This is the type of progress we should hold our governments accountable for.

There is a great deal of work under way to define the right way to do this, like the human development index devised by the UN Development Programme (UNDP), which adds life expectancy and quality of education to GDP. Another, and my favorite, is the happy planet index developed by the New Economics Foundation. The happy planet index adds life satisfaction levels to life expectancy levels and divides the result by the ecological footprint, thus measuring the length and genuine quality of life for present generations divided by the risk to future generations of any damage being done to our capital stocks.[3]

Am I off with the fairies or being gripped by naive idealism? Is such a radical transformation at all possible? Do I really think people would ever support such a profound change away from our current obsession with personal material wealth?

When we consider all this, it's important to remember the scale of the challenge we will face and what a great opportunity for radical shift a good crisis can create. We will be in a head space for change that is nothing like what we face now.

When you wonder if we can do this, consider the personal comparison of a conversation you're having with your doctor about the need for exercise when you're in good health vs. the conversation you have just after you've survived a heart attack. It goes from "Make an effort and you'll feel better and get benefits later" to "If you don't change, you'll die next time." The motivation is quite different. This will be our context.

Nevertheless, when you look at the current reality of politics and social change, it's easy to lapse into negativity and cynicism about our potential. I often have conversations with people who think we will just slide into collapse. They understand the key issue is not the conceptual potential of a steady-state economy or our technical capacity to design and deliver it. The issue is choosing to do so, and they don't see how we are capable of such transformational change.

I understand how observing our politics and our daily consumerism can lead to such an attitude. After all, as we discussed earlier, the main response of world leaders to the so-called global financial crisis, a crisis caused by excessive debt and consumption, was to borrow more money and give it to us so we'd get out and shop more.

However, when I think back over the history of humanity and look at how much we've changed since we evolved from our chimpanzee tendencies and how much we've developed over even just the last few hundred years, I see our potential differently. The change we make is often driven by necessity and a crisis, but the change is generally positive. This transition will be particularly challenging and is more complex than, say, winning a war or inventing new technologies, but it's nevertheless within our capabilities as well as potentially exciting and uplifting.

Despite the evidence of our history, we forget that dramatic and fundamental change in our behavior, culture, and values is not just possible, but is what clearly defines humanity—our ability for conscious and deliberate evolution toward a higher organizational state. This is what we've actually done, and we're about to do some more.

Again, though, the key to understanding this potential is to imagine the context—a crisis where the current way of doing things is finished and the only choice we have left is *how* we would like to change, not whether.

This means we need to start thinking now about what this new economy is going to look and feel like. I don't harbor any delusions that we're going to move to this in the next few years, but we are going to at some point, so the more we consider, debate, and experiment with the ideas involved, the better off we'll be when the time comes. If we choose the right actions now, we can be better off immediately while getting the system better prepared.

Part of this preparation is to take practical action. Actions like those described earlier—shifting the tax base from employment to materials and encouraging part-time work and less consumption. Such actions will reduce the severity of the later crisis as well as giving us valuable insights into what is effective, all while teaching the public and the business community what to expect in the future.

I won't go through any more of the theoretical design of this new economy. It has been well articulated elsewhere. However, while such research is incredibly important, this is not something we can leave to theoretical economists. If this is going to be a human-focused economy, we, the humans affected, need to engage with the ideas and start to define what we want going forward.

Of particular interest and focus should be what we can do today that starts us on the journey and delivers immediate benefits to our lives and our society. Are there such opportunities for personal and collective action, or is there nothing meaningful we can do until society as a whole moves?

The issue of personal vs. societywide action is an interesting question and goes to one of the key challenges that have always faced environmental campaigners. While it is appealing at a personal and social change level to get individuals to change their lightbulbs, lower their impact, and so on, there has always been this nagging doubt, for both those involved in the action and those advocating it, that it doesn't actually make any difference because the scale of the problem is so large and the personal action so small. Some even argue the psychological impacts are negative because it can "serve as a form of absolution that relieves people of the need to engage in the more radical political and lifestyle changes that are ultimately necessary."[4]

The response in its defense is usually two-pronged. First, on a personal level, those acting are empowered by their contribution—that action changes belief faster than the other way around. Second, advocates argue that it sends a signal to the market and to government that there is a desire for change.

Whatever the arguments about the benefits, no one argues that these personal measures have much direct environmental impact on a global scale.

The interesting question in our context, therefore, is whether actions toward a new economy carry the same risk. Will they involve personal sacrifice for negligible real benefit?

So with that historical context and these types of questions in mind, let's consider in some more detail what this new, steady-state economy will look and feel like. How will it be different with respect to the big global issues like poverty? What will it mean day-to-day for those who already have their basic needs met? Are there actions individuals can take now, and what would be the personal impact of doing so?

I can't cover all the issues involved, so I've chosen four to consider as examples as we think about the future: consumerism and shopping; poverty and inequity; business and investment; and, finally, work and communities. So let's dive into our future and see what it feels like.

CHAPTER 16

Yes, There Is Life After Shopping

We'll start with what is arguably the central plank of the global economy. Let's go shopping.

As discussed the data now confirms what many of us have been feeling for a while. Once our basic needs are met, more possessions and more money, for which there's a price to pay in stress, time, and work, actually don't make us any happier or give us more satisfying lives. This is probably the most dangerous and threatening idea in this book. More than terrorism, more than war, and more than communism ever did, this idea strikes at the heart of modern global capitalism. What would happen if we all stopped shopping?

Of course, there's more to the issue of a quantitative economic growth than shopping, but shopping goes to the core of the problem, the solution, and the implications of a steady-state economy for global society. It also takes us out of economic theory and into the implications of all of this in our personal lives.

It goes to the essence of the issue because the global economy is built on a single assumption that is starting to look pretty shaky: that we are motivated to work hard and create more personal wealth to buy more stuff because it will improve the quality of our lives and those of our children.

If this assumption is false, and the data and common sense now say it is, the global economy could face a major crisis just with a change of public mood. This could be the aikido of political revolutions—a small, well-placed move that uses the energy of the attacker to change the whole system.

It is almost impossible to overstate the significance of this potential. This consumption-based economic system has most of the world tied into it, and even those people who aren't aspire to join. It depends on the cycle being whole, and if any part is withdrawn, the system could fall over.

If a trend emerged where people realized that buying more stuff wasn't improving their lives and was instead locking them into a cycle of time-poor lives, unsatisfying work, and endless debt, they might stop. Of course not completely, but buying significantly less would have a far-reaching impact.

This would soon roll out across the system with dramatic consequences. If we stop buying so much stuff, we won't need to work so much to make the money to buy it. We could pay off debt and tear up our credit cards, undermining the business model of most retail banks. If we don't need the money and we don't enjoy our work, we might be less motivated to work as much. If we then don't work so much, we're going to have a lot more time. Ask your friends how many of them could manage to spend 10 percent less on stuff if instead they had an *extra* five weeks' holiday leave every year? Yes, the extra holiday may have to be spent socializing rather than jet-setting but this would still be preferred by most.

The impacts roll on. If we stop buying so much stuff, the growth model of the developing world collapses. The growth we have seen in China and elsewhere is based on a simple idea—make stuff for rich people using cheap labor while stuffing up your local and global environment. With a globalized economy, the impacts quickly spread. If Americans stop buying so much stuff, the Chinese won't be manufacturing it and my own country, Australia, won't be selling mineral resources to China to make all that stuff. If the Chinese aren't selling so much stuff to the United States, they won't have their surpluses to buy U.S. Treasury bonds that finance the U.S. economy. So it would flow on around the world.

The consequences aren't just economic, however, and this is where it gets interesting. If we don't get happiness from buying more material possessions, we'll have to get it from somewhere else. Without the distraction of the emotional drug of materialism, we would look to places like relationships, friendships, and family. We might be more inclined to get involved in our community. Who knows, we might even look inside to discover the source of the unhappiness that shopping was covering up!

If we are less motivated to work for money, we might be choosier whom we work for and what work we do. After all, if meaning isn't coming from stuff, then perhaps it could come from the work we do. It's not hard to imagine what that would mean for companies seeking to attract and retain the best talent—they would find the company's social purpose key to attracting good people. This may make it difficult to recruit people to market chocolate bars!

This may seem far-fetched if you consider it while standing in the middle of Times Square in New York City. I did just this with Rick Humphries, my good friend and a lifelong environmentalist who now works on biodiversity protection for the resource company Rio Tinto. On a visit to the United States, we were on our way home from an evening out and stood there at midnight, looking around at the frenzy of consumerism and marketing going on around us. People going shopping at midnight, flashing signs everywhere screaming at our senses to buy, buy, buy before it's bye bye bye. Rick and I looked at each other and had the same reaction. Sustainability? We're stuffed!

Little did we know that elsewhere in Manhattan, Colin Beavan was pondering the same issue. He was living every day in this citadel of shopping and consumption and wondering what he could do about it.

Colin got it into his head in November 2006 that he would try to live for a year, with his wife, Michelle Conlin, their two-year-old child, and their four-year-old dog, with no net environmental impact. He would reduce his negative impact of waste, CO_2 emissions, and excessive consumption and expand his positive impact through environmental restoration, donations of time and money to environmental groups, and so on, until his family's net contribution to the problem was zero. After convincing his "caffeine-loving, retail-obsessed, TV-addicted" wife to join in, he started to investigate what it would take. He did so not as a moralizing crusade or as some kind of ascetic sacrifice, but as a personal experiment to find out how hard it would be and what impact it would have on him and his family's life. And so No Impact Man was born.

After their first trial week, Colin wrote:

> We got the glimpse of a life with an entirely different rhythm. We began to think that, by depriving us of our Madison Avenue addictions, the no impact experiment might actually make us happier. It was only a seven-day experiment, but it convinced us that living no impact can be done, it can be done pleasantly, and that we could conceivably end up happier rather than sadder—which is why, God help us, we're in it for a year.[1]

A year later and the experience was being turned into a book and then a film, and the blog had attracted 1.8 million visitors. With stories in the *New York Times* and *Time* magazine and TV appearances on shows like *Good Morning America* and *Nightline*, there was clearly something deeper going on than one man's fascination with personal impact.

There is now an emerging movement on this issue and a serious social and consumer trend emerging. Long perceived to be an issue at the margins and relevant only to a fringe part of the market, the issue of changing consumer preferences and a desire for both lower-impact products and fewer products is now firmly entering the mainstream. This has ranged from attacks by religious leaders such as the pope on consumerism to media fascination with efforts to consume less, like Colin and Michelle's, to responses by marketers to this as a consumer trend. There is even advice available on how to market your products to a category called "anticonsumers"![2]

This is occurring naturally as people question their lives and the deception of consumption-driven happiness projected to them every day by marketers. Given that it is already under way, there is no question this anticonsumerism trend will grow exponentially as the Great Disruption gathers momentum. As the world starts to feel increasingly unstable and insecure, the public will come to accept that the cause is an economy built on material consumption and their shopping is where it starts. It will then be a natural development for people to start to focus on shopping and consumerism both at the macro policy level and, more significant, at the personal shopping level.

This is how such trends start. Following a long, slow-building phase, observed as an interesting curiosity by the mainstream, they're then triggered to mass scale by either their own critical mass or an outside event. With the Great Disruption and an economy in decline, people will be forced to experiment and be creative. If, like No Impact Man Colin, they find out their lives have improved anyway, such trends could spread exponentially.

"Shop less, live more" may well become the defining economic and political mantra of the coming decades.

Of course it will build over time; it won't be that we all suddenly wake up and literally stop shopping. Mind you, there have been some who've done just this, giving us important personal lessons and significant insights into public attitudes.

One such example was the participants in the Compact—a group of ten friends in San Francisco who all agreed to buy nothing new for twelve months (food, drink, health, and safety necessities excluded). The idea was in large part a general response to excessive consumerism and advertising pressure, but the group was also motivated by the absurd post-9/11 push that shopping had now become "Americans' patriotic duty."[3]

The concept took off, and groups sprang up around the world. From Australia to France and Iceland to Hong Kong, thousands signed up to participate in this twelve-month shopping-free zone. The experience led to fascinating personal insights for the people involved and an extensive media profile—a small but interesting indicator of the depth of interest and public hunger for a new way.

One of the co-founders, John Perry, told the U.K. *Guardian* newspaper about his reflections on the year: "The real revelation is that it isn't that hard. We all have so much stuff, we could probably live for years without replacing anything. It makes you change the way you look at and appreciate the things you have. We're definitely going to continue."

With the media profile they even faced a backlash. The *Guardian* story[4] continued: "Compact members found themselves attacked by conservatives as 'un-American' and guilty of 'economic terrorism.' One San Francisco shop even offered 'break the Compact' discounts."

While there are important personal insights from people involved in such experiments, the key thing to observe here is not their actual activity, but the fascination of others with it. The backlash against consumerism is, in my view, having watched trends emerge in this area for thirty-five years, a sleeper trend—something to watch carefully as an indicator of what is coming. When it bursts into the mainstream, the implications for the global economy will be profound.

This behavior and people's response to it have a strong and established theoretical underpinning. The research into human happiness and life satisfaction in recent years shows clear and consistent results. Data gathered by people like Professor Martin Seligman at the University of Pennsylvania is being confirmed by others around the world and give us proof of what is actually common sense. We know how to become happier. Get out of poverty, and then focus on community connections, family, love, and active, meaningful lives. All things that are cheap, are easy to access, and, unlike oil and coal, are globally well distributed!

As we covered in the last chapter, the research data that confirms this have been thoroughly tested. And the results are consistent between countries and cultures and within countries over time—as an individual country gets richer, its citizens' lives do not improve.

So given that shopping doesn't make us happy, yet most of us make various levels of compromise in life to get more money to buy more stuff, what do we do to break the cycle? How do individuals take action now, assuming they don't want to go down the path of No Impact Man or the Compact?

Shopping less, working less, and finding new sources of happiness and satisfaction is easy to say but harder to do. This is not made any easier with messages blasted at us all day every day to buy, buy, buy so we'll be happier, sexier, healthier, and all-around more popular and loved. But we can't blame it all on marketing. After many decades in this pointless pursuit, given that we all keep doing it, we can safely assume that most of us are deeply addicted. Therefore, it will be important to accept that we *all* have the problem (vs. making it into a moralizing crusade against shopping) and also that we're going to need some help to give it up.

The good news is that help is at hand. People have been thinking about this and have even formed self-help groups, like the Compact, training manuals, and a humorous gospel choir. Reverend Billy and the Church of Life After Shopping have toured the United States and the United

Kingdom, preaching their anticonsumerism message for over a decade, singing outside shopping malls and exorcising cash registers![5]

On a more practical, everyday level, the lessons of initiatives like No Impact Man and the Compact, combined with the research by Seligman, NEF, and others, are that we can all buy less stuff and feel better for it. Not a morally superior, "save the world" kind of feel good, but a practical, enjoy your life, have more fun, deeper kind of feel good. It's interesting in this context to read the tips section at www.noimpact project.org, the nonprofit set up to promote the ideas behind Colin Beavan's year of no impact. The categories are *more fun, clearer conscience, more money, more time, and better health.* Doesn't exactly sound like much sacrifice involved, does it. There are countless "how to" tips out there. Good places to start include www.noimpactproject.org/change and the Compact's site, sfcompact.blogspot.com.

For motivation and education, take a look at the now legendary animation at www.storyofstuff.com. This twenty-minute *Story of Stuff* by Annie Leonard takes you on an entertaining journey into where all this stuff comes from and the consequences of its manufacture and use. Its message is clear and easy to access—so much so that it has been viewed by twelve million people and been translated into fifteen languages.[6] Well worth a look and fun to do with your kids.

Another set of advice came from the United Kingdom's Government Office for Science, which commissioned the NEF to conduct a review of the interdisciplinary work of over four hundred scientists from across the world. The aim was to identify a set of evidence-based actions to improve well-being, which individuals would be encouraged to build into their daily lives. Nic Marks, founder of the Centre for Well-being at the NEF, commenting on the results, said: "The 'five ways to well-being' are rooted in a wealth of evidence and show that there are simple, positive actions that people can take to improve their well-being. For too long we've measured the health of the nation by how much we are consuming rather than the things that really matter, which is how things are really going for people." The conclusions from this research were distilled into *Five Ways to Well-being*, which focused on connecting with people, being physically active, taking notice of the world around you, learning new things, and giving to others (which includes volunteering). Notice that shopping didn't rate a mention![7]

The science in this area is particularly interesting. According to the NEF: "Studies in neuroscience have shown that cooperative behaviour activates reward areas of the brain, suggesting we are hard wired to enjoy helping one another. Individuals actively engaged in their communities report higher well-being and their help and gestures have knock-on effects for others."

We've been working on all this in my own family and have been experimenting with some simple ideas to guide us. One that has saved us a great deal of money is the seven-day cooling-off period for major purchases. We agree that once we've chosen something we want to buy, not conceptually but specifically the product, shop, and price we're paying, we defer the purchase for seven days. It's amazing how often after thinking about it, we decide against it. A friend in South Africa has a rule where he takes his young kids grocery shopping, and after they've finished, they have to put back 10 percent of what's in the cart. A friend in the United Kingdom has a family rule that any shopping other than furniture-size items can only be done and brought home by bicycle. The effort involved in the two-mile ride quickly reduces the teenagers' consumption levels.

One of the more successful initiatives we've taken at home is to give to our kids as a birthday or Christmas present control over a family experience. We set rules like cost and location and that we all have to go, then let them decide. Their sense of control and the ability to have the whole family join in *their* chosen activity makes for a lot of fun. My eight-year-old, Grace, suffers through the rugby games, but she has her revenge making her big brothers sit through movies about princesses. So as well as creating memorable family experiences, we are teaching tolerance and sharing, not to mention reducing the piles of plastic toys that otherwise mount in the corners of the bedrooms. It's interesting to note that if I test the kids on what presents they remember from previous years, it's more often the experience ones than the stuff we've given them.

There are some significant assumptions and barriers to overcome in our thinking as well. My two young boys, Jasper and Oscar, love playing online computer games. Eleven-year-old Jasper wanted to subscribe to one for $5 a month from his pocket money. I was railing against it, saying what a con it was that these games got you in by being free and then demanded money to play them at a higher level. "Why would you pay money for something like that?" I asked. "It's just an online game." His response came back in flash: "Okay, I'll go and spend it on plastic toys, then." Ouch. Victory to the young fella experiencing the new, low-material-intensity economy. Loss to the old-fashioned father, stuck in his material economy ways. Yes, he subscribed.

So there's a fair bit of new thinking involved in many aspects of these questions. Another one is to recognize the social nature of shopping and how we can not only maintain it, but strengthen it while doing less and different types of shopping. At the community level, there are countless opportunities for this, like "freecycling" networks. These are groups where people give away unwanted goods to other members of their local group who promise to give the goods a decent home—the outcomes include reusing useful stuff, reducing landfill waste, reducing the need to buy new stuff, and, perhaps most important, bringing communities and people together in acts of generosity.

The freecycle idea started when Deron Beal sent out an e-mail to about thirty or forty friends and a handful of nonprofits in Tucson, Arizona. From this small start, the Freecycle Network has grown in just seven years to over seven million people who have joined nearly five thousand local groups in over seventy countries! Every day the network diverts around five hundred tons of waste from landfill. The group's Web site, www.freecycle.org, points out that otherwise carrying away this volume to a landfill would take full garbage trucks piled five times the height of Mt. Everest, just for the last year! And they all feel good about giving things away, as the group's site says: "By giving freely with no strings attached, members of The Freecycle Network help instill a sense of generosity of spirit as they strengthen local community ties and promote environmental sustainability and reuse."

Sure, it's easy to counter these examples of action with evidence of rampant consumerism elsewhere. Rick Humphries and I had those thoughts standing in Times Square. However, my point is not that these new approaches have yet become mainstream, but that they will. There is now enough evidence around the world of a slowly building backlash against consumerism to argue it will soon erupt firmly into the mainstream marketplace.

Shopping less is not the only type of creative consumer activism we are seeing. One of the more fascinating examples in recent times is that of "carrotmobbing," which uses shopping as a positive lever for change. Rather than use the stick of a boycott, the organizers of the "carrotmob" use the carrot of promised customers to drive businesses to change. They approach a range of local retailers and invite bids on what action they will take in return for a sudden flood of customers; for example, "What percentage of revenue on a certain day would you spend on an energy-efficiency retrofit?" The best bid wins, and the organizers then mobilize the group through viral e-mails and the like, and that store suddenly finds a rush of new customers. People were going to buy that stuff anyway, they just changed where they did so on the same day for maximum visible impact. In one case, a local convenience store promised to spend 22 percent on an energy retrofit and the carrotmob delivered customers that tripled their normal daily revenue.

This is a powerful idea, especially if it could be applied to large companies as well. Imagine a global campaign to all buy products from one company for a month. As founder Brent Schulkin says about well-directed consumer power: "We are the economy, we decide who gets rich."

Of course, examples of strong action like carrotmob and the Compact are only a small part of the story. While such approaches will not appeal to everyone, they are, like all bookends of a broader trend, indicative that a larger group is taking less but still significant action in the same direction. There are two categories of such broader actions—a trend toward less consumption overall, as previously discussed, and a shift in consumer expectations of the types of goods they buy and whom they buy them from. Good examples of these include Fair Trade coffee, which has become a dominant market player in many countries, and the rise in organic products.

Studies around this kind of shopping, what is sometimes called the LOHAS market—Lifestyles of Health and Sustainability—indicate a segment in the United States alone worth hundreds of billions of dollars per annum with appeal to over 30 percent of the U.S. consumer market.[8] There is now a booming market for organic food and drink, with the U.S. market growing at around three to four times as fast as the nonorganic market.[9] With such spectacular growth rates, organics have been picked up as a mainstream segment by most major supermarket chains and food manufacturers.

These trends are leading many major global companies to realize they have to find a way to access this market and appeal to these consumers. How can they deliver more value with less material impact? How can they shift their business model to one of services rather than physical products? How can they build their brand as appealing to these new consumers? How do they market to consumers who are anticonsumer?

My conclusion is that we have a major sleeper trend—one that can easily be observed and monitored by looking both at the bookends of the strong anticonsumer attitudes and in the middle of the trend with committed green consumers, well described by the LOHAS market. With the Great Disruption gathering steam, these trends will inevitably grow, with far-reaching economic and social consequences, including many substantial new business opportunities.

So what else is going to happen in this new economy? What will it mean for business, for communities, and for our working lives? And if poverty isn't going to be dealt with via growth, what are we going to do about it?

CHAPTER 17

No, the Poor Will Not *Always Be with Us*

I was brought up in the Methodist Church, which has always had a particularly strong focus on social issues and poverty. My grandfather Jasper Gilding was a minister in the church, and he and my grandma Kathleen lived and breathed those values. As a result, they also manifested strongly in our upbringing, through the attitudes and level of community engagement I witnessed in my parents, Wesley and Ruth.

While we weren't a devoutly religious family, we went to church every Sunday, and my parents spent their working lives in jobs engaged with disadvantaged people, from children's homes to homeless shelters to elder care. One of the interesting side benefits, unusual for a family in suburban Adelaide, was that we often had people staying at our house from far-flung lands, generally visiting students or religious people engaged in social issues. One of these visitors was a Vietnamese monk, Thich Nhat Hanh. Little did I know back in 1965 that he would go on to become one of the world's great Zen masters and peace activists, giving birth to the concept of engaged Buddhism. Nhat Hanh formed a friendship with Martin Luther King Jr., convincing him to publicly oppose the Vietnam War. King nominated Nhat Hanh for the Nobel Peace Prize in 1967.

In a rare interview in 2010, Nhat Hanh, now 84, commented on the issues we are discussing here, saying, "The situation the Earth is in today has been created by unmindful production and unmindful consumption. We consume to forget our worries and our anxieties. Tranquilizing ourselves with over-consumption is not the way."

Very insightful comments but back when I was six years old he was just a kind and gentle man wearing funny clothes! We lived in a simple house in the suburbs, and all this was a natural part of our lives. Perhaps as a result of this upbringing and cultural context, I grew up thinking it was ridiculous that society tolerated so many of our people suffering grinding multigenerational poverty. The older I get, the more ridiculous it seems.

There are deep and complex issues involved here that go to the core of who we are and, more important, who we want to be. They are central to the questions we're covering in this book because as we respond to the coming crisis, our focus is on building a civilized and sustainable society. We can certainly not consider ourselves to be civilized while we accept extreme poverty.

Our solution to poverty has for a long time focused around economic growth. We thought we could lift people out of poverty simply by increasing the amount of stuff and wealth in the whole system, without having to engage in the difficult question of redistribution of wealth—everyone could have more, so everyone could be happy!

Of course, there has long been a significant social movement calling for us to take stronger action to eliminate poverty and realize our full potential as humanity. Joining millions of people around the world who campaign on such issues have been rock star activists like Bob Geldof and Bono, who have engaged the broad public with excellent campaigns like "Make Poverty History." But fundamentally, the response has still been premised on economic growth, the idea that everyone could have more.

The logic and morality of this call to end poverty have grown stronger as we have grown richer. Global economic growth has meant that there is now more than enough to go around. We produce more calories, for example, than are needed to sustain the world population. What is true of food is also true of water, energy, and other resources—economic growth has ensured that today we live in a world of plenty where no one need suffer extreme poverty with respect to global capacity—the problems lie elsewhere.

And yet, as we know and to our great shame, 1.4 billion people continue to live in extreme poverty, generally defined as living on less than $1.25 a day. Free marketeers have long argued that economic growth and global markets would sort this out, and that argument was not without merit. Especially in China and India, economic growth has lifted millions out of poverty and created a new global middle class. The income differential between China and the West has decreased substantially, with GDP per capita increasing in China a huge sevenfold between 1978 and 2004.[1] Throughout this period, China has sustained growth rates that are the envy of the developed world.

But along with these success stories, there are significant failures. The UNDP calculated in 2002 that assuming global progress continued at the same pace, it would take 130 years to rid the world of hunger. Progress is also inconsistent among countries. While the West experienced two decades of sustained economic growth in the 1980s and 1990s, only twenty developing countries managed to experience sustained growth over that period. No fewer than forty other developing countries went through at least five years of stagnation or a fall in per capita income.

While some of this economic growth trickled down, a disproportionate amount stayed at the top. In 2000 the top 1 percent of the world's population owned around 40 percent of the world's wealth, with the top 10 percent owning 85 percent. At the other end, the bottom half of the world's people share just 1 percent of the world's wealth among them.[2] The story on income is no better, with the top 20 percent of people earning 74 percent of it. Despite improvement in some countries, the trends are not all good. Whereas the average African was almost eleven times poorer than the average North American or Australian/New Zealander in 1950, they were over nineteen times poorer by 2000.[3] It seems the economic growth over the last 50 years has defied gravity and floated up rather than trickled down as the theory argued it would. This is not just about inequality and fairness, this is often grinding, brutal poverty. According to UNICEF, in 2001, 51 percent of Ethiopian children under five were stunted because of chronic malnutrition. Such stories and statistics can be found around the world.

Unfortunately, even though economic growth has been fostering some admirable improvements, it clearly hasn't been going far enough. When faced with such absolute and despairing poverty in the context of such massive global wealth, waiting another 130 years to eliminate hunger is not a projection to be proud of. Not to mention the questionable morality of the basic idea—that if we let the rich get richer and richer, little amounts of their leftover wealth would trickle down to the poor, bringing them out of extreme poverty. Explain that to an Ethiopian mother with a child stunted from malnutrition.

Of course, I'm just summarizing here the arguments that have been put forward for many decades. The immorality of poverty, the power of markets and growth to drive change, the need for a fairer distribution of growth, the importance of poor countries having strong economies and open markets, and so on have all attracted significant discussion.

It's time to move on. None of these arguments matter much anymore. That game is up. As we covered earlier, our current model of economic growth, the one that is bringing some of the poor out of poverty, works to make the rich richer as well. Of course, this isn't a practical problem for the poor if it brings them out of extreme poverty. The problem is that the size of the economy needed to achieve this outcome is not possible. So, for example, if we were to aspire to global incomes at, say, EU levels and have them grow modestly at 2 percent per year, with the poor being brought up to that level over the next forty years, the global economy would have to increase to fifteen times today's size by 2050. Remembering we're currently running at 140 percent of the planet's capacity this is of course an absurd proposition.

Even assuming dramatically less progress on poverty than that, we would still be so far past the physical limits that it would remain impossible. Remember, not difficult or inconvenient or challenging. Impossible.

Understanding this profoundly changes the game in many areas, but perhaps nowhere more so than with respect to poverty and inequality. As well as removing the solution we've been investing our hope in, the end of growth has far-reaching impacts on global geopolitics and national social stability. Perhaps most critical—and affecting every country, not just the poor ones—it smashes the general consensus among the public upon which our economic model relies: that the system will ultimately work for everyone if we give it time.

Economic growth has for a long time been the relief valve on the pressure cooker of global society.[4] For the poor, whether defined as those in extreme poverty or those at the bottom end of wealthy countries, the hope of one day being lifted from poverty is what often makes the huge differentials in wealth tolerable. Never having experienced growing prosperity themselves, some of the poorest do not cling to this hope. But their leaders and the developing countries' elite certainly do, and their complete geopolitical focus is on lifting their countries and their people out of poverty through economic growth. They see successes in other countries, and they want their turn. With the end of growth, this source of hope and focus disappears. Do we expect the poor to now accept their poverty as permanent, since no more economic wealth can be created?

In a similar way, the mentality that embraces the principle of economic growth allows us to morally justify the poor in the West as well. The Great American Dream, built upon the foundation of economic growth, suggests that anyone who works hard can improve himself and increase his wealth. In this context, many believe the poor are at least to some degree lazy or incompetent. They are poor by their own actions or lack thereof. Accepting the end of economic growth means that this idea, at best highly debatable, can no longer be argued. If the amount of wealth overall can't increase, you can improve your wealth only by taking away from someone else. The American Dream is dead. The only way to lift the bottom is to drop the top.

Ouch. Not only do we have to face the end of economic growth, but now we have to discuss the most heretical idea of all: redistribution. We'll come back to this shortly.

So the stability of our system has depended upon a gigantic relief valve, which is now broken. To make matters worse, we can reliably assume the unfolding crisis that is forcing the end of economic growth will not only undermine *reductions* in poverty, it will reverse them and drive the poor back down the scale, because of the severe challenges to water and food supply and an increase in climatic extremes.

With disparity rapidly worsening and the escape route closing, pressure in the system will build up until it explodes, unless we take alternative action.

How can we respond? I see two alternatives. One that is put to me when I present on this topic is that we "let nature takes its course," that this process is the system getting back into balance. While people rarely put it to me in these terms, what they mean is we let the poor starve and their countries collapse. Leaving aside the morality of this position, it is inconceivable this could happen without massive disruption globally, including profound and destabilizing global security impacts.

What people don't think through is what that actually looks like. We would not, if we took that choice, have two, three, or four billion poor people quietly going away to die in a far-flung corner of the world. While we can't know just how it will develop, it doesn't take much to imagine how it might unfold.

A global economic crash combined with widespread food shortages, would probably see the desperate slide of nations and regions into chaos. We would see failed states with nuclear arms and countless other weapons being taken over by dictators and terrorists. We would see refugees by the hundreds of millions, if not billions. Yes, some would be too weak or ill equipped to travel far, but many would move first as their countries collapsed around them.

This would not be, as we have seen in past crises, a few million people on isolated roads moving into refugee camps. This would be whole countries of people walking into neighboring states, and they would be desperate, starving people with nothing to lose.

So when we think about "nature taking its course," we should consider what that means and how we would respond at the time. What would we do if whole nations started to collapse, and what would the implications be for the global economy? We could not then deliver widespread aid because the conditions would be overwhelming and highly unstable in terms of security. At its most simple and brutal, would we let whole regions collapse into chaos and draw lines on the map we would "defend"— declaring no-go zones of regions of the world? Would our militaries be able to defend these lines if hundreds of millions of starving, desperate people approached them? How would the politics of the countries that hadn't collapsed respond to such human calamity?

In a globalized world there is nowhere to hide, no barricade high enough, and the whole thing would be live on the TV in your lounge room. It is a short journey from this kind of situation to the global collapse we need to avoid at all costs.

This is why, as we discussed earlier, our militaries are looking at these issues very seriously. They see these trends emerging, and they don't intend to wait until then to think them through.

The respected British defense think tank the Royal United Services Institute concluded in a comprehensive review of the subject in 2008: "In the next decades, climate change will drive as significant a change in the strategic security environment as the end of the Cold War. If uncontrolled, climate change will have security implications of similar magnitude to the World Wars, but which will last for centuries."[5] Take particular note of the last two words—"for centuries."

Another study looking at the relationship between temperatures and civil war in sub-Saharan Africa in recent decades concluded that civil wars there are likely to increase 50 percent by 2030. That level of conflict likely means millions of deaths—and an international impact.[6] A more complete—and more disturbing—picture is provided in Gwynne Dyer's book *Climate Wars*.[7] Dyer, a military and international affairs journalist with a good understanding of the science, portrays the collapse of the European Union in the 2030s as northern African refugees overrun southern Europe and southern Europeans flee to the northern states to escape an expanding Sahara. In his scenario, the 2030s also see nuclear war between India and Pakistan over water resources and a completely militarized U.S.-Mexican border as America seeks to keep out massive waves of immigrants.

Of course, this might unfold in many different ways, some far less dramatic than that, but it is certainly not possible to imagine letting "nature take its course" not having profound impacts on the global economy, including developed countries. The idea that we could pursue a strategy of what Indian ecologist Madhav Gadjil called islands of prosperity within oceans of poverty, is a fantasy that would simply not work in practice.

So we need to consider this option carefully before we assume it is a realistic one.

Personally, I would vote against option one. What is option two, you say? I hope it's better than the first choice!

We have to go back to kindergarten. We have to learn to share with our friends. Unlike in kindergarten, however, now we know that having more toys doesn't make us happy, so we can rest easy that sharing won't decrease our happiness.

The math of this situation is clear. Remember where we started this journey. The earth is full. It is not possible for the future to have nine billion people in a growing quantitative economy. We can argue we should have fewer people, but most of the people we are going to have in this situation are either already born or soon will be. Given that we have limited resources and wealth and can't grow either significantly, we have to share. We have to accept that the only way forward that is acceptable to any of us is to spread the resources we have more equally around the world.

Let's be blunt and clear that this is going to involve those of us in rich countries having less—not just less growth, but less than we have now. Less stuff, less money, less capacity to build wealth and consume. How tragic is this? Not very tragic, really, not even sad. In fact, the lesson learned by those who've tried having less, like Colin Beavan and Michelle Conlin of No Impact fame, and John Perry from the Compact, is that having less actually made them happier. Scary thought given how hard we've been working to have more, isn't it.

If you don't like the idea, then you have to be able to look yourself in the mirror and accept that the world's militaries will be taking control of the process that sees option one unfold. These will be our militaries, our planes, our guns, "defending" us from billions of innocent, starving, desperate people. It will have been our choice, conscious, clear, and premeditated. Sharing doesn't seem so hard, does it?

If we are to choose option two, then we must recognize that our current approach of relying on liberalizing markets and unleashing economic growth is not going to work. We can't afford the risk that the situation will spiral out of control as I have described, because it will then be too late to do anything other than survive.

What we can do right now is launch a significant shift in how we treat poverty alleviation and development. We need to unleash a flood of people, funds, technology, and intellect to rapidly address these issues. The sooner we act, the better our chances of preventing the chaos that we will certainly otherwise face when the Great Disruption is in full swing.

Let's take this away from the practical level for a moment and consider it in the largest possible context. What kind of world do we want? It is incomprehensible that if we put our minds to it, we couldn't fix poverty. I'm not saying it's simple, but putting all the information in the world into a phone in my shirt pocket wasn't simple either, but we did it. Unpacking the human genome wasn't simple, but we did it. So fixing poverty permanently won't be simple and it won't be quick, but we can certainly do it. We have the resources now to do it, we just have to make the decision.

And how cool would it be if we did? Imagine a world where no one was starving, where everyone had basic health care and education, where we could look around the world and say: "You know what? We're doing okay."

What we're going to experience is a profound transformation in values, one that will see us address what has for so long been a blight on our civilization. We'll adopt this course not just because it's the right thing to do, but because when confronted with the Great Disruption, it will be the only socially and ecologically viable option available. This doesn't make the values shift any less important or profound—it just makes the fact that it will happen a lot more certain.

This is not an argument for utopian equality, just for the elimination of grinding, soul-destroying poverty. I can't see any justification that explains a society where some have private jets while some die for the want of a bowl of rice or a glass of clean water. It's just not right.

We should stop it now, while we still have the chance.

CHAPTER 18

Ineffective Inequality

I remember as a teenage activist in the 1970s reading about the works of Karl Marx, I came across the quote "From each according to his ability; to each according to his needs." It struck me then as an eminently sensible, simple idea, and I couldn't understand how any other approach could possibly be a better way to organize our society.

Then and since, we have had the real-world experience of communism, both as a totalitarian oppressive state and in its failure to deliver good economic outcomes while trashing the environment and human rights in the Soviet Union. It seems life is a little more complicated than I thought as a teenager. China's Communist regime has delivered some very considerable gains for its people economically, though at great cost to the local and global environment. Realistically, even those outcomes are due mainly to their adoption of many aspects of Western capitalism, though in their case without the democracy.

So we can safely conclude at this stage that the basic Marxist ideals of the benevolent state and the absence of private ownership are not suited to the reality of human behavior and tendencies.

Does that mean that capitalism instead is the answer to our political and social needs? Do we just let the market rip? That depends on how you define it. There is clear evidence that private ownership and reward for effort are powerful forces for economic and social development, and various applications of them have delivered over the millennia. They clearly tap into some deeply ingrained human tendencies. They are not

223

the only motivators of human activity, but they certainly have significant and often positive impact.

Based on this historical experience, I have confidence that some aspects of market principles and approaches can make a significant contribution to social progress. However, given that market forces as we currently apply them are driving us to the brink of societal collapse, one has to conclude that we have some fundamental redesign work to do if we want to take this approach forward. Our current approach is certainly not working well. Even the avowedly pro-market economist Sir Nicholas Stern argued this when he described climate change as "the greatest and widest-ranging market failure ever seen."

Markets don't work if left alone. They never have and they never will. They need guidance from government on behalf of the people markets serve, as we covered in chapter 11. We appreciate the raw energy of the market tiger, but it needs to be caged and directed. We covered earlier many of the design characteristics for this cage if markets are to play a significant role going forward, like caps on resource use and pollution.

One we haven't yet covered is inequality. As we have seen in recent decades, vibrant markets can create wealth, but they don't distribute it very well; in fact, they tend to concentrate it firmly in the hands of those who already have it.

Don't get me wrong—I'm not advocating that we impose equality for everyone by decree. There are differentials in people's contributions, whether they are driven by skills, character, or effort, and there is nothing wrong with differences in rewards for this, particularly for effort. This difference in reward is *part* of what drives people to work harder, to make an effort to make life better for themselves and their family and, in doing so, often for society as a whole. But to what extent does this motivate the outcomes we desire, how much reward is needed for it to be effective, and what are the side effects of the resulting inequality?

This is a markedly different type of moral question from extreme poverty, which most people believe is just wrong. The morality of inequality, while present, is much grayer. It is a constantly shifting judgment we make as to what's reasonable and fair. At one end, almost everyone would agree that complete equality is unfair and an ineffective way to organize society and motivate people. Likewise, almost everyone would agree there shouldn't be unlimited inequality—that is, there is some point where everyone would say, No, that's too much difference and not fair.

So one side of the issue is what is the *right* level of differentiated reward to motivate individuals to make an effort and to innovate. The other side is how much inequality is too much to be fair and socially effective. At what point does inequality offend our sense of fairness—a moral or ethical issue—and at what point does it create social and political instability—a quality-of-life and economic issue.

Professor Herman Daly points out that the military, civil service, and universities manage to keep ratios between the top and bottom salaries in their organizations within a range of 15/20 to 1 and seem to do okay with no lack of highly skilled, motivated, and competent leaders, yet the corporate spread in the United States is now up to 500 to 1.[1] There appears to be no evidence that such ratios actually encourage performance across the economy. The process of all sides boosting top salaries because the others are is more akin to an arms race among companies, bringing no net benefit to the system as a whole. Such situations clearly won't right themselves and are good examples of where government intervention is required. Yet when restrictions in this area are proposed, senior business figures argue strongly against them, on the grounds that government shouldn't intervene in the market.

This is where we come across one of the paradoxes in our cultural and political attitudes to these issues. This paradox is around the issue of limits.

On the one hand, many of the serious challenges we have been discussing throughout this book are the result of the lack of limits—we have come to accept that all growth is good, that there is no limit to what is reasonable for personal wealth, and that we can dominate nature because our technology will always find ways around the limits we would otherwise face. This belief in the lack of limits has a positive side, perhaps best understood by comparing it with our desire for our children to believe in themselves and their limitless potential. A belief in potential is powerful and important, for societies and for individuals. However, unrestrained it also has a dangerous side, an arrogance and inability to judge risks, with consequences we can clearly see. That's why we impose limits.

While the imposition of some limits remains politically contentious, the paradox is that we do impose limits all the time to make our society "civilized" and have done so throughout history—limits like making non-state-sanctioned violence illegal, imposing contract law to put accountability and enforcement around assumptions of trust, and imposing standards on food safety to protect public health. Despite this, we then sometimes object to other limits as "constraints on our freedom" or "interference in the market"—such as the arguments against capping executive pay or limits on product availability, like what cars we can drive, what guns we can buy, or where we can smoke cigarettes.

What this all means is that there is no credible, central argument against the need to impose some limits or constraints on human behavior. There is no freedom defense for unrestricted violence, and there is no free market defense for selling dangerous food. We accept limits, and we work with them every day. This means the debate is what *new* limits we now need to consider imposing, in the context of the Great Disruption, to continue to make our society stable and civilized and enable its citizens to improve their quality of life. In other words, what areas will the system not self-correct unless we intervene?

We have throughout this book raised many examples where new limits need to be put in place: limits to pollution of our air and water, limits to quantitative economic growth, limits to the consumption of natural resources. These were mostly about environmental constraints and their economic impacts. We are now considering directly social questions—what limits might be needed to make a more stable and effective society in which everyone can flourish.

Is there an argument for greater limits on inequality? What would lead us to impose them? Or should the market in this area be allowed to self-organize, to find a natural level of "effective inequality"?

We currently accept levels of inequality that are off the chart. Do we really believe that CEOs deserve to earn five hundred times as much as their lowest-paid workers? Do we believe our top investment bankers are delivering value to society twenty times as much as our top military commanders? Few actually agree with the current situation, yet we find ourselves in a system we are all part of that is delivering just those results.

Historically, the debate in this area has been framed around relative fairness. High levels of inequality, such as the examples just given, are widely considered unfair. And it's not just the poor that don't like it.

Opinion polls in the United Kingdom and the United States show a strong majority—around 80 percent—believe that income inequalities are too large. This means some very financially comfortable people are not personally comfortable with such high levels of inequality. There is an intuitive sense that such extremes are not right.

Well, like many things we currently accept as normal and find hard to imagine shifting, this is another one that's going to see dramatic change with the Great Disruption. There are two reasons we will accept this change, even though it seems hard to imagine in today's political context.

The first reason is the shift we discussed in the last chapter in relation to poverty—the loss of the pressure relief valve that growth provides. Even though we don't like inequality, we accept it based partly on what is effectively a social contract. We believe each individual has the right to get ahead. In a growing economy, everyone can support this because the pie is getting bigger, so as one person gets ahead it doesn't mean another is forced backward. This makes growth the pressure relief valve for inequality, as argued by Henry Wallich, former governor of the Federal Reserve and Yale economics professor: "Growth is a substitute for equality of income. So long as there is growth there is hope, and that makes large income differentials tolerable."

Without economic growth this contract can't be fulfilled. If the earth is full, someone can have more only if someone else has less. Without the pressure relief valve, reducing inequality becomes a social imperative in order to reduce social friction. But could this happen? Is it even remotely conceivable that, even in a full world, those who have greater material wealth would, in a democratic society, accept having less to enable others to rise up the wealth ladder?

This is certainly hard to imagine in today's political debates. But what if addressing inequality actually increased the quality of life for everyone, even for those we currently see as being at the top of society? Hard to imagine?

Here we come to the second reason we will shift away from such high levels of inequality. This comes from one of the most important pieces of research I've seen in several years, one that has substantially changed my view of how all this will unfold. Up until this point, I thought we were going to have to address poverty and inequality by a combination of moral persuasion and social imperative (to avoid local and global political instability). It appears there is another reason we should do so, one that is likely to be far more influential than moral persuasion.

This new research was presented in the book *The Spirit Level* by Richard Wilkinson and Kate Pickett and was the result of comprehensive analysis by its authors over many years into the impact of inequality on a huge range of social indicators of progress. Its conclusions are startling.

It turns out that the greatest predictor of social ills, across an incredible range of phenomena, is not the absolute level of poverty or disadvantage. It is instead the *degree* of inequality or income difference among people. This is profoundly significant, because we have mostly assumed that actual poverty—lack of wealth—was the cause of social problems. We therefore thought that because economic growth increases wealth, even if unequally, poverty would be reduced and along with it many social problems. This has been one of the key reasons government is so obsessively focused on economic growth as its central objective.

But it seems that absolute wealth is a poor indicator of social progress, whereas relative inequality within our society is a strong indicator. The fascinating thing is how comprehensive this is, impacting life expectancy, obesity, imprisonment rates, teenage pregnancy, mental health, levels of trust in the community, educational performance, status of women, and so on. The differences were not marginal, with most of the indicators being three to ten times worse in more unequal societies. This applied even when none of the subjects in the group being researched were anywhere near what could be considered poor. So, for example, among U.K. civil servants in Whitehall, all well paid by global standards, the bottom of the group had a death rate three times as high as the top of the group, of which only a third could be explained by other causes like obesity and smoking (and some of those were perhaps driven by inequality anyway).

Before you think, "Oh well, then, in whatever society I am in, I better get to and stay at the top of the pile," consider this. The evidence demonstrates that even those at the top are better off if their society is more equal, regardless of their relative level of actual wealth. Studies typically divide society into four income groups—those in the bottom 25 percent, those in the two middle groups, and those in the top 25 percent in terms of income. The studies consistently show that greater equality improves wellbeing even for those in the top 25 percent. It might seem strange at first, but the best way for the wealthiest group to improve their own lives is to improve the lives of those earning less than them!

So here we have the killer blow to economic growth *and* the solution to many of our social issues. First, the killer blow. Inequality, it seems, is an issue with extraordinary leverage on the whole system, and pulling that lever would have substantial social and economic impacts. It will reduce our obsessive focus on economic growth and therefore pave the way for acceptance of its now inevitable demise. Here's why.

We support growth and drive it hard through the political process based on the incorrect assumption most of us hold that having more money and stuff will make us happier—that wealth is the key indicator of our personal success and that more wealth enhances our quality of life.

This is more than a casual connection. In the current model, we are firmly addicted at the personal level to more stuff. The problem is that the process of acquiring it, rather than actually satisfying our needs, drives a self-replicating cycle of dissatisfaction and greater want. We believe more wealth will satisfy us, but what actually happens is that the process actually drives inequality, which increases dissatisfaction, which we try to satisfy with more of the same!

Research in *The Spirit Level* explains this with new data, confirming what has been argued by many others, like Professor Tim Kasser. It seems inequality is one of the greatest drivers to consume. Status competition drives consumption, and inequality exacerbates status competition as we try anxiously to keep up, driven by marketers who exploit our state of anxiety.

On the topic of limits, marketers' attempts to get inside our heads seem to have no boundaries. We have advertisements blaring at us in elevators, one of the few places left in a big city for a moment of quiet reflection on our way to or from a meeting or work. We have radio announcers who transition seamlessly from commentary to advertising in the same voice, tricking us into listening without realizing it's one more push to buy.

Where does all this stop? Maybe they'd like us to rent out our foreheads so they can tattoo their brand there, turning every conversation and walk down the street into a marketing opportunity?

Given what we now know about the environmental impact of consumption and the anxiety that drives it, maybe we should see advertising as pollution, with damaging health impacts like cigarettes, and tax it accordingly, as argued by Professor Tim Kasser. Professor Herman Daly says at least we should disallow it as a cost of production and therefore remove its tax deductibility as a business expense.

While there is much to blame advertising and marketers for in all this, the underlying drivers are not a phenomena of the modern world. The classical economist Adam Smith back in 1776 emphasized our need to live a life without shame. In other words, much of our personal behavior and aspirations are driven by the desire to feel like a respectable and successful member of our community. It's just that of late, we have come to define that by the possession of ever more material goods.

This latter point is what creates the opportunity for marketers. While we cannot argue they are the cause of it, marketers exploit our tendency with very negative results, as argued in *The Spirit Level*, referring to Tim Kasser's work:

> Young adults who focus on money, image and fame tend to be more depressed, have less enthusiasm for life and suffer more physical symptoms such as headaches and sore throats than others (*The High Price of Materialism*, MIT Press, 2002). Kasser believes that people tend to embrace material values when they are feeling insecure (retail therapy, anyone?).
>
> "Advertisements have become more sophisticated," says Kasser. "They try to tie their message to people's psychological needs. But it is a false link. It is toxic."

So as we circle all these issues, the noose begins to close around the neck of economic growth. While it is clear that more stuff doesn't make us happy, most of us don't believe this. We are caught up in the belief that it does, reinforced by all the signals around us in marketing and the media. People with more money than we have appear more popular, more attractive, and more respected. So we consume more because we want to be more like them.

This cycle is driven harder when levels of inequality are higher, and here's the crux of the problem as well as the solution. When we consume, we drive economic growth because we increase the throughput of the quantitative economy. Economic growth tends to increase inequality, which in turn creates a stronger social craving for more, driving us to consume. No amount of consumption can satisfy this craving because the process of growth creates more inequality, which drives the desire more. Therefore we need more income to pursue it further.

We work harder to get more income. As is logical, given the drivers we just described, the more unequal our society is, the more hours we work. This gives us less time for the things that genuinely make us happy, like friendships, community, and meaning. This increases our stress and insecurity and thus increases our desire for more material forms of satisfaction.

To feed this process, governments, at our demand, drive more economic growth to create more jobs with more income, for us and our growing population. To do this, they put in place economic settings that encourage us to consume, reinforcing our anxiety-driven tendency to do so. Marketers then leap to exploit these anxieties and desires and drive consumption harder, convincing us the source of the problem can be satisfied with their product. The more growth we have, the more inequality there is and the more anxiety we feel. Then the cycle starts again.

Did I mention that economic growth is destroying the planet on which the economy and our quality of life depend? But note how we don't even need to use that argument to make the case against economic growth.

So economic growth is dead. It's dead because the planet will not support it. But it's also dead because it's economically and socially irrational—it isn't delivering improvements to the quality of life for the billion or so of us at the top of the global economic tree; in fact, even worse, it's actually now degrading it because of all the social problems inequality is causing. So it appears not only that the old saying that you can't buy happiness is true, but that we've spent a hundred years buying sustained misery, not quite the outcome the advertisers mentioned.

So once more now, economic growth is dead. It will kick and struggle for a while, but it is all over.

That leaves us with some work to do. One key task is to deal with the failure of growth to improve the quality of life for those who've met their basic needs—this means humanity overall has stopped developing. As the authors noted in opening *The Spirit Level*:

> It is a remarkable paradox that, at the pinnacle of human mate-
> rial and technical achievement, we find ourselves anxiety-ridden,
> prone to depression, worried about how others see us, unsure of
> our friendships, driven to consume and with little or no commu-
> nity life.

So we need to get ourselves back on the path of human development, we need to get back on the path our grandparents put us on, of improving our quality of life. (Sorry, Grandma, thanks for the foundation you laid, and yes, we squandered that opportunity, but we'll try to sort it out now.)

How will we do this?

Not with more stuff. The barriers to a better life for people who aren't in poverty are now social and psychological, not material. To address this, we need to create, consciously and deliberately, a more equal society. This is the next logical, self-interested step to improve our quality of life. Here's why.

We now know that inequality is the greatest predictor of social ills, across an incredible range of phenomena. What's really interesting in the earlier analysis of the problem is that it indicates we can start to reverse the downward spiral of growth, inequality, and stressful lives into an upward spiral just as simply, with one lever. While consumerism drives growth, which drives inequality, which drives consumerism, if we increase equality, we decrease consumerism, which decreases growth, which increases equality. Given that doing so would also reduce the political push for growth, it will reduce the negative political response to the Great Disruption as well, thus reducing the risk of social instability a failed growth economy could cause.

Can it really be this simple? Surely we can't just rely on theoretical data for such a profound shift? The data is so strong and so consistent, we can, actually. Besides, it's not theory, it's measurement of how things are across the world. But if you need more evidence, consider this.

World War II in England was a real-world example of putting these ideas into practice. Over the years of World War II we saw rapidly *decreasing* inequality, *decreasing* individual consumption, *decreasing* material living standards, and yet rapidly *increasing* public health, and all with a huge degree of public support. Life expectancy during World War II for civilians increased at more than *twice* the rate of any other years in the twentieth century even as so much death surrounded them. Nor was this just to do with increasing nutritional standards from rationing, because the same thing happened in World War I, when nutritional standards declined. World War I was the only other time in the twentieth century when life expectancy increases matched those of World War II, again more than twice the rate of any other decades. At the end of both the decades of 1911–1921 and 1940–1951, men and women could expect to live at least 6.5 years longer than they could at the beginning.[2]

While material living standards took a hit as civilian production was diverted to war production, and residents of London and other big cities literally had their homes blown apart by German bombing, equality had never had it better. For the duration of both wars, employment skyrocketed and concrete efforts were made to reduce inequality. Part of the implicit "social contract" forged in the war was that in return for the people's sacrifices, the bottom had to be lifted up and minimum standards of welfare had to be guaranteed—the so-called "nation fit for heroes." Under these conditions, real income of the working class rose by more than 9 percent, while the real income of the middle class dropped by 7 percent. In addition to the greater sense of wartime unity that such equality brought with it, we now understand that a familiar process was at work. That process is that increases in equality bring improvements in health—and a whole raft of other indicators—for the great majority of people.

So that's sorted. Really, it is that simple. We just need to decide to do it, and if we do, we'll all be better off.

How do we do this? For a start we could put in place, through a series of policy measures, a shift away from extreme inequality. Herman Daly asks the question "What is the proper range of inequality—one that rewards real differences and contributions rather than just multiplying privilege?"

Writing elsewhere, he gives his answer and sums up the issues as follows:

> Without aggregate growth, poverty reduction requires redistribution. Complete equality is unfair; unlimited inequality is unfair. So we need to seek fair limits to the range of inequality: a minimum income and a maximum income. The civil service, the military, and the university manage with a range of inequality that stays within a factor of 15 or 20. Corporate America has a range of 500 or more. Many industrial nations are below 25. Could we not limit the range to, say, 100, and see how it works?
>
> People who have reached the limit could either work for nothing at the margin if they enjoy their work or devote their extra time to hobbies or public service. The demand left unmet by those at the top will be filled by those who are below the maximum. A sense of community, necessary for democracy, is hard to maintain across the vast income differences in the U.S. When rich and poor are separated by a factor of 500, they become almost different species.
>
> The main justification for such differences has been that they stimulate growth, which will one day make everyone rich. This may have had superficial plausibility in an empty world, but in our full world, it is a fairy tale.[3]

So one key thing we need to do is to recognize that in terms of motivating people, we don't need to pay them five hundred times as much as the lower end of those they are leading. We don't even need to pay them fifty times as much. It's not really a motivation anyway at that level. I've had countless conversations with the seriously rich, and they say it's not the money; that's just the scorecard of progress. So we need to find new scoring systems and ways to celebrate and acknowledge success.

How about contribution to society for a start? And how about we pay our military officers more and our investment bankers less? I know who contributes more to my quality of life.

It's interesting to note that most of us actually want it to be this way. But we've become so caught up with our belief in the system we've been told drives us, we think others don't. In their research for *The Spirit*

Level, Wilkinson and Pickett found that most Americans want to "move away from greed and excess toward a way of life more centred on values, community, and family." However, people feel isolated and see their fellow citizens as different from them, as the ones who are greedy and excessive. So it appears we all secretly want this to happen!

So who does support inequality? Not economists, who by a margin of four to one support governments taking action in this area.[4] Not even the top "go for growth" economists like former Fed chairman Alan Greenspan want it. He called increasing inequality a "very disturbing trend."

It appears there is a clear and in some cases overwhelming majority of people and experts who think we need to have significantly greater equality in our society. Given that the data clearly demonstrates we'll pretty much all be better off down that path, it's time to get to work on making that happen.

Given the global context of having to share wealth in our own self-interest, this direction aligns well at the national *and* global levels.

It seems the answer to the future of human development, to making ourselves happier, and to solving a wide range of social ills including the elimination of poverty is to consciously and deliberately put in place policies and attitudes that make our society more equal.

CHAPTER 19

The Future Is Here, It's Just Not Widely Distributed Yet[1]

We now need to get to work on designing the future. There's a lot to do, but millions of people have turned up to work, excited, committed, and, most important, active and engaged. Every day, many more are joining them.

They're not waiting for permission to get on with it. They're inventing technologies, transforming companies, changing behavior, starting campaigns, and building new organizations—all designed to flourish in and beyond the Great Disruption.

One of the joys of our connected world is that these actions can take off and spread virally, globally, and quickly, being leveraged to build a new way of living and working.

What if the Freecycle Network had seven hundred million rather than seven million members and meant that most of our consumer products doubled their life span, effectively halving the environmental impact of their manufacture while connecting people across communities in conversations about the joy of sharing and not buying so much new stuff?

What if a movement was started to make living for a year with no shopping, like the Compact, become voluntary "planetary service"? It could be the entry ticket to the new economy, just as national "military service" used to be the entry ticket into adulthood and the workforce. After a year of not shopping, the lessons of the ineffectiveness of consumerism would be well ingrained.

What if we started a global movement to buy from local farmers, creating enough market demand to encourage a move back to family farming? This is the dominant way food gets to market in many developing countries, and it's now making a comeback in the developed world, driven by the desire for fresh food, picked when it's ripe and bought from the people who grew it. Even in the United States, a world leader in industrialized agriculture, the number of farmers' markets grew 300 percent from 1994 to 2009, with 5,275 of them now operating across the country.[2] So the trend is under way and could easily be boosted.

What if governments decided to launch a mass mobilization of the public to slash global energy consumption? As well as being a great way to motivate a sense of shared achievement, there are mind-boggling savings on offer. The International Energy Agency modeling shows more than $100 trillion could be saved by 2050 through a focused effort on energy efficiency.[3]

I had my own experience of this market as CEO of a business called Easy Being Green, which was owned by my consulting business, Ecos Corporation. Easy Being Green installed energy-saving equipment like lightbulbs and water saving devices into houses. We had over two hundred mainly young people employed going into thousands of homes every week, saving energy and spreading the message of climate change. We generated and sold carbon credits, reflecting the energy saved, which meant we could provide and install the equipment to householders for free.

There were many things we learned in the process. One was how incredibly motivated and passionate our people were. We had highly skilled university graduates happily employed changing lightbulbs. It might have appeared to be mundane work, but they knew they were acting every day to slow down climate change and doing so for a business that had a clear and positive social purpose—a purpose that was reflected in the culture every day. Another lesson was just how enormous the opportunities are to take simple, cost-effective actions to scale when good policy rewards business innovation. In a little over a year, this amazing team of people installed more than five million lightbulbs and other equipment that would prevent over four million tons of CO_2 pollution from entering the atmosphere—and had fun doing it!

There are many more possibilities. What if large progressive corporations really got mobilized to demand government take urgent action on climate change? There are many strong initiatives already, like the U.S. Climate Action Partnership, with companies as diverse as DuPont, Ford, GE, General Motors, Rio Tinto, and Pepsi. Another one is the Corporate Leaders Group on Climate Change, which produced the Copenhagen Communiqué, in which over five hundred companies called for government action to limit warming to two degrees. These are all good initiatives, but what if these companies behaved as if the economy and their future prosperity and survival were at risk? What if they organized a global market coalition of pension funds, companies, and consumers that was so powerful, it overwhelmed the opposition from other corporations resisting change and forced government to act?

In the future economy, providing new, nonfinancial incentives to employees will be key to attracting and retaining the best people. How about a global movement to have employers agree to cut working hours and income by 10 percent for those employees who want to join a program helping them to cut their consumption by 10 percent? In return, they could get an extra five weeks' holiday or have their weekends start at lunchtime on Fridays. This would boost the number of people with jobs and the number of people smiling on Fridays!

All the key characteristics of the new economy give us opportunities like this today. We can't wait until the crisis is full-blown before we act, or we won't have enough time to build these kinds of solutions, prove they are viable, and generate support for them. As we saw with the interest in initiatives like the Compact and the Freecycle Network, the number of people who understand the scale of the problem we face is growing exponentially, and those people are ready to be engaged with practical actions they can take.

Of all the drivers to change our approach, perhaps in the end we will change mostly because it is just a more intelligent and more rational approach and we are, in the end, intelligent and rational beings.

As the respected and influential economist E. F. Schumacher argued in his seminal book *Small Is Beautiful*, describing what he called Buddhist economics: "A Buddhist economist would consider this approach excessively irrational: since consumption is merely a means to human well-being, the aim should be to obtain the maximum of well-being with the minimum of consumption. . . . The less toil there is, the more time and strength is left for artistic creativity. Modern economics, on the other hand, considers consumption to be the sole end and purpose of all economic activity."

Are we ready for such a radical shift? I think so.

When I first raised these issues among my network in 2005, with my letter "Scream Crash Boom," most people (even those closely involved in the issues) thought I was being extreme with my forecasts of ecosystem breakdown. Now just five years later, system collapse has become a normal part of the conversation as an accepted possibility. So things are moving quickly now. We need to move with them and scale up our expectations of what's possible.

What else is already under way that we can support and expand? One of the key drivers of change will be the financial sector and the role of money. For decades, people have supported investment funds that screen the companies they invest in for various environmental and social criteria. The Social Investment Forum reports that in 2007 in the United States, a total of $2,700 billion was invested using one or more of the three core socially responsible investing strategies—environmental or social screening, shareholder advocacy, and community investing.[4]

These kinds of active investing are now firmly in the mainstream. Where we need to be, though, and will certainly get to, is where there are no special screened funds because all investors consider environmental and social criteria when making decisions, because they realize that these issues are core business questions with significant financial impacts.

Many investors, like David Blood and his team at Generation Investment Management, are already taking this fully integrated approach. They see these issues as normal investment criteria rather than as a special screen—that any good management team would recognize the need to align their strategy and operations with sustainability. As co-founder Al Gore said at their launch:

> Transparency, innovation, eco-efficiency, investing in the community, nurturing and motivating employees, managing long-term risks, and embracing long-term opportunities are integral parts of a company's enduring capability to create value. Business leaders

who align their business strategy and technical development
with sustainability and social accountability will deliver superior
long-term results to shareholders.

It is courageous for people like David Blood to pursue these issues
with such vigor. Most people with his kind of background—he was
previously CEO of Goldman Sachs Global Asset Management—avoid
taking them on too deeply, because doing so can challenge the fundamental beliefs that have defined their careers to that point.

Generation Investment Management is no longer accepting new
investors, as they already have around $6 billion of client commitments.
This money is invested, through their Global Equity Strategy, into
listed companies where Generation believes the company's management and strategy is ready for the trends we have been discussing. It's
interesting to note that these investments did significantly better than
the market overall during the recent financial crisis. Generation also
has around $650 million at work in its second strategy, the Climate
Solutions Fund, investing in businesses that can help address climate
change. When I met with the head of this fund, Colin le Duc, he was
excited about some of the ideas they were investing in and said that the
market is well and truly ready, with the business models and people
ready to address climate. The portfolio includes larger, more established
businesses as well as some younger and more innovative companies.

One of these is RecycleBank, a business that sees reducing the ridiculous amount of waste in our consumer economy as a profit opportunity and is using market principles to remove some of the distortions of
the current system. In a few short years, RecycleBank has involved over
one million people in twenty-six U.S. states and now in the United
Kingdom, saving millions of dollars, trees, and gallons of oil by dramatically increasing recycling rates in the areas it serves. The business
model is simple but ingenious—RecycleBank encourages recycling by
providing reward points to households based on how much they recycle,
then allowing them to trade in their points for rewards at local and
national businesses. It acts like a frequent recycler loyalty program. By
attaching an electronic tag to the bins, the company measures the
amount the house is recycling and automatically credits their account
on collection.

The result is a massive increase in recycling rates—for example, Montgomery, Ohio, saw a 39 percent increase in recycling rates when the program was launched in late 2008. Local governments pay Recycle-Bank to install the program thanks to the millions of dollars in landfill charges they can save. The authorities save money and environmental impact, the company creates jobs and profit, recyclers get raw material, and the households feel good and get rewarded for their behavior. The reason I love this example is that it recognizes that technology alone is not a solution—but technology coupled with behavior change, and designed to promote the latter, can deliver real and lasting results. This is also a fine example of the power of markets to deliver.

Another of Generation's investments is in Ocado, a new supermarket model based in the United Kingdom. This is a potentially disruptive business that exemplifies what we discussed in chapters 11 and 12 about Schumpeter's creative destruction. Based entirely online without any retail stores, Ocado claims their home delivery shopping service has a lower carbon footprint than walking to the supermarket! How's that? Today's "megamarts," with so much retail display space, open refrigerators, and the like, have huge physical and environmental footprints. They are designed to encourage you to purchase more, not for operational efficiency.

By basing their entire operation out of a centralized, automated warehouse, Ocado has completely eliminated this impact. Given that most people don't walk to the supermarkets anyway because such stores tend to lie on the edge of town surrounded by huge parking lots, a single delivery van can take countless cars off the road. Aside from their green credibility, their state-of-the-art logistical system will do some neat things, too, like allowing you to choose a delivery time down to the hour and then sending you a reminder on your phone a couple of hours before with the driver's name and license plate number.

If this model took off, it could drive a significant and positive market disruption with surprising and diverse social and economic impacts. People would no longer have numerous large shopping bags to carry home, and this could tip the scales for many people to get rid of their car or second car altogether. It would destroy the value of the huge investments made in drive-to shopping centers on the edge of town and change the economics of town centers. Given that there's a lot to be said for shopping locally for the environmental and community benefits it brings, this model might rekindle the competitiveness of small, specialist shops close to town that people can walk or cycle to for their small daily items. If people bought online, it would enable far more efficiency in packaging, with function rather than marketing as the main criterion. We should welcome Ocado and business models like it as exciting experiments in new ways of running our economy.

If we want the mainstream investment markets to divert trillions of dollars into these issues, as we'll need them to, we need trailblazers like David, Colin, and their colleagues to show how it can be done successfully. The amorality of money has long been a source of criticism. It cuts both ways, however, because the same tendency that sees big money happily flowing into destructive behavior will see it flood into the transition to sustainability if there's a buck to be made!

Most sustainability-focused investors sit at one end of the sustainable finance spectrum. They have making money as their core objective, with a focus on the social and environmental questions as sources of risk and value. Companies like Generation then sit in the middle of the range, still very mainstream and focused on delivering high returns, but with a clear social purpose agenda and focus. They have something to prove, and making money is how they do it, although it's not an end in itself.

At the other end of progressive financial markets are emerging institutions that are experimenting with not just a different investment focus, but different ownership structures and missions. Triodos Bank, started in the Netherlands in 1980, is a fine example, a pioneer of such approaches and one to watch. Their mission is all about social purpose:

> Triodos Bank finances companies, institutions and projects that add cultural value and benefit people and the environment, with the support of depositors and investors who want to encourage corporate social responsibility and a sustainable society.

Triodos's values and strategy run deep in this area, and they focus all their commercial activities on businesses and projects that have an overt social objective. Their mission continues, stating they seek to "help create a society that promotes people's quality of life and that has human dignity at its core."

I met their CEO, Peter Blom, when I was living in Amsterdam with Greenpeace in 1994. I was amazed then to find such radical thinking in a bank but saw it as a niche peculiar to the Netherlands, long famous for interesting social experiments.

When I had dinner with Peter again recently, I was forced to recalibrate the significance of what they are doing. Their results in 2009 were pretty impressive, with funds entrusted to the group that year up 30 percent to EUR 5 billion, customer numbers up 27 percent in a year, and offices now in the Netherlands, United Kingdom, Spain, Belgium, and Germany. They had also just received the *Financial Times* Global Sustainable Bank of the Year award. Triodos are starting to show the power of what's possible within a business framework when you work with a clear social agenda—what I would call a purpose-centered strategy, as we discussed in chapter 11.

They have long been pioneers, driving change in their sector that others follow. After the global financial crisis led to a push for greater transparency on how banks used people's money, Triodos provided their customers with an online tool that listed all the bank's investments and loans so depositors could see exactly where and how their money was being used—not in general, but specifically which businesses had borrowed it. They even allow customers to search by postcode so they can see if their deposits are being used to help their local economy.

When you meet Peter Blom, he projects like a modern banker with his sharp suit and solid image as the kind of guy you'd trust your money with. When the conversation turns to business, though, you realize you might be talking to the future of banking. He talked about cultural contribution, enhancing the cohesion of communities, and he explored ideas like how they can help build the organic food industry by bringing the value chain together to discuss blockages to mainstreaming. He explained how they had recently established a culture fund to invest with the intent of expanding arts activity. He spoke about how hard it is for artists to get loans for the tools of their trade, such as musical instruments or art studios. He smiled as he described how the risk department had to consider an eighteenth-century violin as security!

He clearly knows how to make money, even though their objective is solid and steady returns rather than the risky spectacular ones that drove the 2008 financial crisis. He gave a little chuckle as he explained that their returns are so solid and consistent, he has to resist demands by pension funds to buy more of the bank's shares—they have a limit on what percentage any one investor can hold to reduce the risk of undue influence on their mission. Triodos further guarantees their independence and strict adherence to their social purpose focus through a shareholding trust that separates the economic benefits of share ownership from control over the bank.

It is true that many of these examples are still marginal relative to the overall size of the markets they play in. In that context, though, it is important to remember how fast this could change. Google, which was started only in 1998 and listed in 2004, had a market cap of $180 billion in 2010. While many activists dislike globalization, this is the upside of a connected world and global market—ideas and companies can transform large parts of an economy rapidly. So who's to say that companies like Triodos couldn't dominate the financial sector in ten to fifteen years' time, in a backlash against the reckless behavior of the current incumbents?

There are many more issues we could cover.

Are there ownership and capital structures that would work better than listed stock exchange markets? While there are clearly some upsides to listed public companies, there are many other models and approaches, some of which are well established and mainstream but lack public attention or market credibility. While the one-degree war will reinforce some current business and investment models in the short term, the realization that growth has truly ended will steadily discredit many existing businesses and old models. That's why I think we'll see some of the approaches on the fringes today become mainstream as the new economy kicks in.

Is there potential for the reemergence of cooperatives, an old idea and still a powerful force in the global economy? Fonterra, the New Zealand milk cooperative owned by eleven thousand New Zealand dairy farmers, now accounts for 20 percent of New Zealand's total exports and 7 percent of the country's GDP. The Swedish forestry company Sodra is owned by fifty-two thousand forest owners and is one of the world's most successful and sustainable forestry and pulp companies, the third largest provider of market pulp for the production of paper and board.

When I met with Sodra CEO Leif Broden, it was clear the company had a culture and strategy based on the interest of its members, who, being forest owners, think in longer time frames than listed company shareholders. Leif is passionate about climate change, proudly explaining that they have recovered so much waste energy from their operations, they now produce more electricity than they use and have become an energy and forestry company. They are investing in windmills on co-op owners' land, giving landowners an additional income source and boosting Sodra's energy production even further. Sodra has long been committed to these issues, having led the industry on totally chlorine-free pulp mills and adopting strict forestry standards using the Forest Stewardship Council's external certification process.

Sodra's environmental leadership gives them a considerable competitive advantage as a trusted partner as they expand around the world. My friend and former Greenpeace colleague Joakim Bergman brought Leif to Australia to meet various environmental NGOs and government representatives when Sodra was exploring investment opportunities in the Australian forestry industry. The environmentalists and government ministers were taken aback to hear the CEO of one of the world's largest pulp companies arguing passionately for action on climate change, the need to eliminate chlorine from pulp manufacture, and the reasons we should protect our forests for future generations. A senior politician commented after meeting with Leif: "That was not the type of conversation we normally have with a CEO!"

Cooperatives like Sodra now employ one hundred million people worldwide, 20 percent more than multinational companies,[5] a strength in the real world that is certainly not reflected in co-ops' market profile or government support.

And how will the nature of work and employment change? Clearly, if we have a steady-state economy, people in developed countries are going to be buying less stuff and needing less money. Given population growth, and a lower throughput economy, this implies fewer working hours in return for lower income. This has far-reaching consequences for many issues, from transport in cities to job design, to government tax revenues, and to work-life balance.

One of the central tenets of modern market economics is constantly increasing productivity of the workforce and technology. While it's hard to argue against this in principle—doing things more efficiently must be good—is it actually improving our lives very much? It rarely translates into sustained higher profits (competitors soon catch up) or higher wages. It generally results just in lower prices, which drives more consumption.

What if improvement in productivity instead translated into fewer working hours? What if the harder and smarter we worked, the less we had to work? Surely that would be a better motivating factor for workers to increase productivity than having the company you work for sell more stuff, more cheaply.

A personal social dividend for productivity is a powerful idea and an inherently rational approach. There is also more to life than efficiency and productivity. As argued by economist E. F. Schumacher in *Small Is Beautiful*:

> Our ordinary mind always tries to persuade us that we are nothing but acorns and that our greatest happiness will be to become bigger, fatter, shinier acorns; but that is of interest only to pigs. Our faith gives us knowledge of something better: that we can become oak trees.

Another big challenge, and an exciting one, is to make our communities stronger, safer, and more connected and trusting. People all over the world are lamenting the loss of community in our cities and towns, as people's lives get overrun by working longer hours to buy stuff they haven't got time to use. What if, for example, through a combination of lower consumption and increased productivity we all spent 20 percent less time at work? Surely our quality of life would improve if this enabled us to slow down and spend more time having a deeper engagement with leisure, culture, and the community?

The reality is we will all need to work less in a steady-state economy. When labor productivity increases, as it does year on year, we can produce the same amount of stuff with fewer people. So at the moment, if we want to keep everyone in work and prevent spiraling unemployment, we need to produce and consume more—so improving productivity means more work, more money, more stuff, and less time to use it. But there's another option, which becomes the only option when we can't produce more stuff anymore. We all work less. We can then have the same number of people in employment, but all working fewer hours per week. It is true we will then have to take more holidays and long weekends or go home at two p.m. I think we'll cope.

Perhaps these lower working hours would enable us to reengage in our communities, making them places that live during the day, vibrant places that are designed for human-scale interaction. Maybe we would use the time to volunteer more, exploring the potential for greater community involvement in key institutions like schools.

I had a powerful experience of the latter when I worked with Mike Hawker, then CEO of Australia's largest insurance company, IAG. Mike was deeply concerned about the breadth and depth of challenges facing disadvantaged communities, and he saw the consequential social problems translating into insurance claims. Not one to just sit around, Mike brought together the CEOs from some of Australia's largest companies to work out how they could contribute. I joined the board and after much discussion, we concluded that education was the most powerful intervention the companies could make, and the Australian Business and Community Network was formed. We made a condition of joining that CEOs involved would personally commit to regularly mentoring the principals of some of Australia's most disadvantaged schools. A few years later, Mike's initiative had resulted in twenty-five companies engaged, with over two thousand of their staff joining the CEOs in various programs at 150 schools. The school principals are amazed to find these major corporate CEOs, normally distant figures they see on the TV news, now sitting in their schools sharing their experience. The passion and commitment of the CEOs are palpable—they take real delight in being able to contribute to the community that has nurtured their careers and success. They also learn a great deal from the school principals about managing in tough situations!

So I have no doubt that extra time can be put to good use. We can also use the extra time to save money and benefit the environment, like getting involved in bartering goods and freecycling, using the process to meet others in our communities and forming relationships that we need for the safer and more connected community we all wish for.

Many studies have shown that more leisure time enhances quality of life, including increased health, fitness, and life satisfaction.[6] The same studies suggest it can also lead to a lower environmental impact of our lives.

Strong communities develop because of well-defined behaviors—behaviors that we understand create "social capital"—connections and relationships that can then be drawn on when needed. Social capital is basically the idea that social networks and connections have value—which could be as simple as borrowing the drill from the neighbor or the fact that having good friends is known to increase our well-being. Just as we might invest in our human capital by giving ourselves or our children a good education, we can also invest in social capital. By deliberately encouraging this, individuals, governments, and city designers can all help build communities that are better connected and therefore more resilient. This means if we're heading into tough times, they will be better, stronger, and safer places to live.

Actions as diverse as street parties, volunteering, Men's Sheds,[7] free-cycling, community vegetable plots, exchange of goods, collective purchases of house upgrades like solar hot water, and car sharing can all reduce environmental impact, save money, build economies, create friendships, and make our lives happier and more satisfying. This can be done in existing communities to build greater strength, or it can provide a set of principles for housing developments deliberately designed to encourage stronger, safer, higher-trust communities. Around the world, town planners, architects, and focused groups like the Cohousing Association[8] are experimenting and promoting this approach. By 2008, there were already 113 cohousing communities built and occupied in the United States.

There are millions of people in community organizations driving these changes in behavior.

I think one of the more interesting organizations is the 1 Million Women campaign, led by suburban mother Natalie Isaacs. Listening to Natalie speak passionately about what got her involved reminds us just how important each and every individual is and what a profound difference we can each make.

Natalie, a mother of four from Sydney's northern beaches, got frustrated at the lack of action on climate by the men in politics in Australia and realized her best response was to do something concrete and practical.

So, with the support of my wife, Michelle, she founded the 1 Million Women campaign with a simple idea. Natalie realized that women were often in influential positions both at home and in the workplace to make things happen. They made 70 percent of consumer decisions in the household. Not one to think small, she thought: "What if we could get one million women across Australia to each commit to reduce emissions by a least one ton by taking simple, easy steps?" She then created a Web site at www.1millionwomen.com.au to makes this task easy, with accessible actions anyone can take, many of which save money and all of which make them feel good.

Within a short time, women all over Australia, from CEOs to suburban mums, became engaged in the idea of women leading action on climate. It took 1 Million Women just a year to have one of the highest membership numbers of environmental organizations in Australia. Every day more women sign up, committing to take direct practical action to start the transformation of our economy.

Women can make a disproportionate difference in this area and are behind many of the interesting new entrepreneurial ventures springing up around the world. They are clearly good at running businesses as well, with recent data[9] showing that women-owned business in the United States grew twice as fast as other types of business between 1997 and 2008. So clearly Natalie is not alone in knowing how to make things happen!

There are many more examples of people showing how creative alliances and thinking can make change happen.

In Australia, a group of men have started the Men's Shed movement. They realized that many men become isolated in their community, especially when not working, and as a result they don't talk about health and emotional issues. Recognizing that "men don't talk face to face but shoulder to shoulder," they thought they'd get them doing things together. So the Men's Shed movement was born to create places for men of all ages to come together and do practical things while making new friends and building community. The movement has taken off, with Men's Sheds being started all around the country and now spreading internationally.

Another creative model is led by Dr. Andrew Venter of the Wildlands Conservation Trust, which now has twenty-five hundred "treepreneurs" in twenty-three communities across South Africa. These "tree-preneurs," including children, are given seedlings of indigenous trees and are asked to nurture them until they get to a certain height. Wildlands then buys back the small trees for credits, which the tree-preneurs take to "tree stores" and exchange for bicycles, clothing, blankets, and food. So while for them money doesn't grow on trees, food, clothing, and bicycles do! Wildlands Trust then plants these trees in urban greening and forest restoration programs, generating further local employment and carbon credits for businesses to buy.

Another great example of market principles being applied on the ground is E+Co, a nonprofit taking a business approach to bringing clean energy to villages to reduce poverty. As they say: "E+Co finds great entrepreneurs. We help them establish clean energy businesses. Then we invest. It's that simple." It clearly works, with projects now operating in Cambodia, China, Costa Rica, El Salvador, Ghana, Guatemala, Honduras, India, Mali, Morocco, Nepal, Nicaragua, Philippines, Senegal, South Africa, Tanzania, Thailand, The Gambia, Uganda, Vietnam, and Zambia.

Over fifteen years, E+Co's investments and advice have supported 1,200 entrepreneurs to bring clean energy to 5.6 million people. In the process they have displaced 22 million liters of kerosene and 670,000 barrels of oil and saved 4 million tons of CO_2 from going into the atmosphere. The really interesting thing is they've done all this with an 8 percent return on funds used.

Individual passion and commitment can make an enormous difference in the world and power great change. Fifteen years ago I met Jack Heath, who had been deeply affected by youth suicide in his family and decided to do something positive in response. A former diplomat and senior adviser to Prime Minister Paul Keating, Jack invited me to join him on the board of his new Australian organization, the Inspire Foundation. Inspire established a youth-driven, Internet-based support service for young people called ReachOut (www.reachout.com). Jack realized that the Internet provided an accessible, anonymous, twenty-four hour and affordable way for young people to seek help and Inspire broke new ground using technology to deliver cost-effective social services, winning numerous awards for doing so in the late 1990s. What Jack also proved was that with the right support, young people can connect and help each other through tough times and the service is now spreading across the world.

This is being supported by Rupert Murdoch, who described Jack as "an extraordinary man." The late Helen Handbury, a major early supporter of Inspire in Australia, was Rupert Murdoch's sister and he is now continuing her work, using his influence to help Inspire spread the support of ReachOut to young people around the world, starting in the United States and Ireland.

There is no doubt that as we enter times of great change, examples like Inspire, 1 Million Women, Freecycling, and many others show the power of the Internet to bring communities of people together virtually to build resilience and connections while driving change in how we behave. What they also show is that individuals, like Natalie Isaacs, Peter Blom, Deron Beal, Mike Hawker, and Jack Heath, can have a great impact when they act on their beliefs and use their passion to make things happen.

It's important to remember how *anyone* can make a difference when they decide to. While these people are in my view heroes they are also just ordinary people who decided to act and as a result are doing extraordinary things. As Jack Heath's wife, Catherine Milne, said of Jack in a national television profile: "He is not a saint but rather a flawed man trying to be good." We are all flawed, we are all ordinary, and we can all make a significant difference *if* we choose to act.

Of course, there has never been a shortage of ideas and talking about how to make the economy more sustainable, communities stronger, and our lives more satisfying. What these examples show is that people have stopped talking and started acting. After thirty-five years of observing great initiatives and projects around the world like the ones just described, I'm convinced we are ready to take such ideas to scale, for three reasons.

The first, as covered throughout this book, will be the physical imperative to change. This cannot be underestimated as a motivator. When our backs are up against the wall, progress will be rapid and barriers that have seemed immovable for a long time will rapidly fall.

The second reason is the power of networks and global connectedness to drive change, incredibly quickly, through communities and around the world. These trends apply to how we change our attitudes toward issues such as consumerism as well as to how we take new technologies and ideas to scale and get them rapidly adopted.

This area was well covered in the book *Connected: The Surprising Power of Our Social Networks and How They Shape Our Lives.*[10] This fascinating and highly regarded research by Harvard professor Nicholas Christakis and the University of California's James Fowler showed the scale of our potential and also the power of individuals changing as a leverage point for group change.

Mathematical analysis of a network of twelve thousand people showed, for example, that you are 15 percent more likely to be happy if someone you are directly connected to (a friend) is happy. It goes further. At two degrees of separation, you're 10 percent more likely to be happy. At three degrees, 6 percent. This might not sound like much, but consider what it means—the fact that a friend of a friend of a friend (someone you've probably never met) is happy makes you 6 percent more likely to be happy. Compared with this, having a salary $10,000 higher makes you only 2 percent more likely to be happy.

What is the relevance of the power of these social networks in our case? Quite simply, it shows how behavioral and attitude change can lead to a cascade of change once people in prominent positions in the social network are converted. When something becomes normal or socially expected, it can spread rapidly. With our social networks now global, it's easy to see how fast an idea like "shop less, live more" could spread.

The third reason the period we are entering will see rapid acceleration in these shifts is that, collectively, the myriad examples like Generation Investment Management, Triodos, Sodra, Ocado, 1 Million Women, and Men's Sheds are actually no longer marginal. While not mainstream in the public consciousness, they are collectively approaching critical mass, and some are already there. Even though government and media focus obsessively on what they see as the mainstream economy—large global corporations—these are just one part of what makes the society and the economy work.

Many more people work in small to medium enterprises than in large companies, more people work in co-ops than in large companies, non-profit community organizations make up a substantial sector of the economy and are growing rapidly, more money was invested in renewable power generation in 2008 and 2009 than in fossil-fuel generation,[11] there is more growth in organic food than in industrialized food, and so on. The future is here, and it's more widely distributed than most of us think.

The main message here is not the many exciting ideas but the extraordinary capacity of human ingenuity to find solutions once we're motivated, along with the power of our social networks and Web-connected world to take these solutions to scale at an amazing pace.

Such a rich field of possibility. This is going to be an exciting period in human history.

And so we approach the end of our story. But before we do, and remind ourselves what's next, let's recap.

The end of economic growth and the realization that climate change is a threat to the future stability of the global economy and society will trigger two parallel responses. The old economy response, defined by actions like those outlined in the one-degree war plan, will appear to take off first and will get the most public and political attention. I believe this will be in full swing by the end of this decade, but it will certainly not be far away. For the immediate future, this will be our most important task. We have to roll out new technologies on a massive scale to prevent the climate from tipping over the edge. We will mobilize mind-boggling amounts of money, people, and focus to this task, and we need to do so as fast as we possibly can. This will be seen as a massive economic transformation. It is true it will be massive, but it will not be a true transformation.

That transformation will start at the same time but build more slowly. This will be the genuine transformation of the economy and society to a steady-state, sustainable economy, built on the pursuit of quality of life, a more equitable sharing of the world's wealth, and learning to operate in harmony with the ecosystem's capacity to support us.

While this transformation won't initially dominate public and political attention like the one-degree war phase, it will be both more profound and more sustained. It will be characterized by a broad social movement that will start building this new economy in a practical sense, while also developing its intellectual framework and political momentum.

This movement will have understood the lesson of climate change—there are limits we can't cross—and will seek to embed this idea deep in our cultural understanding. In this way we will come to understand, slowly at first but building over time, that the physical economy cannot grow and will need to be reinvented and redesigned at all levels.

This approach will not be an underground or marginal part of society. This is why I am so excited about the place we have arrived at in our story. People around the world are waking up every day to where we are and where we have to go.

Some come at it from the point of view of science, seeing the numbers and the physical limits. Others approach it from the economics, recognizing that the economic and financial consequences of moving beyond the limits will inevitably flow back into the economy and have an enormous impact on the value and competitiveness of companies and countries. Some people approach all this from a values perspective, observing at both a personal level and a societal level, that despite extraordinary increases in material wealth over recent decades, lives in the West are not improving in quality. They see trends like California building one new college over the past twenty years while it built twenty-one new prisons, and they know something is profoundly wrong when this occurs in the richest country in the world.

Others come at the issue as academics, studying the data of human development and progress and comparing this against measures of economic wealth. They conclude, now with a strong evidence base, that our current model isn't delivering. They have the data that shows while the average wealth of society is increasing, average quality of life is not improving.

From all these different angles, millions are coming to the same conclusion, and their numbers are growing rapidly. They know we have to change—what we expect, how we behave, and what we aspire to. There can be no technology fix for flawed human values; we have to change the values.

The good news gets better and better. The values and beliefs we need to leave behind are actually ones we don't really like, like aggressive pursuit of self-interest, and the ones we need to emphasize and grow are ones we already have and feel good about—values like having strong communities and leading meaningful lives, like seeing ourselves as part of the ecosystem and living in a world where we look after one another.

With these values in hand, we then have to drive change through our society and economy. We have to build an economy around a simple idea—having happier lives. Not distracted or entertained, but happier in the deeper sense of satisfaction. Of a life being well lived.

This means our criteria for success, at the personal, corporate, and government levels, need to shift away from the idea, now proven wrong, that economic growth and personal wealth are the right central focus because everything flows from that. That game is over. It will die with economic growth. A new game has begun, and we get to write the rules.

So there is only one question left to cover. Where do you fit in?

CHAPTER 20

Guess Who's in Charge?

This is my final chapter, but it is certainly not ours, nor is it humanity's. This is just the beginning of what will be seen by historians as the next step on our long evolutionary journey from apes to our full human potential. It has not been and will not be a smooth ride, but it will sure be a ride to remember.

It appears the newspaper story I read in 1972 was correct. There *are* limits to growth and the trends that story forecast are now unfolding all around us. The question becomes what we will do about it, and this is the final thing I want to discuss with you—where do you fit in? Where on the bus do you want to sit for this, the last leg of that journey?

First, though, some reflection. I lived in Amsterdam for several years in the early 1990s. It is one of my favorite cities in the world, in a country steeped in the stories that symbolize much of our civilization's ebb and flow over the past five hundred years.

I was in a café in Amsterdam one day, pondering the country's history: of art and conflicts, of trade and globalization, of exploration seeking wealth, all with varying levels of tolerance and humanity. Across the canal from me was Anne Frank's house, now a museum honoring the girl whose diary became a classic of world literature, recording her family's experience hiding from the Nazis in an occupied city.

As I sat there, I wondered what my thoughts would have been if I was a resident of Amsterdam in 1938. Suppose I had sat then, in this same café, while a friend told me what he thought was coming. I put myself back there and imagined recounting the conversation. . . .

As we chatted over coffee, Pieter said he believed Germany would, in a few years' time, invade our country, despite our declared neutrality, then rapidly occupy most of Europe, round up and murder millions of Jews, and plunge the world into a war from Europe to the Pacific. He thought this would be the deadliest and ugliest conflict in human history, with unimaginable brutality and suffering leading to over fifty million civilian and military deaths.

At this stage, he couldn't see how we could succeed against this threat, because it would require focus, mobilization, and determination at a level we had never seen before. Pieter imagined a scenario where after Germany invaded our country and occupied most of Europe, it joined forces with the expanding Japanese empire. He continued with his scenario, suggesting that even then, the world's strongest defender of freedom, the United States, would still show no signs of engaging directly in the war. This all seemed incomprehensible to me, but I still shuddered at the thought of it.

Pieter told me the danger was now clear and we needed to act urgently to reduce the risk before the forces against us gained the upper hand, but he was despondent because our leaders were showing no signs of doing so. While he was confident a great alliance would eventually be formed to oppose this threat and a great mobilization would take place, including the United States, victory would then be far from certain because of our late response. He predicted that if we failed, we would enter a dark age of totalitarian rule, with brutal repression and freedom squashed for who knew how long.

Pieter and I discussed it at length, and he urged me to act. He said that while the details were uncertain, the evidence was clear this conflict was coming and I should immediately join the call for action and prepare my family while telling my friends to do likewise.

I cycled home, pondering deeply what he had said. I knew other serious and knowledgeable experts believed this threat was real, but I had also read that many others disagreed, at least with respect to its urgency. Political leaders at home and around

Europe also expressed concern, but they were urging calm. They assured us that yes, this was serious, but it was a quite manageable problem—we should not overreact, as doing so would be expensive and disruptive.

I considered that my children were doing well in school, my family was well settled, my career was nicely on track, and the streets of Amsterdam were calm and ordered. I heard my learned friend's concern, but I found it very hard to accept that a calamity on this scale was more than a remote possibility. If it were that bad, those in charge would surely be responding far more dramatically, wouldn't they?

I went home and discussed it with my wife, feeling rather unsettled. We talked about it, but if we suddenly declared to our friends that we were fleeing the country—indeed, the whole continent—and suggested they join us, they would think us quite mad.

So we waited. Waited to see what unfolded, waited for the situation to become clearer, waited for those in charge to do something if they needed to.

Think of all the millions of people in Europe and the United States who went through a thought process just like this and went about their daily lives, unprepared for what was about to happen despite all the signals around them. How would history have been different if more people had acted earlier and demanded their leaders do more to prepare?

So, back to today. It's hard, isn't it, to hear stories of impending dangers and to know how to respond. It's hard to separate fear from reality, probably from possibly, and the truth among conflicting arguments. While we always complain about the quality of our leaders in politics and in business, we mostly assume they know what they are doing and what's really going on. We assume they will take firm charge if they need to.

We are all challenged by this dilemma. I remember clearly when I wrote the first version of these arguments in my "Scream Crash Boom" letter in 2005, I was very nervous about how people would react. As I sat there about to press the send button, I thought: "Will they think I'm mad? That this time Paul has really lost it?"

I sent it, and while I had many reactions of agreement, I had many that thought I was, while not mad, certainly exaggerating the threat. Some thought it was a shock tactic to get people to respond more urgently. I took this response seriously and went back again and again to challenge myself: Was it really this serious, was I getting carried away with the emotion of it all? And if I was convinced, what was the right thing for *me* to do, given who I am and what skills I have?

Others also agreed with the analysis but didn't know how to respond. It made what they were doing now on the issue seem wholly inadequate as a response. They would say things like this:

> But what can we do? If you're right, maybe we should sell everything and hide in the countryside somewhere and grow food. But then our friends will think we've gone mad when they look around and see the world calmly going about its business while I'm calling the end of the world. And anyway, we can't just walk away, we need to stop this from happening; this is really the most important moment for us all.

Yep, it's just hard. To hold the paradox in our heads—that things are desperately dangerous and urgent but we must act positively and full of hope—is an enormous test for the mind and the soul to act together. The challenge was well expressed by the great American writer F. Scott Fitzgerald: "The test of a first-rate intelligence is the ability to hold two opposed ideas in the mind at the same time, and still retain the ability to function."

So it's hard, but what do you do? Do you run away and grow your food in some far-flung corner of the world, in case we fail, in case humanity can't rise to the occasion? This is, after all, the outcome predicted by some serious experts. What would motivate us to do that? Would it be to save our children and our genes in the belief that if society fails in this historic task, we can rebuild a new world from the ashes of the old?

This is sometimes an appealing thought, even for me. After all, no one can argue I haven't had a go at preventing the situation we now face from emerging. So even I have had days when simply withdrawing has its attractions.

But then I consider the counterargument. That running away could just be fear of failure and the opportunity for a blameless escape, as argued by the writer Paul Williams, who in 1982 wrote the following in his extraordinary poem "Common Sense":

> *On the edge of the dream*
> *we face our deepest doubts.*
> *Now that it all is almost real*
> *a terrible fear of success takes hold*
> *and we grab desperately, uncontrollably, for failure.*
> *One last chance to get off easy.*
> *Who among us really wants to save the world,*
> *to be born again into two thousand more years*
> *of struggle?*
> *How much sweeter to be the doomed generation,*
> *floating gently on the errors and villainy of others,*
> *towards some glorious apocalypse now . . .*
> *Hallelujah! It's not my fault—*
> *Bring on the end times!*

And so we're back at Scott Fitzgerald's paradox, the one we now have to live with, without our heads exploding or our souls aching, at least not too much. We need to fully acknowledge the challenging times and inevitable suffering ahead but stay focused and determined to move forward and past this. Easy to say, harder to do.

So yes, it is challenging to know how to respond to all this and what to do personally. It is easy to see what the world should do, but what should *you* do? After all, the kids are doing well in school, things are calm on the streets, we've got busy lives. Maybe we should just wait until those in charge work out what to do. After all, with all those advisers, resources, and global experts, surely those in charge would make sure we acted dramatically if we really needed to.

Do you really think so?

For decades, those of us trying to change the world have sought to convince those we perceived to be in charge to act. We've argued for stronger regulation, for corporations to behave responsibly, for our political leaders to focus on the long-term interest of our society.

What can I say looking back? The best I can conclude is that it seemed like a good idea at the time, but alas, it didn't work. Why not?

When I left Greenpeace in 1995, I moved into the rarefied world occupied by global corporation CEOs. I engaged them through private conversations as a corporate adviser and personal provocateur and spent time with them in places like the World Economic Forum at Davos and other gatherings like the annual meeting of the Business Council in the United States and the World Business Council for Sustainable Development in Switzerland. I flew in their private jets and had dinner with them in their executive dining rooms.

I was delighted when this began. I thought, "At last, I'm working with the people in charge, the ones who really run the world! Now I can get into their minds, work out how they think, and convince them of the peril facing humanity (and their companies). They will then change the world, and my work will be done."

I spent a good fifteen years of my life working at this. It taught me a lot about how the world works. Convincing them of the peril we all faced was relatively easy. These are, with some notable but rare exceptions, generally decent and very smart people. They respond to logic and science, they have kids, they care about the future, and they want to do the right thing. So convincing them we were in serious danger wasn't the problem.

The problem was they weren't in charge.

If the world were really run by powerful men making decisions in smoke-filled rooms, we could go and knock on the door and explain the problem. We could tell them that things had become so bad that now even *they* were under threat. That would be great. But unfortunately, it's not the way it works.

Our system, the global economy, is a complicated array of interconnected components. Each component is individually managed but works within a system, and while some very smart people try to guide it, no one is, or ever can be, in charge.

Yes, there are places that resemble the apocryphal smoke-filled rooms full of powerful men, where men and women with great influence meet, but they are not in charge. I'm not naive about their power, influence, and self-interest—I've seen them at work using it, for good and for bad. But they are not going to fix this.

The good ones, of whom there are many, will do important things that contribute, pass better laws to incentivize action, make huge investments that take new technologies to scale, encourage consumers to do things differently. But they will do these things as a *reaction* to the system changing around them, not as those in charge of it.

We have a system problem, so we need a system solution. How do we do that?

The only force on earth powerful enough to fix this now is us. The woman entrepreneur bringing energy to her village in India, the organic farmer in Australia locking up carbon in the soil, the CEO in Davos cleverly using his power to shift market attitudes, the scientists taking ice cores in Antarctica, and the mother in China teaching her children how to shop less and live more. All of us, acting collectively.

The world is now connected as never before. Remember how if a friend of a friend is happy, you're more likely to be happy? Well, the same applies to them shopping less, to them being friendly to their neighbors, to them doing work with meaning.

We must remember, the solutions are ready to go; they are the examples I have discussed throughout this book. Solutions working today that deliver energy with zero CO_2 pollution, that build great companies, that deliver water to the urban poor, that create jobs in villages in India, that make communities in America stronger. These solutions are being driven by individuals with passion, people making a difference and making things happen. All we need to do is replicate and accelerate them.

As this unfolds, there will be many different types of action from many different types of people. There is even a clear role for well-directed anger. As well articulated by one of the world's great environmental campaigners, Bill McKibben:

> We definitely need art, and music, and disciplined, nonviolent, but very real anger. Mostly, we need to tell the truth, resolutely and constantly. Fossil fuel is wrecking the one earth we've got. It's not going to go away because we ask politely. If we want a world that works, we're going to have to raise our voices.

McKibben is right. This is a time we need to be clear, loud, and focused in our message. What big oil and coal companies are doing is just plain wrong, and it must be stopped, urgently. The right strategy model for this is Nelson Mandela and the end of apartheid. He was a leader who never once backed way from the rightness of his cause or compromised his goal, but still approached those who opposed him with humanity. This was all the more remarkable remembering that *his* enemies kept him in jail for twenty-seven years and murdered his friends and colleagues. Yet he still worked hard to reach them as human beings. We must advance our cause with determination and strength, but also with the highest integrity.

Most important, we must get on with the job. With all of us in charge, we live in the ultimate global democracy and we vote every minute of every day. We all know what we need to do. Shop less, live more. Raise chickens, and children who think. Build more community, make our lives more connected. Make good companies grow stronger, make bad companies go broke. Elect good political leaders, throw out bad ones. Roll out technologies that work and phase out those that don't.

Most of all, we need to stop waiting for someone else to fix it. There is no one else. We are the system; we have to change. Companies will respond when consumers and investors change their demands. Politicians will drive change when we make them do so.

It won't happen by itself; it will happen because people like us become part of a global movement where we all come together, in a distributed way, in small ways and big ways, to drive a change in thinking, a change in behavior, and a change in our world. Now that we're all connected, if we all act together, we'll change the system.

Will we succeed? Yes, if we decide to.

We must remember to do so, recognizing the threat but living with a lightness of heart and in the opportunity—the exciting, uplifting, civilization-shaping opportunity to make a difference greater than anyone since that ape worked out she could crack open the nut if she used the rock as a tool.

So let's do it. It is time.

Acknowledgments

When a lifetime of activity and a whole movement's history frames one's thinking, the first thing to say is that there are few original ideas in this book. It is more an amalgamation of fifty years of the concepts, ideas, and research of others. So I enthusiastically acknowledge the millions of people engaged on these issues over many decades, and I thank you all for your passion and commitment and for your love of humanity and the planet's extraordinary life force.

In this regard I particularly note Greenpeace, both as its own phenomena and as the home for thousands of courageous campaigners and their groundbreaking activism over four decades. You opened my eyes to limitless possibility as well as making me a global citizen.

I also acknowledge those who in more recent times have called the end of economic growth and have worked so hard to define how we might transition to a new approach. People such as Herman Daly and Tim Jackson, and organizations such as the New Economics Foundation, CASSE, and many others. You were right all along and your time has come.

On a personal level, there are many individuals who have steered me on my course but only a few will be named here. Jim Dixon for haranguing me over many decades on the importance of science. Peter Garrett for expressing faith and providing practical support to a young activist and for decades of friendship since. To all my friends on the Cambridge Programme, including Jonathon Porritt, Polly Courtice, Peter Willis, and others for having the courage to let a provocative, non-academic into the hallowed halls and allowing me to test and hone my thinking with such a powerful audience. To all my colleagues at Ecos and Easy Being Green, far too many to name but you know who you are and what a powerful contribution you all made to the thinking throughout this book.

To Joakim Bergman for endless encouragement and belief, through Greenpeace and life over twenty years, including a firm hand when needed. It is such rocks of friendship and support that define a life well lived. In the same vein, I thank Murray Hogarth and Rick Humphries for sharing life and debating the issues for hours—there are few ideas here that haven't been tested over beer and rugby, perhaps a uniquely Australian process of applying intellectual rigor! Go the gut.

For teaching an activist about business through providing opportunities and wise counsel, but also for your personal commitment to these issues: Jac Nasser, Bruce Blythe, Chad Holiday, Paul Tebo, Ellen Kullman, Mike Hawker, Sam Mostyn, John Pollaers, John Doumani, and countless others. And to Julie Birtles for much personal counsel and many reviews of the original "Great Disruption" letter in 2008. Your strength and passion for transformational change is a wonderful gift.

Sometimes small acts by one lead to major consequences for another. Tom Friedman, a friend and intellectual sparring partner since our walk up the mountain at Davos in 1995, wrote about the Great Disruption in his New York Times column in March 2009. That column triggered the invitation for me to write this book. So without your involvement, Tom, I doubt this book would exist. Thank you for the way you use your extraordinary leverage and brilliant writing to tirelessly push the United States and the world to act on climate, and for making the geopolitical and economic case for doing so.

Inspired by Tom's column, my editor, Peter Ginna, and my agent, Pilar Queen, both approached me. I thank you both for all your efforts to make this project happen. Peter, your confidence in my ideas and your courage to take them to the mainstream, along with your professional guidance, have been crucial and greatly appreciated.

Another who deserves special acknowledgment is Professor Jorgen Randers. I thought I had been focused on these issues for a long time until I met Jorgen—who started writing *The Limits to Growth* before I started high school. Never losing good humor or the curiosity for new ideas—and never displaying what would be understandable bitterness at being right but ignored for forty years—says a lot for your character and humanity. Your time has finally come and *The Limits to Growth* will now be recognized for its accuracy and its profound historical significance.

To Paul Ferris and Michelle Grosvenor for reviewing countless drafts and for probing and researching to provide rigor and a critical eye to my ideas and opinions. Being challenged by fearless but caring critics made this book much stronger.

Finally and most of all, to my wife and soul mate Michelle and to my life's most important outcome, my children—Callan, Asher, Jasper, Oscar, and Grace. Michelle, you know you have always been half my story; loving, pushing, propping up, and slapping down as needed. Mostly for always being there. To my little ones, some of whom are now bigger than me and all of whom soon will be. This is really for you, in every way. You will live with the consequences of our actions longer than I, and your children longer than you. I know you will do your best for them, as I have done for you. I hope and believe it will all turn out well.

Notes

Chapter 1: An Economic and Social Hurricane

1. There is, of course, subjective judgment in defining quality of life, heavily influenced by one's own relative situation. Median world income in 2007 was $1,700. While this would seem very low to many, it is over twice the generally accepted definition of poverty at $2 per day and well above the definition of extreme poverty at $1.25 per day. So around half the world's people, or over three billion of us, live above this $1,700 per year level—more than double the defined poverty level. Another way of considering it is that as of 2009, half of the world's population was defined as "middle class" for the first time—that is, they had roughly one third of their income left for discretionary spending after basic food and shelter. I therefore choose one billion, the top third of those defined as middle class, as an estimate of the number whose lives are reasonably "comfortable" with respect to basic needs, in global terms.

Chapter 2: The Scream— We Are Their Children's Children

1. "Scream Crash Boom" is available in full on my Web site, www.paulgilding .com.
2. Henry David Thoreau, *Walking* (Rockville, Maryland: Arc Manor, 2007). and *Journal* (August 30, 1856). Available online at http://www.library.ucsb .edu/thoreau/.
3. Peter Matthiessen, "Environmentalist Rachel Carson," *Time*, March 29, 1999.
4. William Darby, "Silence, Miss Carson!" *Chemical and Engineering News* 40 (October 1, 1962): 60–62.
5. Michael Smith, "'Silence, Miss Carson!': Science, Gender, and the Reception of *Silent Spring*," *Feminist Studies* 27, no. 3 (Autumn 2001): 733.

6. See http://www1.umn.edu/ships/pesticides/library/monsanto1962.pdf.

7. Priscilla Coit Murphy, *What a Book Can Do: The Publication and Reception of* Silent Spring (2005), 24–25 (Massachusetts: University of Massachusetts Press, 2005).

8. "The Cities: The Price of Optimism," *Time*, August 1, 1969.

9. *Newsweek* editorial, March 13, 1972.

10. Graham Turner, *A Comparison of the "Limits to Growth" with 30 Years of Reality*, Commonwealth Scientific and Industrial Research Organization, 2008 (Canberra, Australia: CSIRO, 2005). Available online at http://www.csiro.au/files/files/plje.pdf.

11. Ingrid Eckerman, *The Bhopal Saga—Causes and Consequences of the World's Largest Industrial Disaster* (India: Universities Press, 2005).

12. I first heard of this phrase in 1999 when used by John Passacantando, then of Ozone Action and later of Greenpeace.

13. Naomi Klein, *No Logo* (New York: Picador, 2002), 343.

Chapter 3: A Very Big Problem

1. Principle 15, Rio Declaration on Environment and Development, 1992. Available online at http://www.un.org/documents/ga/conf151/aconf15126-1annex1.htm.

2. Article 2, Framework Convention on Climate Change, 1992. Available online at http://unfcc.int.

3. Naomi Oreskes and Erik Conway, *Merchants of Doubt: How a Handful of Scientists Obscured the Truth on Issues from Tobacco Smoke to Global Warming* (New York: Bloomsbury Press, 2010).

4. Greenpeace International, *Koch Industries: Secretly Funding the Climate Denial Machine*, 2010; see http://www.greenpeace.org/kochindustries for the full report.

5. Naomi Oreskes, "The Scientific Consensus on Climate Change," *Science* 306, no. 5702 (December 2004): 1686, doi:10.1126/science.1103618.

6. William R. L. Anderegg et al., "Expert Credibility in Climate Change," *Proceedings of the National Academy of Sciences* 21 (June 2010), doi:10.1073/pnas.1003187107.

7. These reports include those by the U.K. House of Commons Science and Technology Select Committee, an independent international panel set up by the University of East Anglia, and the Independent Climate Change Email Review. All concluded that the e-mails did not undermine the findings of climate science or the "rigour and honesty" of the scientists involved. The reports are available at http://www.cce-review.org; http://www.uea.ac.uk/mac/comm/media/press/CRUstatements/SAP.

8. The full reports and summaries are available online at http://www.millennium assessment.org.

9. See http://www.guardian.co.uk/environment/2010/may/17/saving-fish-stocks-cost-jobs.

10. World Bank and the Food and Agriculture Organization, *The Sunken Billions: The Economic Justification for Fisheries Reform*, 2008. Available at http://worldbank.com.

11. Joshua Bishop (ed.), *TEEB—The Economics of Ecosystems and Biodiversity Report for Business*, Appendix 2.1, available at www.teebweb.org.

12. International Energy Agency, *World Energy Outlook 2009*. Available at http://www.iea.org.

13. The papers can be found on their Web site, www.stockholmresilience.org. See Johan Rockström et al., "A Safe Operating Space for Humanity," *Nature* 461 (September 24, 2009): 472–475.

14. Walter K. Dodds et al., "Eutrophication of U.S. Freshwaters: Analysis of Potential Economic Damages," *Environmental Science & Technology* 43, no. 1 (2009): 12–19.

15. Robert Costanza et al., "The Value of the World's Ecosystem Services and Natural Capital," *Nature* 387 (May 15, 1997): 253.

16. See www.footprintnetwork.org.

17. WWF and Global Footprint Network, *Living Planet Report 2008*, and the National Footprint Accounts 2009 data tables, available at www.footprintnetwork.org.

CHAPTER 4: BEYOND THE LIMITS—THE GREAT DISRUPTION

1. See the UN Population Division Web site for world population projections, at esa.un.org/unpp.

2. Australian Treasury and Department of Climate Change and Water, *Australia's Low Pollution Future: The Economics of Climate Change Mitigation*, 2008. Available at http://www.treasury.gov.au/lowpollution future/.

3. Dominic Wilson and Anna Stupnytska, "The N-11: More Than an Acronym," Goldman Sachs, Global Economics Paper No. 153, 2007. Available at http://www.goldmansachs.com.

4. John Hawksworth, "The World in 2050: How Big Will the Major Emerging Market Economies Get and How Can the OECD Compete?" PwC, 2006. Available at http://www.pwc.com. PwC's figures are based on purchasing power parity (PPP), where amounts are adjusted to take account of how many goods or services one unit of currency buys. For example, $1 at market exchange rates buys a lot more in China than it does in the

United States and slightly less in Scandinavia than it does in the United States. PPP is a useful measure for our purposes, since it has been closely linked with consumption and thus ecosystem demands. This accounts for much of the difference between PwC's estimates and the others I have referenced, all of which were based on nominal US$.

5. Stefan Giljum and Christine Polzin, "Resource Efficiency for Sustainable Growth: Global Trends and European Policy Scenarios, background paper for the UN Industrial Development Organization's *International Conference on Green Industry in Asia* (September 2009), available at http://oxford.academia.edu/ChristinePolzin/Papers/.

6. Tim Jackson, *Prosperity Without Growth?* (U.K. Sustainable Development Commission, 2009), 48.

7. WWF and the Global Footprint Network, *Living Planet Report 2008.*

8. Paul R. Ehrlich and John P. Holdren, "Impact of Population Growth," *Science* 171, no. 3977 (1971): 1212–1217.

9. Gurdev S. Khush, "Green Revolution: Preparing for the 21st Century," *Genome* 42, no. 4 (1999): 646–655.

10. National Academy of Sciences, *Carbon Dioxide and Climate: A Scientific Assessment*, Washington, D.C.: National Academy of Sciences, Climate Research Board, 1979. Available at http://www.nap.edu.

11. David Archer, "Fate of Fossil Fuel CO_2 in Geologic Time," *Journal of Geophysical Research* 110 (2005), doi:10.1029/2004JC002625.

12. Tim Jackson, *Prosperity Without Growth?: The Transition to a Sustainable Economy*, U.K. Sustainable Development Commission, 2009. Available from their Web site at www.sd-commission.org.uk.

CHAPTER 5: ADDICTED TO GROWTH

1. John Stuart Mill, *Principles of Political Economy*, book IV, chapter 6 (1848). Available online at http://www.econlib.org.

2. See, for example, Tim Jackson, *Prosperity Without Growth?: The Transition to a Sustainable Economy*, U.K. Sustainable Development Commission, 2009. Available from their Web site at www.sd-commission.org.uk.

3. Unnamed caller on ABC Radio 702, Sydney, Australia.

CHAPTER 6: GLOBAL FORESHOCK—THE YEAR THAT GROWTH STOPPED

1. National Snow and Ice Data Center, http://nsidc.org/news/press/2007_seaiceminimum/20070810_index.html.

2. James A. Screen and Ian Simmonds, "The Central Role of Diminishing

Sea Ice in Recent Arctic Temperature Amplification," *Nature* 464 (April 29, 2010): 1334–1337, doi:10.1038/nature09051.

3. See http://bio-fuel-watch.blogspot.com/2010/04/large-scale-soy-farming-in-brazil.html; also see http://www.scientificamerican.com/article.cfm?id=biofuels-bad-for-people-and-climate.

4. Lorenzo Cotula et al., "Land Grab or Development Opportunity?: Agricultural Investment and International Land Deals in Africa," FAO, IIED, and IFAD, 2009. Available at http://www.fao.org/docrep/011/ak241e/ak241e00.htm.

5. Shepared Daniel with Anuradha Mitta, "The Great Land Grab: Rush for World's Farmland Threatens Food Security of the Poor," Oakland Institute, 2009. Available online at http://www.oaklandinstitute.org/pdfs/Land Grab_final_web.pdf.

6. Joachim von Braun and Ruth Meinzen-Dick, "'Land Grabbing' by Foreign Investors in Developing Countries: Risks and Opportunities," IFPRI Policy Brief 13, 2009. Available at http://www.ifpri.org/publication/land-grabbing-foreign-investors-developing-countries.

7. Horand Knaup and Juliane von Mittelstaedt, "The New Colonialism: Foreign Investors Snap Up African Farmland," *Spiegel Online International*, August 30, 2009.

CHAPTER 8: ARE WE FINISHED?

1. H. Damon Matthews and Andrew J. Weaver, "Committed climate warming," *Nature Geoscience* 3 (2010): 142–143.

2. This is actually a myth, but the concept is well understood in popular culture.

3. The report was obtained by the *Observer* newspaper and reported on in that paper on February 22, 2004.

4. Anthony Storr, *Churchill's Black Dog, Kafka's Mice, and Other Phenomena of the Human Mind* (New York: Ballantine Books, 1990).

CHAPTER 9: WHEN THE DAM OF DENIAL BREAKS

1. John A. Romley et al., *The Impact of Air Quality on Hospital Spending*, RAND Health, 2010. Available at http://www.rand.org/pubs.

CHAPTER 10: THE ONE-DEGREE WAR

1. Paul Gilding and Jorgen Randers, "The One Degree War Plan," *Journal of Global Responsibility*, vol. 1, issue 1 (2010): 170–188. Available online at http://www.emeraldinsight.com/journals.htm?articleid=1860356.

2. H. Damon Matthews and Andrew J. Weaver, "Committed Climate Warming," *Nature Geoscience* 3 (2010): 142–143.

3. Steven J. Davis, Ken Caldeira, and H. Damon Matthews, "Future CO_2 Emissions and Climate Change from Existing Energy Infrastructure," *Science* vol 328, no. 5997 (September 2010): 1330–1333.

4. Economic History Association Web site, http://eh.net/encyclopedia/article/tassava.WWII.

5. Robert G. Ferguson, "One Thousand Planes a Day: Ford, Grumman, General Motors and the Arsenal of Democracy," *History and Technology* 21 (2005): 149.

6. World Resources Institute, Climate Analysis Indicators Tool, available online at http://cait.wri.org/cait.php?page=yearly (accessed May 11, 2009). These percentages are based on 2005 emissions, excluding Land Use, Land Use Change and Forestry.

7. We ran our assumed emission scenario (along with an IPCC "business as usual" scenario) through the C-ROADS model with the kind help of Lori Siegel. See T. Fiddaman, L. Siegel, E. Sawin, A. Jones, J. Sterman, *2009: C-ROADS Simulator Reference Guide*, Ventana Systems, Sustainability Institute, and MIT Sloan School of Management, www.climateinteractive.org.

8. McKinsey & Co., *Pathways to a Low-Carbon Economy* (2009), shows how for every year of delay, the peak atmospheric concentration of CO_2e could be expected to be 5 ppm higher for the same level of action. Available online at http://www.mckinsey.com/clientservice/ccsi/. Stern also argues the economic value case for "strong and early action" in Nicholas Stern, *Executive Summary, Stern Review on the Economics of Climate Change*, 2006. Available online at http://www.sternreview.org.uk/.

9. Dollars or euros per ton of CO_2e is a measure of the estimated cost to take actions to achieve a ton of CO_2e reduction. The McKinsey study referred to categorized various actions (for instance, energy efficiency, nuclear power, solar panels, auto efficiency) into various cost categories.

10. See Prince's Rainforests Project, *An Emergency Package for Tropical Forests*, March 2009, http://www.princeofwales.gov.uk/content/documents/Report%20%20March%202009.pdf.

11. In this paper we assume there will be some six thousand major power plants in operation in 2018 (against some five thousand today). We assume that one thousand of these are closed down during the C-war in 2018–2023 (reducing emissions by 5 $GtCO_2e/yr$) and that a further one thousand plants will be retrofitted with CCS equipment (reducing emissions by a further 2 $GtCO_2e$ by 2023). A big CCS plant sequesters on average 2 $MtCO_2/yr$—roughly 1 in a gas-fired utility and roughly 3 in a coal-fired utility.

12. CCS refers to various technologies designed to capture the carbon emitted

from burning coal in power plants, then concentrating it and transporting it to underground basins, where it can be locked up indefinitely.

13. See http://www.desertec.org.

14. See Mark Z. Jacobson (Stanford University) and Mark A. Delucchi (University of California, Davis) in "A Plan to Power 100 Percent of the Planet with Renewables," *Scientific American*, November 2009, where an article summarizes their full study.

15. See V. R. Cardozier, *The Mobilization of the United States in World War II: How the Government, Military and Industry Prepared for War* (1995), especially chapter 10 (Jefferson, N.C.: McFarland, 1995).

16. Gilding and Randers, "The One Degree War Plan," *Journal of Global Responsibility*, vol. 1, Issue 1 (2010).

CHAPTER 11: HOW AN AUSTRIAN ECONOMIST COULD SAVE THE WORLD

1. *New York Times*, December 18, 2008.

2. For an overview of DuPont's performance and approach see: Scot Holliday, "A Case Study of How DuPont Reduced Its Environment Footprint: The Role of Organizational Change in Sustainability," dissertation at The George Washington University, Washington, D.C (2010).

3. See various papers at http://www.isc.hbs.edu/soci-environmental.htm, including a twenty-year review of Porter's hypothesis at http://www.isc.hbs.edu/PorterHypothesis_Montreal2010.htm.

CHAPTER 12: CREATIVE DESTRUCTION ON STEROIDS

1. A U.K. review by the Parliamentary Office of Science and Technology finds that coal power typically generates in excess of 1,000 grams CO_2e per kWh, versus 4.64 for onshore and 5.25 for offshore wind. That is, about 200 to 1, or a 99.5 percent reduction. See http://www.parliament.uk/documents/post/postpn268.pdf.

2. From Al Gore, *Our Choice* (New York: Rodale, 2009), p. 57.

3. http://www.foreignpolicy.com/articles/2010/08/05/the_ministry_of_oil_defense

4. See Mark Z. Jacobson (Stanford University) and Mark A. Delucchi (University of California) in "A plan to power 100 percent of the planet with Renewables," *Scientific American*, November 2009, where an article summarizes their full study.

5. Renewable Energy Policy Network for the 21st Century (REN21), *Renewables 2010: Global Status Report*, 2010. REN21 is a network of governments,

international organizations including the International Energy Agency, international NGOs, and industry. Available online at http://www.ren21 .net/. See also UNEP, "Global Trends in Sustainable Energy Investment 2010 Report," available at http://sefi.unep.org/english/globaltrends2010 .html.

6. United States Energy Information Administration, statistics available at http://www.eia.doe.gov/energyexplained/index.cfm?page=electricity _home#tab2.

7. See summary article at http://www.businessspectator.com.au/bs.nsf/Article /IEA-cleantech-low-carbon-energy-technology-emissio-pd20100705 -73F5M.

8. http://www.climatespectator.com.au/commentary/sizing-low-carbon-economy.

CHAPTER 13: SHIFTING SANDS

1. See http://www.nytimes.com/2009/07/05/opinion/05friedman.html.

2. See http://www.guardian.co.uk/environment/2010/feb/18/worlds-top-firms-environmental-damage.

CHAPTER 14: THE ELEPHANT IN THE ROOM

1. *A Steady-State Economy*, commissioned by the Sustainable Development Commission, April 24, 2008, http://www.sd-commission.org.uk/publications .php?id=775.

2. Ibid.

3. Representative Barber Conable is credited as the source of this quote.

4. See http://www.climatespectator.com.au/commentary/sizing-low-carbon -economy.

CHAPTER 15: THE HAPPINESS ECONOMY

1. Adam Smith, *An Inquiry into the Nature and Causes of the Wealth of Nations*, 5th ed., edited by Edwin Cannan (London: Methuen & Co., Ltd., 1904).

2. Centre for the Advancement of Steady State Economics, http://steadystate .org.

3. See http://www.happyplanetindex.org.

4. Paper by Professor Clive Hamilton and Professor Tim Kasser, presented at Oxford University conference 2009, 4 degrees and beyond, http://www.clive hamilton.net.au/cms/media/documents/articles/oxford_four_degrees_paper _final.pdf.

CHAPTER 16: YES, THERE IS LIFE AFTER SHOPPING

1. See http://noimpactman.typepad.com/blog/2007/02/the_personal_im.html.
2. See http://www.drewsmarketingminute.com/2008/09/how-to-market-t.html.
3. See http://www.commondreams.org/headlines01/0929-04.htm.
4. See http://www.telegraph.co.uk/news/worldnews/1538555/The-year-of-living-frugally-how-10-friends-survived-without-shopping.html.
5. See http://entertainment.timesonline.co.uk/tol/arts_and_entertainment/music/article6281684.ece and Reverend Billy's site at www.revbilly.com.
6. See http://www.latimes.com/news/science/environment/la-me-story-of-stuff-20100713,0,2775603,full.story.
7. See http://www.neweconomics.org/projects/five-ways-well-being.
8. See http://www.lohas.com/forum/lohas8/market/index.html.
9. See http://www.ota.com/pics/documents/2010OrganicIndustrySurveySummary.pdf.

CHAPTER 17: NO, THE POOR WILL *Not* ALWAYS BE WITH US

1. Barry Bosworth and Susan M. Collins, "Accounting for Growth: Comparing China and India," *Journal of Economic Perspectives* 22, no. 1 (Winter 2008): 45–66.
2. United Nations University World Institute for Development Economic Research, *The World Distribution of Household Wealth* (2006), available online at http://www.wider.unu.edu/.
3. Angus Maddison, *The World Economy: A Millennial Perspective* (OECD, 2001), available online at http://www.theworldeconomy.org/.
4. I first heard this analogy in a conversation with Charles Secret from the New Economics Foundation.
5. Royal United Services Institute, "Delivering Climate Security: International Security Responses to a Climate Changed World," *Whitehall Papers* 69 (2007, published April 2008).
6. Marshall B. Burkea et al., "Warming Increases the Risk of Civil War in Africa," *Proceedings of the National Academy of Sciences* 106, no. 49 (2009).
7. Gwynne Dyer, *Climate Wars: The Fight for Survival as the World Overheats* (Toronto: Random House Canada, 2008).

CHAPTER 18: INEFFECTIVE INEQUALITY

1. See http://www.thesolutionsjournal.com/node/556.
2. Richard Wilkinson and Kate Pickett, *The Spirit Level: Why Greater*

Equality Makes Societies Stronger (New York: Bloomsbury Press, 2010) and Richard Wilkinson, *Unhealthy Societies: The Affliction of Inequality* (London: Routledge, 1996).

3. Ibid.

4. Daniel B. Klein and Charlotta Stern, "'Economists' policy views and voting," *Public Choice* 126 (2006): 331-342.

CHAPTER 19: THE FUTURE IS HERE, IT'S JUST NOT WIDELY DISTRIBUTED YET

1. Adopted from a quote by author William Gibson.

2. See http://www.ams.usda.gov/AMSv1.0/ams.fetchTemplateData.do?template=TemplateS&navID=WholesaleandFarmersMarkets&leftNav=WholesaleandFarmersMarkets&page=WFMFarmersMarketGrowth&description=Farmers%20Market%20Growth&acct=frmrdirmkt.

3. See http://www.iea.org/press/pressdetail.asp?PRESS_REL_ID=395.

4. See http://www.socialinvest.org/resources/sriguide/srifacts.cfm.

5. See http://www.ica.coop/coop/statistics.html.

6. *State of the World 2010*, Worldwatch, "Transforming Cultures: From Consumerism to Sustainability," article by John de Graff, http://blogs.worldwatch.org/transformingcultures/wp-content/uploads/2009/11/SOW2010-PreviewVersion.pdf.

7. See http://www.mensheds.com.au.

8. See www.cohousing.org.

9. See http://www.womensbusinessresearchcenter.org/research/keyfacts.

10. See http://connectedthebook.com.

11. Renewable Energy Policy Network for the 21st Century (REN21), "Renewables 2010: Global Status Report" (2010). REN21 is a network of governments, international organizations including the International Energy Agency, international NGOs and industry, available at http://www.ren21.net/. See also UNEP, "Global Trends in Sustainable Energy Investment 2010 Report," available at http://sefi.unep.org/english/globaltrends2010.html.

Further Reading

Here are just a few examples of the many books, papers, and Web sites dealing with the issues covered in this book.

My Web site
My Web site www.paulgilding.com allows you to contact me, sign up for my regular commentary, the *Cockatoo Chronicles*, and to obtain papers such as "The One-Degree War Plan."

Paul Roberts, *The End of Food* (Boston: Houghton Mifflin Harcourt, 2008).
This book provides excellent insight into what will arguably be the most profound consequence of the Great Disruption—the future of food.

Tim Jackson, *Prosperity Without Growth: Economics for a Finite Planet* (London: Earthscan, 2009).
Tim Jackson's very readable book is essential for anyone seeking to understand why we must and how we might transcend economic growth. The United Kingdom's now-disbanded Sustainable Development Commission first published an earlier version of this book in the form of a free report titled "Prosperity Without Growth?"

David MacKay, *Sustainable Energy Without the Hot Air* (Cambridge, England: UIT Cambridge, 2009)
This excellent overview of low carbon energy pathways in response to the climate challenge can be downloaded for free or purchased on paper at www .withouthotair.com.

Gwynne Dyer, *Climate Wars: The Fight for Survival as the World Overheats* (Toronto: Random House Canada, 2008).
An overview of future geopolitical risks and conflict scenarios viewed through the lens of climate change and sustainability.

Richard Wilkinson and Kate Pickett, *The Spirit Level: Why Greater Equality Makes Societies Stronger* (New York: Bloomsbury Press, 2010).
A fuller explanation of the issues covered in the chapter on inequality.

Herman Daly, *Beyond Growth: The Economics of Sustainable Development* (Boston: Beacon Press, 1997).
Herman Daly is the world's foremost post-growth economist. His work will appeal to those who are interested in understanding the economics in more detail. He's the author of numerous books and papers. *Beyond Growth* is a good place to begin delving into his work.

Donella Meadows, Jorgen Randers, and Dennis Meadows, *Limits to Growth: The 30-Year Update* (White River Junction, VT: Chelsea Green, 2004).
The book that started so much, updated with thirty years of reality.

Clive Hamilton, *Growth Fetish* (London: Pluto Press, 2004).
Clive Hamilton neatly sums of up the problems of our obsession with growth in this book: buying things we don't need, with money we don't have, to impress people we don't like.

The New Economics Foundation
This U.K.-based organization is consistently at the forefront of understanding our challenges and proposing creative, workable solutions to them. Their publications are all available free online at www.neweconomics.org.

The Center for the Advancement of the Steady State Economy (CASSE)
A U.S.-based organization dedicated to advancing the concept of a no-growth, steady-state economy. They provide a Web-based overview of the implications for various aspects of everyday life and society, and suggestions of measures that could start the transition to a steady-state economy. www.steadystate.org.

The Footprint Network
The home of the idea that the economy is operating at over 140% of capacity and increasing every day. This site has all the data and methodology. www.footprintnetwork.org.

Index